Foreword

NCSS members who receive this bulletin shortly after its publication in December will discover a very special holiday treat. *Social Education* has long published many fine articles on social studies in the elementary schools. This anthology contains some of the best, but by no means all, of the excellent articles on elementary social studies to appear in *Social Education* during the past seven years.

The anthology is timely, not only because it arrives during the holiday, but also because elementary school social studies seems beset these days with unusual uncertainty. The need to cut school budgets, coupled with slogans accompanying the "back to basics" movement, threatens the place of social studies in the elementary grades in some communities. Concern about apparent declines in reading competence and mathematics skills has encouraged a handful of educators and some parents to urge that other aspects of elementary education be diminished in order to emphasize the "three R's." Such people seem to believe that children's social learning can be postponed or left to other agencies. What a drastic change this idea is from that of earlier times, when social studies, with its emphasis upon citizenship development and character education, was viewed as the core of the curricular program and set the instructional agenda for other subjects!

We must trust that notions about reducing the role of social studies will not become pervasive and will, in fact, recede as the implications of such thinking become more apparent. In the meantime, it is important for the National Council for the Social Studies to speak out forcefully on behalf of social studies in the elementary schools. The articles contained in this anthology contribute significantly to our case.

NCSS has been fortunate that there have been three talented educators who have volunteered their time and accepted the responsibility for editing the Elementary Education Section of *Social Education* since it began in 1966. The current editor, William Joyce, and Frank Ryan, are the co-editors of this anthology. I wish to congratulate them for their accomplishment. I want also to draw attention to those NCSS members who serve on the Board of Advisors to the editor of the Elementary Education Section. Their judgments led to the initial appearance of the articles that follow; their advice has helped create this anthology. Above all, I am grateful to the authors who offered their ideas to *Social Education* and who permitted us to reprint them in this anthology.

To the members of the Publications Board and to the NCSS publications staff, especially Dan Roselle and Joe Perez, congratulations for another fine job during a tremendously busy year. And (I nearly forgot) thank you for the fine holiday gift.

December, 1977

Howard D. Mehlinger
President, NCSS

Introduction

In November, 1966, the Elementary Education Section first appeared in *Social Education*. Edited initially by John Jarolimek and later by Huber Walsh, this section of the journal has been published four times annually since its inception. Partial funding has been provided by the Mary G. Kelty Fund.

During their tenure as editors of the Elementary Education Section of *Social Education*, John Jarolimek and Huber Walsh established and maintained high standards of quality. Not only did they publish scholarly, provocative articles that spoke to the needs and concerns of teachers, supervisors, and teacher educators, but they were also eminently successful in ensuring that the articles were written in an understandable, functional style.

The extent to which this tradition has persisted can be judged by the articles that have been published in the Elementary Education Section over the past five years. Assisting the current Elementary Education Editor is a Board of Advisors consisting of classroom teachers, supervisors, school administrators, and college instructors. These highly competent educators suggest themes for future issues, identify prospective authors, and review manuscripts; on occasion, they serve as guest editors and authors. Although the Board of Advisors is an active, working group, final responsibility for this section of *Social Education* rests with the authors and with the Elementary Education Editor.

In recent years we have received from our readers numerous expressions of support and requests for reprints of articles. Many readers tell us that they make extensive use of our articles in elementary social studies classes, in teacher education classes, and in in-service programs. Indeed, growing numbers of college instructors have requested that we publish an anthology of articles on elementary social studies for their use in pre- and in-service teacher education classes. These encouraging reactions prompted the publication of this anthology.

In the fall of 1976, a committee consisting of several members of the Board of Advisors for the Elementary Education Section of *Social Education* convened for the purpose of selecting articles for publication in this anthology. After evaluating all articles published in this section from January, 1970 to May, 1977, the committee identified what it believed to be the most significant articles published during this period. The Committee based its selections on these criteria:

iv

Social Studies and the Elementary Teacher: Promises and Practices

An Anthology Edited By
William W. Joyce and Frank L. Ryan
Michigan State University   University of California, Riverside

BULLETIN 53

In collaboration with the 1976-77 Board of Advisors of
the Elementary Education Section of *Social Education*.

Ellen Burchfield*
Huntsville (Ala.) Public Schools

Arthur Ellis*
University of Minnesota

Arlene Gallagher*
College of Our Lady of the Elms

Leslie Hundley*
Kirkwood (Mo.) School District

Myra Herlihy*
Geneseo, New York

Alan J. Hoffman*
Georgia State University

Theodore Kaltsounis
University of Washington

Edith King
University of Denver

James M. Larkin*
University of Pennsylvania

Millie Reed*
Kentucky Department of Education

Sister Judith Shanahan
Archdiocese of Indianapolis

Margo Sorgman
University of Utah

Jan Stolte
Lansing (Mich.) Public Schools

Huber M. Walsh*
University of Missouri, St. Louis

Ronald Wheeler*
College of William and Mary

James Wirth
Montgomery County (Md.) Public Schools

* Advisory Committee for the preparation of this book.

NATIONAL COUNCIL FOR THE SOCIAL STUDIES

Library of Congress Catalog Card Number: 77-93070
ISBN 0-87986-014-6
Copyright © 1977 by the
NATIONAL COUNCIL FOR THE SOCIAL STUDIES
2030 M Street, N.W. Washington, D.C. 20026

1. Does the article speak to current, significant issues in the field of elementary social studies?
2. Does the article contribute new research knowledge, new approaches to teaching, or new information about curriculum development?
3. Does the article stimulate the reader's intellect and inspire the reader to evaluate and/or apply the information?
4. Does the article communicate effectively?
5. Does the article contain those enduring qualities that command the attention of today's social studies educator?

While members of our committee were selecting articles for inclusion in this anthology, they observed that some articles—particularly those published several years ago—contained sex specific pronouns (*He* when referring to a student or school administrator, *she* when referring to an elementary teacher, etc.) and other comparable references. We did not delete this material, because of our conviction that competent scholarship dictates that articles selected to be reprinted in an anthology should be published *as they were originally written*. The only exception to this policy concerns the authors' professional titles and institutional affiliations. Wherever possible, we have updated this information, in the hope that it will provide the reader with current information regarding the authors.

We wish to acknowledge with gratitude the valuable contributions made by the authors of the articles, and by the members of the advisory committee for the preparation of this book. We appreciate the insightful reviews rendered by John Dunn, Timothy Little, Gary Manson, and Stanley Wronski. We are also deeply indebted to Ruthann Bratt, who competently managed the secretarial tasks involved in this publication. Finally, we wish to thank our own institutions, Michigan State University and the University of California at Riverside, for the support they provided.

William W. Joyce
East Lansing, Michigan

Frank L. Ryan
Riverside, California

Contents

Foreword by **Howard D. Mehlinger** iii

Introduction by **William W. Joyce and Frank L. Ryan** v

Dedication ix

I. **Instructional Strategies and Techniques** x

A. Strategies

1. The Student as a Researcher

   Ronald Wheeler   Instructional Implications of
   and **Kevin P. Kelly**   Historical Research
                               for the Elementary Grades   2

   John R. Lee   Some Thoughts on
                               Descriptive Research Procedures
                               for Children   7

   Alan J. Hoffman   A Case for Using Survey
                               Techniques with Children
                               (with Some Reservations)   11

   Arthur K. Ellis   The Utilization of Experimental
   and **David W. Johnson**   Research Methods by
                               Teachers and Students   17

2. Values Clarification

   Sidney B. Simon   Values-Clarification vs.
                               Indoctrination   24

3. Simulation

   R. Garry Shirts   Simulations, Games,
                               and Related Activities
                               for Elementary Classrooms   31

B. Techniques

1. Learning Activities

   Jack R. Fraenkel   The Importance
                               of Learning Activities   37

2. Using Learning Centers

   James M. Larkin   The Learning Center
   and **Jane J. White**   in the Social Studies Classroom   44

3. Utilizing the Community

   David G. Armstrong   A Framework for Utilizing
   and **Tom V. Savage, Jr.** the Community for Social
                               Learning in Grades 4 to 6   65

C. Applications to Teacher Education

1. Modules

   Michael L. Hawkins   The Use of Modules in
                               Teacher Education   73

2. Microteaching/Videotaping
Mario D. Rabozzi   Microteaching/Videotaping
Experiences in the
Methods Course   81
3. Prototype, Simulation, Protocol Materials
Wayne L. Herman, Jr.   Performance Competencies:
Lessons Using a Prototype,
Simulation, and Protocol Materials 87

II. **Instructional Topics, Programs of Study, and Textbooks**   96

A. *Topics*

1. Moral Education
Richard K. Jantz   The Role of Moral Education
and Trudi A. Fulda   in the Public Elementary School   98
2. Law
Arlene F. Gallagher   Premises for Law   106
3. Consumerism
Timothy Little   A Simulation To Lunch
a Study of Law and Consumerism 112

4. Career Education
Lorraine Sundal Hansen   Career Development
and W. Wesley Tennyson   as Self Development: Humanizing
the Focus for Career Education   118
5. Ethnic Studies
James A. Banks   Developing Racial Tolerance
with Literature
on the Black Inner-City   128
6. Global Education
Charlotte J. Anderson   Global Education in
and Lee F. Anderson   Elementary Schools: An Overview 135

B. *Programs*

1. Man: A Course of Study
John·G. Herlihy   Man: A Course of Study
An Exemplar
of the New Social Studies   141

C. *Textbooks*

1. Evaluation
Arthur S. Nichols   Evaluating Textbooks for
and Anna Ochoa   Elementary Social Studies:
Criteria for the 'Seventies   145

III. Instructional Environments   150

A. The Hidden Curriculum

Frank L. Ryan   Implementing the Hidden
                                 Curriculum of the Social Studies   152

B. Integrated Teaching

Beverly Jeanne Armento   Let's Get it Together:
and Judith Preissle Goetz A Case for Integrated Teaming   157

C. Open Classrooms

Vito Perrone   Social Studies
and Lowell Thompson   in the Open Classroom   163

D. Early Childhood

Bernard Spodek   Social Studies for Young Children:
                           Identifying Intellectual Goals   170
Vincent Rogers   Reaction   179

Location of Authors' Articles in Social Education   182

About the Editors

A former elementary teacher, William W. Joyce is Professor of Education at Michigan State University, where he teaches undergraduate and graduate courses in elementary social studies. He has served as Chairperson of the College and University Faculty Assembly of the National Council for the Social Studies and has been a member of various NCSS committees. His publications include an elementary social studies textbook published by Follett, four professional textbooks, and various instructional media for use in elementary social studies classes. His most recent publication is *Teaching Elementary Social Studies Through the Human Experience* (Holt, Rinehart and Winston, 1978), which he co-authored with Janet Alleman-Brooks. Currently he is editor of the Elementary Education Section of *Social Education*.

Frank L. Ryan is Professor of Education at the University of California, Riverside. He has taught in the elementary grades of the San Diego City Schools. In 1976 the NCSS awarded him the Exemplary Research Citation. He is a co-author of an elementary social studies series, *Windows on the World* (Houghton Mifflin), author of *Exemplars for the New Social Studies* (Prentice-Hall, 1971), and co-author (with Arthur K. Ellis) of *Instructional Implications of Inquiry* (Prentice-Hall, 1974); and he serves as consulting editor to the *Journal of Educational Research*. Since 1972 he has served on the Board of Advisors to the Elementary Education Section of *Social Education*.

Dedication

We dedicate this publication to John R. Lee (1923-1976). A long-term member of the Board of Advisors for the Elementary Education Section of Social Education, Dr. Lee was Professor of Education at Northwestern University, Evanston, Illinois. Those of us who are his former students and colleagues will never forget the impression he made on our lives. Truly, he exemplified the highest standards of our profession.

SECTION I
Instructional Strategies
and Techniques

The articles in this section focus on classroom instruction. They are organized into three broad categories: strategies, techniques, and applications to teacher education.

Discovery teaching, inquiry, and learner involvement have great significance in the first set of articles, which view the student as a researcher. It is especially noteworthy that within each of these four articles specific theoretical considerations are developed and then translated into specific classroom applications. Lee presents a generalized plan for guiding students to pose questions and collect the relevant data, and includes an application of the plan to analysis of textbooks for sexist tendencies. Historical and sociological procedures that young learners might use to gather and interpret data from their immediate environment are presented in articles by Wheeler and Kelly and by Hoffman. Similarly, Ellis and Johnson present explicit examples of how students can conduct social science experiments by manipulating specific variables, collecting and analyzing data, and drawing inferences.

Values clarification is one of several instructional trends from the 1960s that continues to attract serious attention in the 1970s. The specific values-clarification applications offered by Simon have great relevance for teachers, since they can be supplemented by such related procedures for working with value conflicts as role playing and "magic circle" discussions.

Shirts offers encouragement to teachers who are considering the possibility of designing their own simulations in order to meet specific instructional needs; this possibility seems especially appropriate for primary grade teachers.

Fraenkel, after developing the premise that different types of learning activities serve different functions, delineates four categories of learning activities and offers specific examples for each. The perceptive reader will recognize in her or his own experience numerous examples of the learning activities proposed by Fraenkel and reflected in the many suggestions for learning centers offered by Larkin and White. Learning centers may be thought of as one vehicle among many possibilities for presenting social studies materials. Similarly, among many potential settings available for implementing social studies instruction, Armstrong and Savage offer a framework of community-focused social studies.

The final articles of Part I are representative of how multiple instructional procedures might be employed in a variety of settings to assist pre-service and in-service teachers in acquiring the instructional competencies required to implement current social studies programs.

Instructional Implications of Historical Research for the Elementary Grades

Ronald Wheeler and Kevin P. Kelly

Recent Trends in Historical Research

In the past ten years the "social science" approach to historical studies has gained a major degree of acceptance within the historical profession. This approach is not simply a revisionist position offering new "correct" reinterpretations of older, more traditional historians. Rather it cuts across the board and affects various schools of thought because it offers all historians a new methodological slant—a new way of dealing with their traditional concerns. Moreover not only does it aid historians in their task of explaining past human behavior, it also sharpens their focus on the process of historical change, forcing historians to deal with it with more precision.

The social science-oriented historian adopts interdisciplinary interests borrowing heavily from sociologists, anthropologists, and others. In his choice of subject matter, the historian studies the family and the processes of urbanization and modernization. The anthropologist's holistic approach to the study of communities is inspiring historians to re-examine past communities. But subject matter is only one way in which the historian learns from the social scientist. More important is his acceptance of the basically scientific methods of the social scientist. Increasingly historians adopting this approach strive to establish explicit models of explanation—models which provide hypotheses verifiable through precise testing. Vague notions about causation such as the democratization of the frontier have been replaced with explicit models of economic growth.

No development is more important to the growth of this approach to history than the application of the computer to historical investigation. The

RONALD WHEELER is Associate Professor of Education and KEVIN P. KELLY is Assistant Professor of History at the College of William and Mary, Williamsburg, Virginia.

computer makes it possible for the historian to handle large amounts of data in a way impossible to an earlier generation of scholars. Although nineteenth-century census schedules have long been available the nature and amount of information contained in them could only be utilized effectively by the computer. Personal estate inventories which have long been used by colonial American historians to illustrate the life style of the colonial gentry can now be systematically examined to determine the actual distribution of wealth, changes within that distribution, and most importantly, to correlate these changes to other social and economic events of the period. Legislature roll-call votes, city directories, southern plantation account books, vital statistics of births and deaths, and much more are now added to the historian's more traditional sources of information like personal letters, diaries, and newspapers.

These new sources of information reinforce the historian's scientific methodology. The vast bulk of these data is quantifiable and as such is ideally suited to statistical analysis. The use of statistical procedures to uncover trends, provide correlations and determine levels of probable significance has not relieved the historian of his basic job of explanation, but it has greatly advanced his ability to frame explicit hypotheses which can be tested. The result is a history more clearly focused on the processes of historical development.

Perhaps no historical inquiry demonstrates more thoroughly the interdisciplinary and scientific approach than the study of the family. For a long time, historians felt the family to be only of antiquarian interest and left its study to genealogists. But now, guided by sociologists who long identified the family as a basic unit of social organization and anthropologists who explored the importance of kinship networks, historians are beginning to re-examine the family. Basic questions to the historian of the family concern size and demographic characteristics of families, the shape of intrafamilial structure (i.e., extent of parental authority over children) and relationships between families in society.

It is not possible in this brief article to survey all of the great amount of work being done by the social science-oriented historians. However, it is hoped that this overview has provided the reader with at least the flavor of the latest developments in the field. Those interested in delving into the literature should consult the *Journal of Social History,* the *Journal of Interdisciplinary Studies* and the *Historical Methods Newsletter.*

Instructional Implications

Too often history has been taught as a bland mixture of unrelated facts about people, places and events. Fenton suggests that "a student who learns facts and generalizations about the past without becoming involved in the process of inquiry—and most students in American schools do exactly this—does not study history."[1] In other words, to really study history, a student must do the things an historian does. What does an historian do? To put it simply, historians sift through old documents, diaries, books, letters and the like to search for answers to questions. It is hard to imagine an eight- or nine-year-old child equally engrossed in similar activities. The emerging social science approach to history, however, has the capability of allowing young learners to study history in a potentially more exciting and meaningful way. Instead of studying the causes of the Civil War, or who discovered America, quantifiable indicators of life styles can be introduced, giving the child a sense of the flow of social change. A student can experiment with sources and conclusions of data he has generated and readily imagine himself and his own life style in comparison to the past.

Historians now studying the family use concepts and inquiry techniques borrowed from the sociologist and anthropologists. The focus of these investigations is not on the great or near-great people or events in American History, but rather on a pervasive social institution. While a child may never have heard of Thomas Jefferson or Bunker Hill, he does have direct, concrete experience as a participating member of a family unit. His teacher can tap this experiential base by asking a series of questions designed to identify the problem or problems to be investigated. A lead-in to the "family" investigation might be to ask the class what things they know about the family. Predictable responses might include: families live in houses, apartments, cities, farms, etc.; there is a mother or father or both in a family; some members of the family work; and there are usually brothers and sisters in the family. Next, the teacher could focus on family size by asking each student to state the first names of his brothers and sisters. The teacher tallies the responses on the chalkboard.

Suppose the class finds that most of the students are members of two-children families. What does that tell them? First, it establishes an average family size for their class, but, more important, this information serves as a springboard for investigating the past. Now the students might be interested in finding out the average family size for their parents, grandparents, and even great-grandparents.

When the students start to consider family size at different intervals of time they are beginning to grapple with precisely the same kinds of questions that professional historians are interested in. Questions like: Does family size change through generations? If so, why? What variables might affect change? An historian might go directly to published U.S. census reports in attempting to answer some of these questions, but in the classroom a more appropriate procedure would be for the teacher to have the students generate their own data. Together the teacher and students can construct a questionnaire to be taken home and completed by the students' parents and other members of their families. Drawing on the material the students have already been exposed to, the class may decide that other questions ought to be included in the questionnaire in addition to those about family size. The final questionnaire might ask for the following information about students' parents, grandparents, and great-grandparents:

- Where were they born?
- When were they born?
- Where have they lived?
- What was or is their occupation?
- Did they always have the same occupation?
- How many brothers and sisters do they or did they have?

When the students return the completed questionnaires to school there are multiple possibilities for their use. Certainly a first step in processing these data would be for the teacher to help the students enumerate, group and label questionnaire items. For example: How many grandparents were from four-children families? Five-children families? What kinds of work did grandparents do? How many grandparents are in each work category? After these data have been processed the student can make some descriptive statements about the family. Suppose, for example, that the students find that most grandparent families had five children, were farmers, and were not born in the state where the school is located; and that most parent families had three children, were city dwellers, and were born in the state where the school is located. Knowing this, the teacher can guide the students to arrange these data chronologically. Once a time line is developed the students can examine relationships among these data; e.g.: Are there changes in family size, location, and occupation through generations? What are the similarities and differences? Do any patterns emerge? Based upon the hypothetical class findings listed above, the students might observe that when we compare parent and grandparent families the average family size is declining and that more families are living in cities than in rural areas. The teacher might have the students speculate as to whether or not there is any connection between parent and grandparent family size and location. He could ask: What would be the advantages of having a lot of children if you were a farmer? Would a large family be a disadvantage if you lived in the city? Perhaps some students might reach a tentative conclusion that children are important to the economic well-being of the farm family. In this investigation the students deal with a number of variables (i.e., categories of data) simultaneously. In this case the variables are family size, location and time. Such activities are crucial for children to begin to realize that historical events are the result of multiple causes rather than of a single cause.

Thus far the students have abstracted quantitative data from the original personal statements on the questionnaires. To humanize some of the abstract ideas that the students have been dealing with, a variety of activities could be interwoven throughout the study of the family. Some possibilities might include:

1. Students could bring to class photographs of themselves, parents, grandparents and great-grandparents. Family trees can be developed and displayed on the bulletin board and in student-made books.

2. Students' grandparents could talk to the class about commonplace things that they did when they were the students' age. For example: Where they went to

school; what subjects they studied; what were their favorite sports, foods, books, music, etc.; and how they traveled from place to place.

3. Grandparents or parents could demonstrate to the class skills that were necessary when they were young, such as making bread, shucking corn or plucking chickens.

4. Using a local *City Directory* from either parents' or grandparents' era, students could re-create "Mainstreet"—e.g., any major thoroughfare. (City directories list shops and homes and pinpoint their relative location.) Let one group of students outline "Mainstreet" on a large sheet of white construction paper and then use blocks, paper cartons and the like to simulate shops and homes. Have another group of students do the same thing, except this group uses a recent *City Directory* and re-creates "Mainstreet" today. After the groups have completed their projects let them compare the two "Mainstreets," noting similarities and differences. If changes are observed, let the students discuss why they think they occurred. Parents, grandparents, older people, photographs, maps, pictures and direct observation would be helpful in verifying the accuracy of both the re-created streets and the inferences made during the discussion.

5. Students could examine pictures and advertisements in old catalogues, newspapers and magazines to draw inferences about the tools, food, clothing, furniture, machines, and so on that might be found in the shops and homes along "Mainstreet." Historical societies, city libraries, and newspaper companies are often good sources for these data.

The "family" investigation and related activities are illustrative, rather than exhaustive, of the possible applications of the social science approach to the study of history. The *City Directory* activity is only one way students can begin to study urban history. Another approach would be to have students select certain occupations in their city and compare them at different points in time using the "Yellow Pages" of old telephone books.[2] By plotting these locations on a city map, students could determine patterns of residential, commercial, and industrial growth through time. Likewise, oral histories can be constructed from interviews with older people that illuminate the past. Through the inclusion in their social studies program of the kind of lessons just described, teachers can begin to involve students in an aura of historical inquiry activities.

Footnotes

[1] Edwin Fenton, "A Structure of History," in Irving Morrissett (ed.), *Concepts and Structure in the New Social Science Curricula* (New York: Holt, Rinehart and Winston, Inc., 1967), p. 51.

[2] Adapted from Frank L. Ryan and Arthur K. Ellis, *Instructional Implications of Inquiry* (Englewood Cliffs, N.J.: Prentice-Hall, Inc., 1974), pp. 32-34.

Some Thoughts on Descriptive Research Procedures for Children

John R. Lee

A first-grade girl looks out the classroom window, walks over to the bulletin board, selects one card from each of four groups of cards, and pins her selections on the daily weather chart. One card shows an umbrella and rain. The second shows a thermometer and the word COOL. The third shows a small tree bending slightly in the wind. The last shows thick gray clouds.

This girl has observed and described the weather outside. Her description involved four elements of weather. She has shown it is raining, it is cool, the wind is blowing briskly, and the sky is cloudy and sunless. As she sits down, she says, "I like it when it rains. It makes the grass greener."

She has demonstrated certain skills, she is developing concepts about weather and its component elements, and she has expressed an attitude toward rainy weather. Without a white coast and a maze full of rats, without a computer and a chalkboard filled with formulas, without a Ph.D. and a foundation, she has engaged in a bit of descriptive research.

Obviously, she described something, and, obviously, she described something she observed. But can we call this research? The answer is *yes* if you can accept certain limitations. Her variables were loose operational categories (the sun is shining or it is cloudy). Her measuring instruments were simple (before she came inside, the air on her skin felt *Hot, Warm, Cool,* or *Cold*). Her sample was not randomly selected (it is raining *here*). Her question was simple (what's the weather?). The facts she reported triggered a hypothetical "rain makes the grass greener." Thus, her descriptive research could have led to further investigation of a related idea.

At the time of his death in October, 1976, JOHN R. LEE was Professor of Education at Northwestern University, Evanston, Illinois.

If you can accept these limitations, then you can accept that a "careful hunting for facts or truth" is a sufficient definition for research by children in the elementary grades. A Nobel Laureate in physics and the father of the operational definition once said, "The scientific method, as far as it is a method, is nothing more than doing one's damnedest with one's mind, no holds barred."[1]

Doing one's damnedest requires objective observation and clear, accurate description. Children from the ages of five through eleven observe and describe constantly in their everyday life. As kindergarten through sixth-grade pupils, these same children, with guidance from their teachers, can become even more effective observers and describers. For example:

A second-grade girl says, "I want to be a patrol boy someday."
A boy says, "You can't. Only boys can be patrol boys."
A teacher asks, "Are you sure of that ? How can we find out?"

The pupils fire away, "We can look at all the patrols and see" . . . "We can look in our books" . . . "We can ask Mrs. Potts. She runs the safety stuff" . . . "I'll ask my brother. He's on the patrol" . . . "We can ask the principal. He thinks he knows everything."

Groups are formed to follow up on these (and any other) suggestions. The teacher asks each group, "What will you do? What will you look for? What will you ask? When will you do this? When will you tell the rest of us what you found out?"

The groups set about their tasks. On the way home, pupils check the patrols they pass. The identification process isn't difficult: Is it a boy or a girl wearing the orange belt? The book-lovers pore over their textbooks, looking for pictures showing safety patrols. Older brothers and sisters are questioned. A surprised Mrs. Potts answers questions. The principal can't be found; he had to go to a meeting downtown.

The reports come in. There are seven safety stations. There are two safety boys—always boys—at each station. Mrs. Potts confirms these facts: yes, seven stations; yes, two boys at each station; yes, only boys. Yes, all are sixth graders. The book examiners found eight pictures in three books; all pictures showed only boys on patrol duty.

"I told you so!" cries our second-grade boy. "Only boys can be patrol boys!"

Our second-grade girl is no patient Griselda, "I don't care! I want to be on the safety patrol when I get to sixth grade."

What has gone on here? An interesting question was raised. Plans for gathering information were discussed. Observations were conducted. Information was noted and remembered. The situation was described. The facts were now known to these second graders.

The comment made by the girl after the facts were known indicates this class was now faced with the same problem many descriptive researchers must face. Description provides hard data, but these data describe a *status quo.* The facts tell us what a situation is; they don't tell us how the situation came about, or how we think it ought to be, or how we might go about changing an unsatisfactory *status quo.*

Almost all descriptive research ends with conclusions or interpretations leading to harder questions of a problem-solving nature. For this second-grade teacher, the obvious next questions become: Why are *all* safety patrol members boys? Why can't girls be members of the safety patrol? The principle trumpets itself: good research spawns more research.

Elementary school social studies programs are filled with topics susceptible to descriptive research. What kinds of containers and carriers can be found in use in our school? What is needed for people in local stores to produce goods and services? What examples of sexism can we find in the textbooks we read? What happens if pupils share in making rules for their classroom? What does it feel like to be discriminated against? Do all library books tell the same story about the life of Jane Addams or the life of George Washington?

The teacher who wants to lead pupils to conduct descriptive research needs to consider certain general ideas. First, research should be conducted in a climate where there is freedom to fail—pupils must feel psychologically safe to state a hunch, to test it, to err, and to say they have erred. Second, just as pupils must learn to use a textbook, they must have the opportunity to learn to do research—pupils must be guided as patiently and carefully to learn new methods as they are guided to learn new subject matter. Third, the general principles of readiness, motivation, practice, organization, and transfer apply as much to learning to do research as to other, more traditional topics and procedures—guiding research is a case of applying known principles of learning rather than seeking wholly new principles.

What happens with the topic of sexism in, say, a fifth grade? The question has been raised: Why do our textbooks put down women in so many ways? The first step is inquiry into the accuracy of the question. Thus, the research question becomes: Is it true that our social studies textbook puts down women?

Plans are laid. The fifth-grade social studies texts in the room will be examined. From this pilot study should come two products: first, hard facts for the books of one grade; and, a set of questions that will focus research in other textbooks of other grades.

The texts are examined (observed) and examples of put-downs are identified:

- here are pictures of Abraham Lincoln's parents. Under the father's picture is the caption, "His father was Mr. Thomas Lincoln." Under the mother's picture, "His mother was Mrs. Thomas Lincoln." Why not ". . . Mrs. Nancy. . . ?"
- two sentences from the text, "The brave farmers planted crops in the frontier forests. Their wives and children worked with them." Weren't the women and children farmers?
- from a section on Thanksgiving. A class is shown giving a play. The caption notes that boys are playing "hunters, farmers, Indians." All the girls are playing "mother."

- from an economics section. "This man is producing goods. This woman is helping to produce goods." Why is he producing while she is helping to produce?
- a city council is shown considering a new zoning law. All the "councilmen" are men.

From these and many other examples, the class concludes that women are put down in both text and pictures. The class also draws up a set of questions (a measuring instrument) to aid them in examining texts from all the earlier grades:

- Are women always shown as mothers while men are shown doing many interesting things?
- Is the man always shown as the money-maker in a family?
- Is the man shown in the more important job while the woman is shown as his helper (doctor and nurse)?
- Are all married women shown as mothers?
- In showing work done in the home, are there male jobs and female jobs? Is there any sharing of jobs?
- Are boys shown to be doing something active while girls are shown watching the boys?
- Are the stronger, bolder, taller, more active characters always boys?
- Are the smaller, cleaner, best dressed, more quiet characters always girls?
- Do such words as explorers, discoverers, pioneers, settlers, farmers, workers, representatives, and leaders mean men but not women?

This set of questions might not be inclusive enough for adult researchers, but a teacher can always ask what else the investigators might find. And, if the question is asked, then some class members will find other evidence.

These questions lead to observation. Evidence is found and recorded. The situation is described and the research question is answered. Then the original "why" question can be raised again for further research. The functions of descriptive research were met: hard facts bearing on an interesting question were produced; the researchers developed an understanding of how one type of knowledge is generated; and the research led to further productive research questions.

What this inquiry took was letting the pupils do *their* damnedest, no holds barred, to find answers to a question they considered important and interesting.

Footnotes

[1] Percy W. Bridgman, "Prospects for Intelligence," *The Yale Review*, V. 34 (1945), p. 450.

A Case for Using Survey Techniques with Children (with Some Reservations)

Alan J. Hoffman

Would you believe that most women age 30 and older think that women in general "nag" more than men? Would it surprise you to learn that men of all ages agree that women "nag" more than men, but that females below age 30 believe you can't decide "nagging" tendencies on the basis of sex differences? Sixth graders in a suburban school district outside Atlanta, Georgia tend to believe the above statements, at least as they apply to their community, and, what's more, they have some research collected from an opinion survey to support their beliefs.[1]

This experience in sampling opinions was the first for these children and their teacher. Perhaps recounting this experience might help readers who may wish to attempt it. Some suggestions and cautions for doing a survey with children are included. A primary-grade example of a sex role difference "survey" is also included as well as some other suggested topics in which use of a survey could be incorporated.

Why Sample Opinion?

Children (adults too) often express opinions which state or imply that everyone agrees something is true. One week prior to a unit on the changing role of women throughout history, the teacher listened and recorded opinions she heard her children express, particularly those which stated differences based on sex type. A few examples were:

"Girls are so weak; let me open the window."
"Boys are so impatient! Mrs. Hoffman said we'd see the film after lunch."
"Nag, nag. Where'd you learn that from . . . your mother?"

ALAN J. HOFFMAN is Associate Professor of Education at Georgia State University, Atlanta, Georgia.

After a brief historical study of the changing role of men and women, the teacher discussed some of the attitudes some people once held toward women. Were these valid differences? She then read to the class some of the statements she had heard students make about sex differences. Were these opinions of all people? Of all people in this class? Students soon discovered that this was not necessarily the case.

The teacher then explained that one way to answer some question concerning attitudes, opinions, and beliefs would be to ask everyone involved. Students soon saw the difficulties involved, particularly when you were talking about large groups of people (money, time, energy).

She explained that when you only take the opinion of some of the people involved with a particular issue, the procedure is called *sampling*. One of the problems in sampling is deciding whether the sample will be accurate; that is, representative of the whole group, the *population*.[2]

Children were then told about some of the reasons surveys are conducted. Consumer market sampling, voter opinion surveying, and some research in the physical and social sciences were mentioned. The children were told that the type of research they would be doing would be a simplified procedure that a sociologist might do.

Starting the Research

Children were led to make some educated guesses (called hypotheses by behavioral researchers) about what they might find concerning attitudes about women today. A few of their many hypotheses were:

Older people will feel that males and females are basically different when it comes to performing certain jobs. Young people won't be so sure.
All people will feel that women are the worst naggers and the nosiest.
All people will feel that men are stronger and better at sports.

The opinion survey was then constructed. Children were encouraged to state questions which were not heavily biased. A few items drawn from the questionnaire used in the survey are shown at the right.

Administering the Questionnaire

The children took the questionnaire first. All responses were then placed in a sealed box in the room. Then the class, with the help of its teacher, constructed a cover letter which would accompany each questionnaire. The letter briefly described the unit the children were studying and explained that the interviewer (the student) knew the value of allowing the interviewee to remain anonymous. An envelope supplied by the student was provided with each questionnaire. The interviewee was instructed to fill out the questionnaire and then place it in the envelope and seal it.

Children were each asked to get the opinions of four people, preferably two males, two females. They were encouraged to sample the opinions of parent-guardians, relatives, friends, hopefully getting the opinions of several

Questionnaire (Sample)

Person responding, please answer the following completely. Incomplete questionnaires cannot be used in our data analysis. Thank you!

Circle one:

sex—male   female

age—10–20   21–30   31–40   41–50   51–60   61–70
            71–above

In your opinion, do men or women perform each of these activities better? Check your answer.

Activity	Men	Women	No Difference
Cooking			
Teaching			
Making Decisions			
Cutting Hair			
Politicians			
Managerial Position			
Driver (bus, car, taxi)			
Medical Work			

Do you feel that one sex is more likely to show any of the following traits?

Trait	Men	Women	No Difference
Practical			
Intelligent			
Open-minded			
Patient			
Nagging			
Independent			
Polite			
Nosey			

age groups. It is important to note here the need for a relatively safe and successful sample. Children can later learn the frustration of standing at a shopping center on a rainy afternoon sampling the opinions of an unenthusiastic electorate.

Analyzing and Drawing Conclusions

Tallying the responses can be a nightmare. Help the youngsters to organize the data for tallying. On page 14 are parts of two tally sheets used in the study. Tallying in red for one group (for example, men in this study) and blue for another group can help in comparing the data. In this study 182 responses were returned from 255 sent out.

MALES

TRAIT	RESPONSE CHOICE	10 - 20			21 - 30	
		MEN	WOMEN	NO DIFFERENCE	MEN	WOMEN
Practical		④ IIII		⑭ THL THL IIII	② II	
Intelligent		② III	④ II	⑬ THL THL III		
Open-minded		② II	③ III	⑬ THL THL III	① I	
Patient		① I	⑤ THL	⑫ THL THL II	① I	③ III
Nagging			⑪ THL THL I	⑦ THL II		⑤ THL
Independent		⑦ THL II		⑪ THL THL I	③ III	① I
Nosey		① I	⑨ THL IIII	⑧ THL III		⑥ THL I

FEMALES

TRAIT	RESPONSE CHOICE	10 - 20			21 - 30	
		MEN	WOMEN	NO DIFFERENCE	MEN	WOMEN
Practical		② II	④ IIII	⑯ THL THL THL		③ III
Intelligent		③ III	① I	⑱ THL THL THL III		
Open-minded		① I	⑥ THL I	⑮ THL THL THL	① I	①
Patient		② II	⑩ THL THL	⑩ THL THL		② II
Nagging		① I	⑧ THL III	⑬ THL THL III	① I	⑥ THL I
Independent		② II	② II	⑱ THL THL THL III	② II	① I
Nosey			⑨ THL IIII	⑬ THL THL III	① I	④ IIII

This is not the time to lay chi-square on your children! Tell them there are many sophisticated ways to analyze the data which they may learn later in high school or college and then reduce analysis to things like means, medians, and modes. Since the number of responses may vary with age groups and with regard to male and female, using percentages proved helpful. This is also a good time to include graph and chart skills.

In looking at the results, probing questions can lead children to not only check the accuracy of certain hypotheses they have made, but can also lead to better refinement of them as evidenced by their views on "nagging," mentioned at the beginning of the article. An excellent evaluation question would be to ask children for advice about how the questionnaire might be constructed differently if the teacher should decide to have next year's class do a survey.

A Primary-Grade Example

Obviously, attempting to use a survey with first graders requires some modification from the lesson previously presented. Again, however, the teacher began by collecting certain "truth" claims; e.g., "big boys don't cry," "good little girls don't cause trouble," "girls are smarter."[3]

She then explained to the class that different people have different opinions about what girls and boys are like, or should be like. She created an atmosphere of curiosity concerning how alike and how different their feelings might be.

Attitudes of the children were surveyed by having the children place a boy doll and then a girl doll along a poster board continuum with choices ranging from very weak to very strong. Attitudes about intelligence, cleanliness, tendency to cry, complain, fight, and follow directions as they related to sex-role stereotyping were also sampled.

Children helped in tabulating the results. This was accomplished by constructing the sheets so that only one item for one sex was recorded by each group. Naturally some cross-checking was necessary.

While the analysis of data was somewhat limited, some children were able to see the influence of others, particularly their parents and older brothers and sisters, on how they came to feel. This was partially accomplished by having children take home their survey and discuss it with members of their family.

While the steps involved in utilizing the survey technique were essentially the same for this primary teacher, there was a need for simplifying the process regarding the stating of hypotheses, survey construction, data collection, and analysis.

Other Suggested Topics

All of the social science disciplines present areas in which children could sample opinions. A few examples follow:

History—Trace historical background of relatives of the children. How many family generations can people recall?

Anthropology—Survey the different religions in your class/school/community. How does this background compare with others in the United States?

Economics—Find out about attitudes of consumers on use of credit cards, cash, checks, etc.

Geography—Study the moving patterns of people both inside and outside your community.

Political Science—Select an issue of current local/national interest and find out what your class, other classes, or the community may think about it.

Conclusions

The steps outlined in the article represent an attempt to involve students in seven important steps of problem solving; namely:

1. Forming hypotheses and making predictions
2. Writing questions and questionnaire
3. Sampling
4. Administering questionnaire
5. Tabulating results
6. Analyzing data
7. Forming conclusions and generalizations and reviewing methods employed.[4]

The data collected from a two-page questionnaire will convince any teacher and youngster of the value of a computer! At last word, the children doing the sex-role difference study were still going strong in analyzing the data they collected.

Footnotes

[1] Many thanks are extended to my wife, Nancy Hoffman, sixth-grade teacher, Jolly Elementary School, Dekalb County, Georgia, and to her students, for their efforts in constructing, administering, and analyzing a survey on sex role differences.

[2] Later in the data collection procedure, children were helped to see that their sample was somewhat *biased*. The sample was selected to enhance success in collection. It was made up of selected parents, relatives, and friends and had not been selected *randomly*; that is, by chance.

[3] Many thanks are extended to Gloria Lapin, first-grade teacher, Evansdale Elementary School, Dekalb County, Georgia, for her efforts in conducting and reporting this survey.

[4] These steps are outlined and developed in Herbert M. Blalock *et al.*, *Sociological Resources for the Social Studies*, Boston: Allyn and Bacon, 1969. See particularly the booklet entitled *Testing for Truth: A Study of Hypothesis Evaluation*.

The Utilization of Experimental Research Methods by Teachers and Students

Arthur K. Ellis and David W. Johnson

What do you do when what you know about teaching is contradictory? Take the case of Jeannette. Jeannette was working hard individualizing her social studies curriculum because she believed that students would achieve more and like social studies better if they worked individually on their own materials and at their own pace. Then she attended a workshop on structuring learning and found out that most research studies indicated that cooperation among students produced more learning and better attitudes than did individualization. Being committed to individualization and a rather skeptical person, she decided she would have to see it for herself in order to believe that cooperation would be more effective for teaching than is individualization.

In order to find out how cooperation among students compared to working individually, Jeannette knew she would have to organize her classroom so she could systematically observe the behavior of her students under controlled conditions. Deliberate and controlled observation is necessary for objectivity. Her classroom had to be arranged so that any observer of the students would see the same results. This intersubjectivity testifies that the observation is uncontaminated by any factors except those common to all observers.

Next, Jeannette decided what aspects of student behavior she would observe. Student achievement in a social studies unit and student attitudes toward learning social studies were picked. She decided that if cooperation among students resulted in higher achievement and better attitudes than did individualization, she would change her methods of teaching.

After some reflection Jeannette realized that observing whether or not

ARTHUR K. ELLIS is Associate Professor of Education and DAVID W. JOHNSON is Professor of Educational Psychology at the University of Minnesota, Minneapolis.

cooperation was related to achievement and attitudes was not enough. She wanted to know whether cooperation or individualization would *cause* student achievement and the acquisition of positive attitudes. Simply observing that cooperating students were achieving more would not prove that cooperation causes achievement. It might be that the brighter and more motivated students liked to cooperate and, therefore, they were achieving more, not because of the cooperation but rather because they were brighter and more motivated. There might even be a chance that high achievement causes cooperation among students! Just observing that cooperation and achievement are found together (i.e., are correlated) would not prove any superiority of cooperation over individualization. In a correlational relationship it is not clear which variable "causes" the other or if in fact some third variable (such as intelligence) is "causing" the observed relationship. Besides finding a correlation Jeannette realized that she would have to prove that the "cause" variable changed before the "effect" variable and that some extraneous variable such as intelligence or motivation was not responsible for the results of her observations.

In experimental research one distinguishes between the independent and dependent variables being observed. An *experiment* is a situation in which one observes the relationship between two variables by deliberately producing a change in one and observing whether this produces a change in the other. The *independent variable* is the one the experimenter changes directly. In Jeannette's case the independent variable is cooperative interaction among students or individual efforts on the part of students with no interaction with others. The *dependent variable* is the one whose value is affected by the change in the independent variable; its value is dependent on the value of the independent variable. In Jeannette's case the dependent variables are student achievement and student attitudes toward social studies.

Jeannette has two independent variables (cooperation and individualization) and two dependent variables (student achievement and student attitudes). She now has to *operationalize* these variables by describing what behaviors she will observe as indices of the variables. *Cooperation* can be operationalized by defining it as students working together on one group lesson for which all members will receive the same score or grade while demonstrating certain skills such as communicating, helping, and sharing. *Individualization* can be operationalized by defining it as students working alone on an individual lesson for which each will receive an individual score or grade while demonstrating certain skills such as ignoring other students, working independently, and using only one's own resources and materials. Student *achievement* can be operationalized as the (1) number of social studies projects completed, (2) the quality of each project, and (3) scores on an examination on the material covered, the exam being given individually to the students working on individualized projects and cooperatively to students working on cooperative projects. Student *attitudes* can be operationalized as the score on a series of questions asking how much students like social studies. Once the independent and dependent variables are clearly operationalized, Jeannette can make a decision about the design of her experiment and the way in which students are assigned to cooperative or individualized projects.

The type of design Jeannette uses for her experiment and the way in which she assigns students to be in one condition or the other are closely related. The best type of design looks like this:

1. Randomly assign half the class to the cooperative condition and half to the individualized condition.
2. Give clear instructions as to how they are to work on the social studies projects, how they will be evaluated, when their work will be evaluated, and how long the experiment will last.
3. Provide all the materials and resources each group or each student will need.
4. Have them begin work while you observe to ensure that their behavior is appropriate to the conditions (i.e., students assigned to cooperative groups are not working individually or students assigned to work individually are not cooperating with each other).
5. Measure student achievement and attitudes on a daily, weekly, and final basis.
6. Compare the results to see if there is a difference between the students in the cooperative condition and the individualized condition.

One of the important aspects of conducting a valid experiment is to eliminate all possible sources of error in the observations. Random assignment of students to the cooperative or individualized conditions is the best way of ensuring that any differences found in achievement and attitudes are due to the way in which students learned and not due to intelligence, background, motivation, previous experience with similar projects, or other possible differences between the students in each condition. If Jeannette let students choose which way they wanted to complete the projects, for example, brighter or more knowledgeable students might all choose to be in one condition or the other, thus introducing an error due to ability or previous learning in the experiment. Sometimes it is possible to rank the students in the class on previous learning and ensure that the two conditions have equal numbers of high, medium, and low "previous-learning" students, but there are so many factors which might influence student achievement and attitudes that it is much safer to randomly assign students to each condition. If subjects are not randomly assigned, then the results of the experiment should be viewed with skepticism and doubt.

Other sources of error include the teacher's attitudes toward cooperation and individualization, the overall atmosphere of the school and the community, and the nature of the students' previous experience. The results of Jeannette's experiment would be much more convincing if she is able to get several teachers in several different schools and school districts to conduct the same experiment at the same time using the same operationalizations of the independent and dependent variables.

Once the experiment is over, Jeannette can analyze the results by finding the mean or average for the students in the cooperative condition and the students in the individualized condition. Through comparing the two means and the amount of variance in scores within each condition Jeannette can find the probability that the results are due to chance or due to the influences of working cooperatively versus working individually. Such a procedure is a "t-test" and can be found in introductory statistics books. Due to limited space it will not be explained here.

From the results of the t-test Jeannette will know the likelihood that her findings are due to chance versus the way in which learning was structured. She then needs to interpret what her findings mean and make a decision about what learning situations they can be generalized to and how the future teaching will be affected. The issue of generalization includes thinking about what teachers, what subjects, what students, and what schools the results can be applied to. It is important in making a decision about how to use the results of the experiment to compare them to the results of similar experiments conducted by other people. If Jeannette's results are similar to most of the other research studies and indicate that cooperative learning produces more achievement and better attitudes than does individualized instruction, then she can have confidence that her results are valid. If, however, they indicate that individualization is more effective than cooperation, Jeannette must decide how her study differed from the other studies and whether her results are free from error and more valid than the results of the other studies in the area. Then she can make a decision about what implications the results have for her teaching.

Having gained a measure of insight into the processes of experimentation, Jeannette decided to let her fifth-grade students attempt some experimental inquiry in their social studies. She felt that the conduct of experiments by the students themselves would give them an idea of how knowledge of human behavior is often generated. After a brief discussion in which she noted the procedures used in experimental design, Jeannette asked the students whether they could list some questions which could be researched through experimental inquiry.

> *Teddy:* Will the whole world ever get blown up?
> *Joshua:* Which is better—third grade or fifth grade?
> *Robyn:* When we played the "observation" game, you said it trained us to be good observers. We could do an experiment to find out.

The class decided that, given certain limitations in the areas of resources and controls, Teddy's question, though intriguing, would be unmanageable. Some students pointed out that Joshua's question dealt with preferences and could possibly be an interesting survey topic but that it would still need to be more narrowly defined.

The class decided that Robyn's question would be fun to research since it involved a game as a way of learning the social science skill of observation. Students noted that at least two different research questions could be posed.

Table 1

Outline of Experiment to Test Effects of Observation Game

Question: Does the observation game teach the skill of observation?

Hypothesis: The group that plays the observation game will have a higher average score on an observation test than the group that doesn't play the game.

Procedure: Each second grader in Room 2-A was randomly assigned to either the experimental group, which played the observation game, or the control group, which listened to short stories. Each day for four days the students in the experimental group played "Observation" for fifteen minutes while the control group heard stories for that amount of time. The "teachers" were two fifth-grade students who alternated each day between the two groups to minimize the effect of the instructor. There were fourteen second graders in each group.

Materials: *Experimental Group*
Eight picture cards depicting people doing various things, e.g., one card shows Indians harvesting corn and pumpkins. For each card there are ten questions which seek data about the card. To play the game, students are shown a card and told to look at it for one minute. Then the card is taken away and students are asked to answer questions about the picture on a score sheet. Two cards were used each day for the four days.
Control Group
Four animal stories. One story was read to the group each day.

Test: On the fifth day the entire class played the observation game. They used two new cards and the test consisted of twenty questions, ten about each picture.

Analysis: The average (mean) score was computed for each group. Table 2 illustrates the results obtained.

Inference: The observation game is a way to learn the skill of observation.

"Does the game teach the skill of observation?" or "Does the game teach the skill of observation better than some other way of teaching it?" Because this was a first attempt, the students decided to keep things simple and use the first question. They decided to conduct the experiment in a second-grade classroom. Table 1 illustrates the outline of their experiment.

In this case, Jeannette was content to let her fifth-grade researchers eyeball the difference in mean scores because she felt that a t-test would be too complicated for them. However, she mentioned the existence of such a test to the students and indicated to them that it is not always possible to know whether a difference in mean scores is significant merely by eyeballing the scores. Actually, electronic calculators, increasingly available, would greatly simplify the computations necessary for the t-test (see Table 2, p. 22).

Table 2
Scores of 2-A Students on Observation Test

Experimental Group		Control Group	
Student	*Score*	*Student*	*Score*
1. Peter A.	17	1. Tom C.	11
2. Martha A.	15	2. Robert E.	13
3. David C.	15	3. Alice H.	8
4. Terry E.	13	4. Jon H.	10
5. John G.	19	5. Melissa K.	18
6. Laurie H.	16	6. Stephanie M.	11
7. Dick M.	10	7. Hank M.	6
8. Mandy M.	17	8. Jane P.	15
9. David N.	16	9. Fred S.	12
10. Jeff P.	20	10. Stan S.	10
11. Cherie R.	16	11. Michael T.	13
12. Tina R.	15	12. Dana T.	12
13. Ralphy R.	11	13. Rhonda W.	5
14. Jim W.	14	14. Kristie Y.	8

Average (Mean) = 15.3   Average (Mean) = 10.8

Table 3
Experimental Study on the Effects of the
Rick/Janet Spelling Method

Question: Does the Rick/Janet Spelling Method yield results superior to those obtained by the regular spelling workbook?

Hypothesis: Students in the Rick/Janet spelling group will have higher scores than students in the workbook group.

Procedure: The students in Mrs. Annenberg's third-grade class were placed by random in two groups. One group studied spelling words for fifteen minutes each day for four days using the Rick/Janet Method. The other group studied the same words for the same amount of time. On the fifth day, both groups took the same test on the words.

Analysis: Student scores for each group were randomly paired and coded on a matrix.[1] When a student in the Rick/Janet group had a higher score than his/her paired partner, a square was filled diagonally down to the right. When a student in the workbook group had a higher score than his/her paired partner, a square was filled diagonally down to the left. No square was filled where partners tied. The results show that the workbook method yielded higher scores and the hypothesis was rejected.

Another teacher, Jack, was interested in having his students conduct experimental research in social studies. The class decided to test the effects of different ways to learn. Their experiments included "learning math alone versus working in pairs," "the Rick/Janet Spelling Method versus the workbook way," "solving riddles with training versus solving riddles with no training," and "the effects of information on sexist attitudes of boys and girls."

Table 3 outlines the experiment on the effects of the Rick/Janet spelling method (see p. 22).

Table 4 shows the test scores for each group, and Table 5 illustrates the matrix used to analyze the data statistically (below).

Table 4		Table 5	
Paired Test Scores for		Comparison of Test Scores:	
Both Spelling Groups		Rick-Janet Method vs. Workbook	
Pairings Based on Random Assignments			
Rick/Janet Group	Workbook Group		
17	19		
17	18		
18	25		
23	21		
20	16		
16	18		
18	21		
16	20		
21	21		
20	25		
10	25		
15	19		
15	20		
19	12		
21	16		
16			

In one sense, these experiments were all rather crude. They involved simple designs and analyses. Yet in another sense, the conceptual framework of experimentation was there in each case: the controlled situation, the manipulation of variables, and the analysis of cause and effect relationships occurring as a result of certain treatments. In each case, new information was generated, and kids and teachers were in a position of seeing how knowledge based on research comes to be.

References

1. Campbell, Donald T., and Julian Stanley, *Experimental and Quasi-experimental Designs for Research,* Chicago: Rand McNally and Company, 1963.

2. Isch, John, "How To Find Out If There Is a Relationship Between Two Things or If There Is a Difference Between Two Things," unpublished manuscript.

3. Ryan, Frank L., and Arthur K. Ellis, *Instructional Implications of Inquiry,* Englewood Cliffs: Prentice-Hall, Inc., 1974.

4. Wald, A., *Sequential Analysis,* New York: John Wiley and Sons, 1947.

Footnotes

[1] Our thanks to Professor John Isch for the translation of this statistical procedure.

Values-Clarification
vs.
Indoctrination

Sidney B. Simon

Whatever happened to those good old words we once used when we talked of values? Remember how comfortable it was to say *inculcate?* It was a nice, clean, dignified, closely shaved word if there ever was one. Then there was the old standby, *to instill*—usually followed by "the democratic values of our society." Doesn't anyone instill anymore? And what about the word *foster?* In schools, not so very long ago, we used to "foster" all over the place. But nobody does that much anymore. What has happened to the old familiar jargon of value teaching?

What happened was the realization that all the inculcating, instilling, and fostering added up to indoctrination; and despite our best efforts at doing the indoctrinating, we've come to see that it just didn't take. Most of the people who experienced the inculcation, instillation, and fostering seem not the much better for it. They appear to play just as much hanky-panky with income taxes as anyone else, and concerned letters-to-the-editor are not written by them in any great profusion. They pollute and defoliate; move to the suburbs to escape integration; buy convertibles with vinyl tops that collapse in roll-over accidents; fail to wear seat belts; and commit all kinds of sins even while they are saying the very words that have been dutifully inculcated, instilled, and fostered in them. It *is* discouraging.

At this point, one might ask: "Is it all that bad?" "Aren't they also among the good people who go to the polls in November, read the current events weeklies, and pay their Bankamericard charges on time?" Yes, of course. But in these troubled, confused, and conflicted times, we need people who can do much more than that. We desperately need men and women who know who

SIDNEY B. SIMON is Professor of Humanistic Education at the University of Massachusetts, Amherst, Massachusetts.

they are, who know what they want out of life, and who can name their names when controversy rages. We need people who know what is significant and what is trash, and who are not so vulnerable to demagoguery, blandness, or safety.

The indoctrination procedures of the past fail to help people grapple with all the confusion and conflict which abound in these baffling days. For example, in values-clarification, we apply a strategy which is deceptively simple. We ask students to spend some time listing the brand names in their home medicine cabinets. Just think of your own medicine cabinet as you are sitting reading this. What's in it? How many creams, ointments, and salves have you been sold? Do you use a brand-name, buffered product instead of plain old aspirin? How did you get started on that? What about the spray cans? How many are in your aerosol arsenal? What did you use before the product you now spray? How did all those brand names get there? Who bought them? What was the motivating force? How did you learn what to value as seen in your medicine cabinet? As long as you have the door to your cabinet open, why don't you pull out the cosmetic tray? How vulnerable are you to avoiding the hysteria surrounding all of us about getting a wrinkle? Getting old has become such a negative value. Who are the people who fear it?

In place of indoctrination, my associates and I are substituting a *process* approach to the entire area of dealing with values in the schools, which focuses on the process of valuing, not on the transmission of the "right" set of values. We call this approach *values-clarification,* and it is based on the premise that none of us has the "right" set of values to pass on to other people's children. Yes, there may be some things we can all agree upon, and I will grant you some absolutes, but when we begin to operationalize our values, make them show up in how we live our days and spend our nights, then we begin to see the enormous smugness of those people who profess they have the right values for others' children. The issues and hostility generated around hair length and dress and armbands are just the surface absurdity.

More dangerous is the incredible hypocrisy we generate when we live two-faced values and hustle the one right value to children. Think about the hundreds of elementary school teachers who daily stop children from running down the halls. I close my eyes and I see them with their arms outstretched, hands pressing against the chest of kids who put on their "brakes" in order to make the token slowdown until the teacher ducks into the teacher's room for a fast cigarette before all the kids get back to hear the cancer lecture. Think of those teachers preaching to children about the need to take turns and share. "We wait on lines, boys and girls, and we learn to share our crayons and paints in here. And, I don't want to see anybody in my class being a tattletale—except in cases of serious emergency, naturally." The words are all too familiar. I have used them in the old days. I have also seen myself cut into the cafeteria lunch line ahead of third graders. (Take turns? Well, not when we have so few minutes for lunch and always so much to do to get ready for afternoon classes.)

The alternative to indoctrination of values is *not* to do nothing. In this time of the anti-hero, our students need all the help we can give them if they are to make sense of the confusion and conflict inherited from the indoctrinated types. Moreover, we all need help in grappling with the chaos of the international scene, with the polarization of national life—not to mention the right-outside-the-door string of purely local dilemmas.

An approach to this problem is to help students learn a process for the clarification of their values, which is a far cry from indoctrination. The theory behind it can be found in *Values and Teaching* (Louis E. Raths, Merrill Harmin, and Sidney B. Simon, Columbus: Charles E. Merrill, 1966). In the remainder of this article, I will describe some of the strategies we are presently using to help students learn the process of values-clarification and begin lifelong searches for the sets of personal values by which to steer their lives.[1]

Five Value-Clarifying Strategies and their Use

Strategy # 1—Things I Love to Do

Ask students (teacher does it with them) to number from 1-20 on a paper. Then suggest they list, as rapidly as they can, 20 things in life which they really, *really* love to do. Stress that the papers will not be collected and "corrected," and that there is no right answer about what people *should* like. It should be emphasized that in none of values strategies should students be forced to participate. Each has the right to pass. Students may get strangely quiet; and, at first, they may even be baffled by such an unschool-like task as this. Flow with it, and be certain to allow enough time to list what they really love to do. Remember, at no time must the individual's privacy be invaded, and that the right of an individual to pass is sacrosanct.

When everyone has listed his 20 items, the process of coding responses can be started. Here are some suggested codes which you might ask the students to use:

1. Place the $ sign by any item which costs more than $3, each time you do it.
2. Put an *R* in front on any item which involves some RISK. The risk might be physical, intellectual, or emotional. (Which things in your own life that are things you love to do require some risk?)
3. Using the code letters *F* and *M*, record which of the items on your list you think your father and mother might have had on their lists if they had been asked to make them at YOUR age.
4. Place either the letter *P* or the letter *A* before each item. The "P" to be used for items which you prefer doing with PEOPLE, the "A" for items which you prefer doing ALONE. (Stress again that there is no right answer. It is important to just become aware of which are your preferences.)
5. Place a number 5 in front of any item which you think would not be on your list 5 years from now.
6. Finally, go down through your list and place near each item the date when you did it last.

The discussion which follows this exercise argues more eloquently than almost anything else we can say for values-clarification.

Strategy #2—I Learned That I. . . .

This strategy fits in with the one above. After students have listed and coded their 20 items, the teacher might say, "Look at your list as something which tells a lot about you at this time in your life. What did you learn about yourself as you were going through the strategy? Will you please complete one of these sentences and share with us some of the learning you did?"

> I learned that I. . . .
> I relearned that I. . . .
> I noticed that I. . . .
> I was surprised to see that I. . . .
> I was disappointed that I. . . .
> I was pleased that I. . . .
> I realized that I. . . .

The teacher must be willing to make some "I learned that I. . . ." statements, too. And they must not be platitudinous, either. Every effort is made for the values-clarifying teacher to be as honest and as authentic as possible.

"I learned that I. . . ." statements can be used after almost any important value-clarifying strategy. It is a way of getting the student to own the process of the search for values. It should be clear how diametrically opposed "I learned that I. . . ." statements are from indoctrination, although it is possible to misuse this or any clarification strategy to get kids to give back the party line. On the other hand, using this strategy can begin to build that lifetime search for personal meaning into all of our experiences.

Strategy #3—Baker's Dozen

This is a very simple strategy which teaches us something about our personal priorities. The teacher asks each student to list 13, a baker's dozen, of his favorite items around the house which use PLUGS; that is, which require electricity.

When the students have made their lists, the teacher says, "Now, please draw a line through the three which you really could do without if there were suddenly to be a serious power shortage. It's not that you don't like them, but that you could, if you had to, live without them. O.K., now circle the three which really mean the most to you and which you would hold onto until the very end."

It should be clear that again there is no right answer as to what "good" people *should* draw lines through and circle. The main thing is for each of us to know what we want and to see it in the perspective of what we like less.

Strategy #4—"I Urge" Telegrams

The teacher obtains blank Western Union telegram blanks. Or simply has students head a piece of paper with the word *Telegram*. He then says, "Each of you should think of someone in your real life to whom you would send a telegram which begins with these words: I URGE YOU TO. . . . Then finish the telegram and we'll hear some of them."

A great many values issues come out of this simple strategy. Consider some of these telegrams:

> *To my sister:* "I urge you to get your head together and quit using drugs." Nancy. (All telegrams must be signed. It is our affirmation of the need to name your name and to stand up for what you believe in.)
>
> *To my Sunday School teacher:* "I urge you to quit thinking that you are the only person to know what God wants." Signed, your student Rodney Phillips.
>
> *To my neighbor on the North Side:* "I urge you to see that we have no other place to play ball and that you not call the cops so often." Signed, Billy Clark.

One of the things that students working with values-clarification learn to do is to find out what they really want. "I urge telegrams" help do that. Just think of the people in your own lives to whom an "I urge telegram" needs to be sent. The second thing students working with values-clarification learn to do is to find *alternative* ways of getting what they need and want. Take the case of Billy Clark's neighbor. The class spent some time brainstorming ways of approaching that neighbor. They talked about how to negotiate with a grouch, and how to try to offer alternatives in your drive to get what you want.

"I urge telegrams" are used several times during the semester. The students keep them on file and after they have done five or six, they are spread out on the desk and "I learned statements" made from the pattern of the messages carried by the telegrams.

Students also learn to use the "I urge you to. . . ." model to get messages across between student and student and between student and teacher.

An assignment I like to use, related to the "I urge telegram," is to have each student get a letter-to-the-editor published in a magazine or newspaper.

Strategy #5—Personal Coat of Arms

Each student is asked to draw a shield shape in preparation for making a personal coat of arms. The teacher could go into the historical significance of shields and coats of arms, but the exercise is designed to help us learn more about some of our most strongly held values and to learn the importance of publicly affirming what we believe; that is, literally wearing our values out front on our shields.

The coat of arms shield is divided into six sections (see p. 29). The teacher makes it clear that words are to be used only in the sixth block. All the others are to contain pictures. He stresses that it is not an art lesson. Only crude stick figures, etc., need be used. Then he tells what is to go in each of the six sections:

> 1. Draw two pictures. One to represent something you are very good at and one to show something you *want* to become good at.

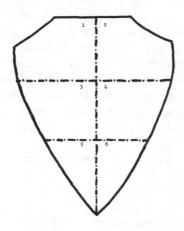

A Personal Coat of Arms

2. Make a picture to show one of your values from which you would never budge. This is one about which you feel extremely strong, and which you might never give up.
3. Draw a picture to show a value by which your family lives. Make it one that everyone in your family would probably agree is one of their most important.
4. In this block, imagine that you could achieve anything you wanted, and that whatever you tried to do would be a success. What would you strive to do?
5. Use this block to show one of the values you wished all men would believe, and certainly one in which you believe very deeply.
6. In the last block, you can use words. Use four words which you would like people to say about you behind your back.

The teacher can do several different things at this point. He can have the students share among themselves in little trios or quartets. He can also get the pictures hung up on the walls and get people to take each other on gallery tours to share the coats of arms. A game could be played which would involve trying to guess what the pictures represented. The class might try to make a group coat of arms to represent their living together in that classroom. In any case, the value expressions elicited in this nonverbal way are very exciting and lead to discussions which range far and wide. Incidentally, this strategy is a good one to use with parents to illustrate to them the power of the values-clarification methodology. It makes a meaningful exercise for an evening PTA meeting.

The Coat of Arms strategy illustrates quite well some things common to all of the values-clarification strategies. The teacher sets up an interesting way of eliciting some value responses. He establishes that there is no right answer. The strategy is open-ended and allows students to take the exploration to whatever level they want to take it. Finally, there is a chance to share with each other some of the alternatives that emerge from our searching. This whole process allows each student to focus on areas where he has some work yet to do in order to keep growing. The Coat of Arms can be done several times during the school year and the various shields compared and seen as measures of a student's search.

Conclusion

The five strategies used as illustrations of what values-clarification is must raise some serious questions in the minds of readers who have more conventional views of what the social studies should be. For one thing, I have used no standard subject-matter content: there is no history, no geography, etc. Yet, if one thinks through what the outcomes of a course will be making use of the five strategies, he will see the student emerging with a deeper sense of who he is, what he wants, what is precious, and what is of most worth in his and others' lives. Has the social studies ever done more than that?

Values-clarification demands that we take a new look at what we have been calling the social studies. I feel more and more strongly that the most severe problem facing all of us is *HOW TO GET PEOPLE TO LOOK AT THE LIVES THEY ARE LEADING*. How can we get fathers and mothers to see that high college-entrance scores are not the end of a high school education? How can we get people to see that getting a high-paying job is not the final reward of a college degree? How can we get men and women to take on some larger share of their personal responsibility for the rampant racism in our nation? Or for allowing a senseless war to continue indefinitely? When will educators make a contribution towards helping people examine the headlong pursuit towards accumulating more and more material possessions and enjoying them less? Or what can we do about keeping our students from making drab and dreary marriages or being trapped into pointless jobs which they hate to go to each morning? It boils down to a concern for values, and yet we must not fall into the trap of believing that if only we could give boys and girls the right set of values to believe, they would avoid the mistakes of the rest of us. Nonsense!

Indoctrination is not the answer. The only thing that indoctrination did for people in the past was to help them postpone the time when they began the hard process of hammering out their own set of values. Values simply can't be given to anyone else. One can't value for other people. Each individual has to find his own values. One can memorize all the platitudes he wants, but when it comes to living and acting on the values, he needs to carve them out of carefully reflected experience. The skills necessary for doing this can be learned in values-clarification.

Perhaps when the reader and author acknowledge how little help they received from their own education about making sense out of life, maybe then they will be willing to help other people's children learn the *process*, a lifetime process, of searching for a viable set of values to live by and perhaps even to die for.

The author is convinced that he can leave his own children no greater inheritance than the gift of knowing how to negotiate the lovely banquet of life ahead of them. That is indeed something of value.

Footnotes

[1] Most of these strategies are from Sidney B. Simon, *et al.*, *Values Clarification* (New York: Hart Publishing Co., Inc., 1972).

Simulations, Games, and Related Activities for Elementary Classrooms

R. Garry Shirts

"I'll start with a hint—strawberry is a Queen Anne."

"Is cherry a Queen Anne?"

"Yes."

"Is beet a Queen Anne?"

"Right again."

"Is a Queen Anne any red fruit or vegetable?"

"Tch, tch, tch. It's against the rules to guess the rule. You can only ask if such and such is a Queen Anne. I'll give you another hint, though: Tree is a Queen Anne."

"Tree is a Queen Anne? Oh no, it can't be!"[1]

So goes Barry Barnes' introduction to the games and activities developed for primary school children at the Far West Laboratory.[2] Following the Queen Anne game, he shows the teachers a rectangular box (looks like an old cheddar cheese carton) with a lid that slides back. Inside are cards with numbers on them. He slides the lid back and exposes the numeral three.

"What do you think the next number will be?"

"I say four."

"No, it will be two."

After almost every number from one to twenty has been guessed, he slides back the lid and exposes the number 6. More guesses, but everyone finally agrees that the next number will be 9. He pulls back the lid. It's twelve. And now everybody knows the pattern. Everyone, that is, except one or two art teachers who still look a little puzzled in the back of the room. Then he asks the group to tell him what the next letters in this series will be: OT, TF, FS, SE. Can you do it?[3]

R. GARRY SHIRTS is Director of Simile II, Del Mar, California.

Following this he challenges them to a contest. He has nine numbers written in a tic-tac-toe figure hidden from view. For every number he has to tell the group, he gets a point; for every number they guess, the group gets a point. He wins the first contest, and from then on it always ends five to four in favor of the teachers.

2	4	6
3	5	7
4	6	8

These are only a few of the numerous games, puzzles, and related activities that have been developed for elementary children[4] at the Laboratory, which can be applied in a wide variety of classroom situations.

The NASA game is another simple game to execute, yet it can produce surprisingly sophisticated discussion in children. They are asked to assign a numbered priority to fifteen items for inclusion on a moon expedition, first as individuals, then by consensus in groups.

Frederick Goodman[5] gives sixth-grade students some marbles, a stack of blocks, and a few directions, and in a short time they are building coalitions, establishing governments, police systems, and political machines. A game with profound implications for our time, yet very simple to execute.

Rex Walford, in his book *Games in Geography*,[6] presents examples of different types of geographical games, most of which require only a piece of paper and a pencil. They are oriented towards the geography of England, but can easily be adapted to reflect local or regional concerns.

Jay Reese[7] of Eugene, Oregon, has created a game called *Explorers*. He drew a grid of three-quarter inch squares on a sheet of 3 × 4 foot tagboard. Each vertical line of the grid was numbered and each horizontal line was lettered. On a smaller grid an imaginary continent was drawn which was kept out of the sight of the students. The class was divided into groups which represented explorers from different nations. They were to start on the right-hand side of the area and explore the unknown region to the left. Each team could move three grids per day. At the end of each day the teacher drew on the large map, using his smaller master map as a guide, whatever they would have seen in their travels that day; e.g., water, coastline, or nothing because of poor visibility. When they discovered the coastline they had to decide whether to stop and settle the area or to continue exploring the continent. Those groups that decided to settle the area were required to obey a set of laws imposed on them by the mother country. Inevitably, there were disputes with the other exploring countries and the mother country.

Not all of the games and simulations require so little equipment and advance preparation. For instance, the Community Land Use Game (CLUG)[8] has been used successfully by sixth graders. It is a classic game that has spawned several generations of land use games. To use it one would have to do more than the usual amount of studying and preparation. Yet the learnings that can come from the game are so useful it would be a shame not to expose the children to the game merely because it required extra work for the teacher.

These are but a very few examples of games and simulations that have been created the last few years. Until now, it has been very difficult to get information about what is available, but in the fall of 1970 *The Guide to Simulation Games for Education and Training*[9] was published. It gives full particulars on games currently available. I would highly recommend that your school library buy a copy. It is the "Sears and Roebuck catalog" for the simulation and game field.

Games are not new to elementary teachers. They have been using them in their classes for years, but simulation is a relatively new activity that has somehow gathered great clouds of mystery around it. No two "experts" can agree on what simulation and related terms mean. But for the sake of discussion it is necessary to venture a ball park definition. The essence of simulation is the creation of an experience which models a process or condition in the real world. If the simulation is a model of a process that is gamelike, such as the stock market, a political contest, or a war, then the simulation takes on gamelike characteristics. Role playing is one form of simulation in which a person simulates being in the position of another person. However, role playing and simulations are generally considered to be different processes. The difference is that in role playing the forces to which the participant reacts largely come from the initial description of the situation, the person's imagination, or from the other people in the role playing exercise, whereas in a simulation, the participant is also bound by reality as it is represented in the rules and structure of the simulation. In other words, the participant in role playing has great freedom; he can imagine any condition, make any decision, or create and shape the situation as he wills without suffering "tangible" consequences to his actions. By contrast the environmental forces created by the rules and structures of the simulation put one in a position of "living" the consequences of his actions: he may be thrown out of office, win or lose an election, make a profit for his corporation, not be allowed to pass Go, be defeated in battle, fail to get a job, or suffer any one of a variety of results depending on the nature of the simulation.

Building Your Own Simulation

When considering what simulations to use in the classroom, it is helpful to think of them as belonging to three categories. In Category I we have those simulations which require special training or a computer before they can be used by a "stranger" (person other than the developer). The second category contains simulations which are easily exported; they do not require special training or computers in order to be used by a stranger. In the third category are those simulations that require the presence of the developer.

Developing a simulation for one's own use is quite a different matter from developing one that can be exported. In the home-grown simulation or game, the teacher or some other person serves as an umpire determining the consequences of the action of the participants on the basis of his knowledge and experience. When a problem arises, the teacher thinks through the experience with the students and arrives at an answer that allows the simulation to continue. He models reality out of his personal experience and knowledge. Because he is free from the hard work and inhibiting effects of formalizing the model in writing, it is possible to develop simulations in the classroom which are surprisingly rich in detail, content, and process.

Furthermore, I would predict (if it were possible to measure) that there is no correlation between the level of a simulation's complexity and its effectiveness as a teaching device. Indeed, when considering elementary students it may well be that there is a negative correlation: that the students learn more from the less complex than the complex experience. On the other hand, I am confident that the *designers* of the more complex simulations learn a great deal more than the designers of the Category III experiences, but that is another matter.

The main point here is that the teacher-designed simulations, even when they are relatively less complex than commercial versions, may be just as instructive and valuable as those experiences which have cost thousands of dollars to build and years to design. If you add to this the enjoyment and learning that results when one creates his own experience, then the answer to the frequently asked question "Should we try to design our own simulation experiences?" becomes yes, yes, most emphatically, yes.

There are several approaches to building a simulation. One is to turn the entire classroom into a simulated environment. For instance, each year Wesley Stafford, now teaching in Africa and formerly of the La Mesa-Spring Valley School District in California, had his students land on a deserted island or an unknown planet and build a complete government and culture from the ground up. The year I visited him, the students were living on a heretofore unknown planet. They had labored for weeks over a constitution for their new civilization, trying to find one which was fair to all concerned yet made it possible to accomplish something. They invented their own language, which was used during a certain part of each day. The face of the clock and all other numbers in the room were changed to a base five numbering system which was adopted as their official measure and which several of the students became especially adept at manipulating. To protect themselves from alien visitors a password was developed (the principal was turned away several times until he got next to some of the students and learned the magic words). The room itself was decorated by the students to reflect the new environment. One entered through a cave and was confronted with a "live" volcano and a mural on the wall depicting the flora and fauna of this new world. The total simulated environment approach created a strange feeling in adults who visited the class for the first time, as they heard children speaking a different language, reading time from a weird clock, and having to say a strange password before entering. Possibly the feeling is similar to those of the child as he tries to navigate in the adult world.

The mechanics of building a simulated environment were dealt with by the class and the teacher as they developed. Some of the ideas came from the students, some from the teacher. The teacher had the final say as to whether or not an idea would be implemented, but he rarely had to invoke that power. The students agreed to, and did, in fact, work extra hard to accomplish their regular work so they could devote themselves to their simulated environment. It is likely that the required work faded from their memories within weeks of the ending of school but I doubt that many have forgotten the year they spent on another planet.

The ungraded class of Doreen Nelson at the Westminster Avenue Elementary School in Venice, California provides us with another approach. Using a cardboard base, styrofoam, and other materials gathered from the classroom, home, and industries in the area, the class rebuilt their neighborhood as they would like it. First, they recorded representative structures of the area on film. Then with a couple of architectural students as consultants and a lot of thinking, planning, and creative fun, they constructed a new environment to reflect their wishes. All cars were eliminated and replaced by a monorail and a system of conveyor belts. More area was available for parks and playgrounds and in general an esthetically pleasing environment was created. All construction plans had to be passed by a democratically chosen planning commission, city council, and a nine-year-old mayor.

Donald Love and associates of the Meadowbrook Intermediate School in Poway, California, were interested in having their students develop an understanding of some basic principles of economics. One class was given the scissors, brushes, and the duplicating machine, another class the paint, paste, and art paper, and the third class, construction paper, duplicating paper, and spirit masters. When any of the three classes undertook a project that involved materials which they did not own, it was necessary for an economic transaction to take place. At first, every transaction resulted in an elaborate haggling session worthy of the best skills of the proverbial horse traders. Then the students became annoyed with the amount of time required to carry on such transactions and developed a standardized rate of exchange, i.e., 32 sheets of construction paper equals 18 spirit masters, but that also quickly proved cumbersome. Then one class hit upon the idea of printing money, which they did. It looked like a breakthrough, but the other two classes would not accept it for payment. But the idea caught on and it was decided that there should be one currency for all three classes. It then became obvious that a government was needed to control the amount printed, whom it was distributed to, etc.

Unfortunately, these experiences cannot be packaged and exported to classes all over the nation. They depend on the creativity, interest, and experience of the specific teachers and their classes. However, it is possible for teachers to take the basic idea and create their own world, and of course that is what we are encouraging here.

To help you build games, you will probably want to pursue the appropriate chapter and references to game building in the books cited in the following section. A word of caution, however. Frequently, when I point out to a teacher that he has created a simulation-type experience, the response is, "Oh, I'm sorry, I didn't know that was what I was doing. I was just trying to create a good experience for the kids." Had he known that there were people who were "experts" in creating and analyzing such experiences, he probably would not have felt that he had the right to undertake the task. We are conditioned to honor and sanction the "territorial" privileges of special knowledge, and new disciplines generally develop a specialized jargon and rites of membership to protect their new territory. So accustomed are we to respecting these "territorial" privileges—medical doctors are the only people who can practice medicine, lawyers are the only ones who can practice law, plumbers are the only ones who can plumb—we are frequently shamed out of using our creative talents. This is not to say that special knowledge can't be helpful, but it is better to attempt a creative act in ignorance than to refrain from trying because of lack of knowledge.

Reading List

In addition to the books already cited for special information, I would suggest as general background a small pamphlet edited by William Nesbitt called *Simulation Games for the Social Studies Classroom*,[10] or Alice Kaplan Gordon's *Games for Growth*.[11]

If you are a primary teacher and have not been exposed to the fantasy-filled fun of theater games, I urge you to order Viola Spolin's *Improvisation for the Theater*.[12]

If you are interested in role playing, and perhaps even more importantly in values, I would strongly recommend Fannie and George Shaftel's *Role-Playing for Social Values: Decision-Making in the Social Studies*.[13]

Footnotes

[1] In this game a Queen Anne is any word with a double letter. In other games a Queen Anne might be any item that can be defined by a general rule.

[2] For more information, write to Far West Laboratory for Educational Research and Development, 1 Garden Circle, Berkeley, California 94705.

[3] NT for Nine, Ten.

[4] An additional source of information for children's games is the free catalogue distributed by Creative Publications, P.O. Box 328, Palo Alto, California 94302.

[5] Instructions for "They Shoot Marbles, Don't They?" can be obtained from Frederick L. Goodman, Department of Education, 4023 University School, University of Michigan, Ann Arbor, Michigan 48104.

[6] Rex Walford, *Games in Geography*. London: Longmans Green Ltd.

[7] For more information write to Jay Reese at 3235 West 17th Avenue, Eugene, Oregon 97402.

[8] Players' instructions available Free Press (Macmillan Co.), 866–3rd Ave., New York, New York 10022.

[9] David W. Zuckerman, Robert E. Horn, Paul A. Twelker, *The Guide to Simulation Games for Education and Training*, Information Resources, Inc., 1675 Massachusetts Avenue, Cambridge, Massachusetts, 02138.

[10] William Nesbitt, *Simulation Games for the Social Studies Classroom*, Foreign Policy Association, 345 East 46th Street, New York, New York 10017.

[11] Alice Kaplan Gordon, *Games for Growth*, Science Research Associates, College Division, Palo Alto, California.

[12] Viola Spolin, *Improvisation for the Theater*. Evanston, Illinois: Northwestern University Press.

[13] Fannie R. Shaftel and George Shaftel, *Role-Playing for Social Values: Decision-Making in the Social Studies*. Englewood Cliffs, New Jersey: Prentice-Hall, Inc.

The Importance of
Learning Activities

Jack R. Fraenkel

The 1960's witnessed a tremendous burst of activity in the social studies. New materials, books, films, filmstrips, records, pictures, manuals, pamphlets—all appeared in abundance. A major assumption of the producers of these materials (along with several professional organizations, private institutions, government agencies, most of the lay public, and many teachers) was that the key to improving social studies teaching lay in the reorganization of subject matter. Operating under the same assumption, several organizations or groups of social scientists also tried during these years to improve instruction in their fields at the public school level. A number of books were published in which individual social scientists presented their interpretations of the newer insights and understandings of their disciplines.[1]

Let us consider this assumption for a moment. For the most part, the subject matter of the social studies consists of facts, concepts, and generalizations drawn from the disciplines of history and the social sciences—traditionally geography, political science, and economics; more recently anthropology, sociology, and social psychology.[2]

The manner in which each of these various elements is arranged is often called the *structure* of a discipline,[3] even though it appears that there is no "one" structure for any given discipline upon which all scholars can agree. Theoretically, however, the essential concepts and generalizations (and ways of developing them) in one discipline (e.g., sociology or economics) often differ from those in another (e.g., political science or geography).

We therefore find included in social studies courses, in both elementary and secondary schools, information that consists of concepts (e.g., culture,

JACK R. FRAENKEL is Professor of Interdisciplinary Studies in Education at San Francisco State University, San Francisco, California.

cooperation, values, goods, services, change); generalizations (e.g., the daily activities of a people reflect their individual and group values); and specific facts (e.g., population statistics) from each of the social science disciplines, as well as from other sources. These constitute the subject matter of the social studies that students are expected to learn.

To focus on subject matter alone as the key to instructional improvement in the social studies is, however, to deal with only part of the problem. Social studies, like all subjects, consist of both content (e.g., modern man's alienation) and process (e.g., learning activities related to the theme of alienation). They go hand in hand. One cannot learn something about economics, for example, unless one learns it *in some way*. One cannot learn to think unless one thinks about *something*. One does not become skilled in working with people unless one works with them on *some task* involving *some data*.

The selection and organization of social studies content serve only to *impart* knowledge. The selection and organization of learning activities, on the other hand, facilitate *the use of* such knowledge. It is through the learning activities by which students become both spectators and participants in the world around them that they acquire the competencies to assimilate, understand, and work with the knowledge they amass.

Teachers need to concern themselves, therefore, not only with *what* they expect students to learn, but also *how* they expect them to learn it. Knowledge alone, whether it be knowledge *of* (e.g., the reasons why people revolt), or knowledge *how* (e.g., to play a musical instrument), does not, in and of itself, encourage students to think; does not change attitudes and predispositions; does not build certain kinds of skills. These objectives are achieved primarily by the ways in which this basic content is translated into learnable tasks for students in the classroom.

What Is a "Learning Activity"?

Learning activities are experiences designed to engage students with certain subject matter. The purpose of such involvement is to motivate students to think about and use subject matter, to maximize their individual learning, and to stimulate their interest so that their schooldays will be eventually succeeded by self-directed continuing education. The most appropriate type of activity, of course, depends on the nature of the subject matter and the objectives that teachers and students wish to attain. In some cases, the most appropriate activities will consist of certain student *behaviors*, such as interviewing, describing, discussing, or explaining. In other cases, the most appropriate activities will involve the creation and development by students of certain *products*, such as essays, reports, maps, or models. In still other instances, participation by students in certain *experiences*, such as viewing a film, attending a concert, going on a field trip, or visiting a factory, will be more suitable (see Figure 1, p. 39).

For example, if a teacher wishes to have his students gain some insight into the nature of war, its causes and effects, he needs to ask, "What particular subject matter can help provide such insight?" Let us suppose that he and his

Figure 1		
Types of Learning Activities		
Behaviors	**Products**	**Experiences**
Interviewing	Maps	Viewing a sunset
Describing	Charts	Listening to a record
Discussing	Models	Attending a ballet
Listing	Outlines	Visiting a factory
Grouping	Reports	Smelling a flower
Explaining	Diagrams	Tasting a food
Predicting	Essays	Watching a demonstration
Hypothesizing	Murals	Browsing in a library
Summarizing	Poems	Seeing a play
Choosing	Songs	Holding a kitten
Rating	Photographs	Painting a picture
		Playing a musical instrument
		Riding a bicycle
		Talking to an elderly person
		Playing a game
		Walking through a park

students decide that an understanding of why the Spanish-American War of 1898 occurred will be particularly illustrative. The teacher must then ask himself, "What student behaviors, products, and/or experiences will most effectively promote such understanding?" Will it suffice if students are able to identify several of the *immediate* causes of the war? Or should they also be able to identify several of the *underlying* causes as well? Perhaps the ability to *identify* causes by itself is not enough to insure understanding. Perhaps students should also *explain why* these were causes. Perhaps they should *compare and contrast* the causes of the Spanish-American War with the immediate and underlying causes of the American Revolutionary War, the American Civil War, and the War in Vietnam. Perhaps the Spanish-American War should be compared with other wars than these.

Consider another example. Suppose a teacher is interested in opening students' eyes to how individuals faced with a choice between two compelling alternatives *feel*, hoping thereby to help them acquire an empathy for individuals in conflict situations. What subject matter is illustrative here? Harry Truman's account of his agonizing decision to drop the atomic bomb on Hiroshima and Nagasaki? John F. Kennedy's *Profiles in Courage?* Richard Wright's *Black Boy?* Perhaps the *Autobiography of Malcolm X?* Whatever his choice (or the class's), he must again determine what behaviors, products, or experiences might promote the insight he desires. Will it suffice if students simply *read* or *see a film* about the actions of such individuals (e.g., Richard Wright in *Black Boy*)? Should they *make inferences*, based on a character's actions, about his feelings? Perhaps they should *discuss* the character's feelings? Perhaps they should *act out* the character's feelings through role-playing? Perhaps they should be asked to imagine themselves in a similar situation and then to *discuss* what they think their own *feelings* might be. Perhaps none of these. But if none of these, what instead?

Different Types of Learning Activities Serve Different Functions

Whether behavior, product, or experience, not all learning activities serve the same function. For example, some provide for *intake* of information. Activities of this kind may include reading, observing, interviewing, listening to records, and viewing films. These kinds of activities are essential for students, since they must have information to work with or think about before they can be expected to engage in intelligent action. They must have data before they can do anything with it. Raw data alone, however, are but perception. Data must be organized and internalized in anticipation of being used. Thus, the necessity for a second type of learning activity which facilitates *organization* of information. Examples of this type of activity include charting, note-taking, graphing, map-making, outlining, and preparing time-lines. Such activities help students to organize and thus make sense out of the material to which they have been exposed.

A third type of learning activity helps students to *demonstrate* what they have learned. Such activities as discussions, sociodramas, murals, writing, and role-playing enable students to display the skills they possess, to demonstrate how well they can think, and to indicate how well they understand the actions, problems, and feelings of others.

A fourth type of learning activity encourages students to *express* themselves by *creating* or producing an *original* product. Expressions of this type of learning include composing a poem or song, writing an original essay, building an original model, illustrating an idea by means of dance or drawing. Though they overlap to some degree, the essential difference between creative and demonstrative activities is that demonstrative activities ask students to illustrate the degree to which *they understand* data they have previously acquired and organized. Creative activities, on the other hand, encourage students to use their newly acquired understanding to produce *a new and different* product, or to render an original performance (see Figure 2, p. 41).

A realization of the idea that different kinds of learning activities serve different functions should help us design learning activities that will assist students to learn in a variety of ways. In too many classrooms, students are engaged for the most part in the same kinds of activities every day—they listen to teachers talk (most teachers talk far too much![4]); they read; they write. These kinds of activities are obviously very important. But different students learn in different ways. And many students do not learn very well at all via talk and the printed word. They need to be more directly or actively involved. It is for this reason that direct activities, such as field trips, role-

Figure 2
Examples of Learning Activities in Each Category

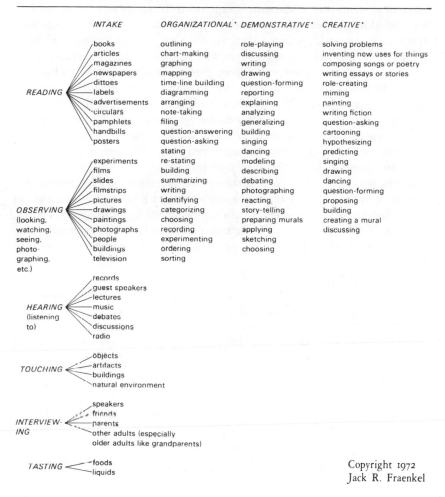

	INTAKE	ORGANIZATIONAL*	DEMONSTRATIVE*	CREATIVE*
READING	books articles magazines newspapers dittoes labels advertisements circulars pamphlets handbills posters	outlining chart-making graphing mapping time-line building diagramming arranging note-taking filing question-answering question-asking stating	role-playing discussing writing drawing question-forming reporting explaining analyzing generalizing building singing dancing	solving problems inventing new uses for things composing songs or poetry writing essays or stories role-creating miming painting writing fiction question-asking cartooning hypothesizing predicting
OBSERVING (looking, watching, seeing, photo- graphing, etc.)	experiments films slides filmstrips pictures drawings paintings photographs people buildings television	re-stating building summarizing writing identifying categorizing choosing recording experimenting ordering sorting	modeling describing debating photographing reacting story-telling preparing murals applying sketching choosing	singing drawing dancing question-forming proposing building creating a mural discussing
HEARING (listening to)	records guest speakers lectures music debates discussions radio			
TOUCHING	objects artifacts buildings natural environment			
INTERVIEW- ING	speakers friends parents other adults (especially older adults like grandparents)			
TASTING	foods liquids			

* Some activities legitimately fit into more than one category, depending on the purpose behind the activity.

playing, sociodrama, committee work, drawing, painting, dancing, taking photographs, making maps, working in the community—in short, any and all activities that involve *doing* things as well as receiving information—are so important for students to engage in as teachers develop new activities in class. Students need to learn from books and other printed materials, to be sure, but they also need to learn from audio-visual media, from discussing, from observing, from interviewing, from taking things and ideas apart, from putting things and ideas together, and from feeling.

If there is one thing that we know about how individuals learn, it is that different students learn differently. Some students learn easily, all or some of the time, through reading; others need to see, hear, or touch the objects with which they are working. Some students are able, part of the time, to work effectively by themselves; others often need the stimulation of group participation. Some students understand more clearly if they can express what they have absorbed in an unusual way (for example, a "letter to the editor"); others grasp a relationship more clearly when they organize their data into tabular or chart form.[5] It is important, therefore, that we take steps to insure that students have open to them as many ways to learn as possible. But all four types of activities—intake, organizational, demonstrative, and creative—are essential if learning is to take place.

Let us consider an example. Imagine that a teacher and his sixth-grade class have decided to investigate the contemporary problem of alienation in the United States. The teacher hopes that the students will be able to express orally or in writing their beginning impressions of how an alienated person feels. In what kinds of activities might he begin to engage students in order to fulfill this objective?

PROBLEM: Alienation

OBJECTIVE: Students will express orally or in writing their beginning impressions of how an alienated person feels.

PROCEDURE:

1. Play the record "She's Leaving Home" from the album *Sgt. Pepper's Lonely Hearts Club Band.*[6] Ask the class if they can identify the artist and the song (Intake).

2. Ask the class to listen to the record again, only this time to follow the lyrics that are reprinted in the beginning of Chapter I in *Alienation: Personal Problem or National Tragedy?*[7] Ask them to reflect on what the song is talking about and then answer orally or in writing the following questions:
   a. What is the song about?
   b. Why is the girl in the song leaving home?
   c. How does she feel? What makes you think so?
   d. How do her parents feel? What makes you think so?
   e. How would you describe the relationship which exists between the girl and her parents?
   f. What might produce such a relationship? (Organizational)

3. Discuss each of these questions with the class, encouraging students to offer their opinions. Point out that there are no right or wrong answers to these kinds of questions (Demonstrative).

4. Encourage the class to write a short passage of their own, compose a poem, draw a cartoon, or a sketch, etc., in which they describe a situation in which they or some individuals they know have experienced feelings similar to the girl's (Creative).

5. Summarize the class's response to questions "e" and "f". Now ask the class to read the rest of Chapter I, pointing out that in the remainder of the chapter are recounted two additional and somewhat different situations which, when consid-

ered along with the song, are both similar and different in several ways. Ask the class, as they read, to look for some of these ways (Intake and Organizational).

6. Have each student make a list of the similarities and differences that he has identified, and then ask the class to compare the lists. What differences do they notice? How would they explain these differences? (Demonstrative and Creative)

7. Now ask the class to hypothesize as to what factors encourage alienation in people (Creative).

This learning activity sequence includes all four categories of activities—intake, organizational, demonstrative, and creative—described above. It is but one example of how the objective in this particular case might be accomplished. The point to stress, however, is that the teacher helped students obtain data necessary for the task at hand (the intake), helped them to organize these data in their own way so that they could use them later, provided an opportunity for them to demonstrate (and the teacher to realize) their understanding of the data and what they meant to them, and then encouraged them to express their understanding in an original product, creation, or task. In the past, many social studies (and other) teachers have concentrated unduly on activities that provide for intake, while overlooking or minimizing organizing, demonstrating, and creative opportunities. It is the organizing, demonstrating, and creating types of learning activities, however, that allow students to take in and use what they have learned. Teachers who expand their repertory to include a rich mosaic of many different kinds of learning activities are likely to find their students enjoying the social studies more and increasingly capable of varying their educational experience. And that's one of the things we teachers are after, isn't it?

Footnotes

[1] See the volume produced by the American Council of Learned Societies in collaboration with the National Council for the Social Studies, *The Social Studies and the Social Sciences*. New York: Harcourt, Brace, and World, 1962. Also, Erling Hunt (editor), *High School Social Studies Perspectives*. Boston: Houghton Mifflin, 1962; William T. Lowe, *Structure and the Social Studies*. Ithaca, New York: Cornell University Press, 1969; John U. Michaelis and A. Montgomery Johnston, *The Social Sciences—Foundations of the Social Studies*. Boston: Allyn and Bacon, 1965; Irving Morrissett (editor), *Concepts and Structure in the New Social Science*. New York: Holt, Rinehart and Winston, 1967; Irving Morrissett and W.W. Stevens, Jr. (editors), *Social Science—The Search for Rationale*. New York: Holt, Rinehart and Winston, 1971; Raymond H. Muessig and Vincent R. Rogers (editors), *Social Science Seminar Series* (6 volumes). Columbus, Ohio: Charles E. Merrill Books, 1965.

[2] Whether it should be so drawn, at least exclusively, is a subject of considerable debate. See Fred Newmann, "Questioning the Place of Social Science Disciplines in Education," *Social Education*, November, 1967, pp. 593-596; and James P. Shaver, "Social Studies: The Need for Redefinition," *ibid.*, pp. 588-592.

[3] Bruner, Jerome S., *The Process of Education*. New York: Vintage Books (Random House), 1960.

[4] Floyd, W.D., "An Analysis of the Oral Questioning Activity in Selected Colorado Classrooms," unpublished doctoral dissertation. Colorado State College, 1960. Floyd taperecorded 31 one-hour class sessions in various elementary schools. He found that 71 per cent of all words spoken were by the teacher.

[5] Taba, Hilda, *Curriculum Development: Theory and Practice*. New York: Harcourt, Brace and World, 1962.

[6] Lennon, John and Paul McCartney, "She's Leaving Home," from the album *Sgt. Pepper's Lonely Hearts Club Band*. Copyright, 1967. Northern Songs, Ltd.

[7] Urick, Ronald V., *Alienation: Personal Problem or National Tragedy?* Englewood Cliffs, New Jersey: Prentice-Hall, Inc., 1970.

The Learning Center
in the
Social Studies Classroom

James M. Larkin and Jane J. White

I. Rationale for Learning Centers

The open classroom, programmed reading, the lecture method, the unit, team teaching, the inquiry method, individualization, modular scheduling—all are manifestations of fundamental concerns: How can valued knowledge be transmitted? How can the learner become an active chooser and orderer of his/her own experience? We propose an alternative organizational tool: the Learning Center. We think that it is a powerful alternative, precisely because it functions to allow many of the variables crucial to the teaching/learning situation—realization of cognitive objectives from traditional systems of knowledge, realization of affective objectives, learners actively "making meaning" for themselves, learners choosing areas they wish to study, utilization of a variety of methods of study, the development of skills of working with others—to be actualized in the elementary school program.

The concept of a Learning Center is not new: it is merely a model (similar to the unit method of teaching) that becomes a new restructuring, a pulling together, an integration of what has been done for many years by excellent classroom teachers. Physically a Learning Center is a designated area of the classroom containing a specific number of learning stations (perhaps sequentially ordered) where resources (selected by the teacher as shaper of the environment and contributed to by the students as active transactors) are provided to guide individuals and groups of children in specific learning activities. As an organizing mechanism, Learning Centers can be utilized in traditional classrooms, individualized classrooms, open classrooms, and team teaching classrooms. Basically, Learning Centers are a major tool for all

JAMES M. LARKIN is Associate Professor and Director of Teacher Education at the Graduate School of Education, University of Pennsylvania, Philadelphia. JANE J. WHITE is a coordinator of student teachers at the University of Maryland's Baltimore campus.

teachers intent on sharing the teaching/learning experience with children, but before this can happen, the teacher must perceive of himself or herself and the child as co-creators of knowledge, and active teaching/learning individuals.

II. Planning for Using Learning Centers

A. The Theme or Problem Area. A Learning Center must have as its central focus a problem, idea, or theme worthy of sustained examination by students. This problem, idea, or theme becomes the *generic nexus*, or the central topic of study that generates a variety of sub-topics and permutations; collectively these constitute the substance of the center's activities. In elementary social studies classrooms we specifically recommend themes of an interdisciplinary nature. We submit that, for young children, such themes are most appropriate as they benefit from the varied resources of the social science disciplines and provide greater leverage for the student's individual interest and abilities to be realized. In this way, the social sciences are used as resources and allow the theme or problem area to be investigated, to govern the attendant inquiry of the student.

A Learning Center developed around the problem area of the "Automobile and Its Impact on American Life" could include: the assembly line, Henry Ford's life, the internal combustion engine, population growth (history), the interchangeability of parts, growth of unions, wage rates, strikes and vertical industries (economics), the interstate highway system, maps, travel and recreational industry (geography and economics), automobile prices, and status, design, mobile isolation, housing, school and commercial planning, location and development (sociology), and finally pollution, noise level, and junked cars (human beings and ecology).

The theme or problem area should be selected in terms of its intellectual depth—its ability to help students organize both their personal experience of the world and their investigation and synthesis of that which they do not know. The theme should have the potential power to challenge the present intellectual constructs of the class while generating a variety of lines of investigation to initiate and maintain student involvement.

Themes selected because of their potential interest for students usually directly relate to their daily lives. Teachers should regard such themes as being open to investigation and inquiry by everyone and should present issues wherein each child can be his or her own special expert on the basis of his or her data collection. The topic "Families" using some methodology from sociology may have students surveying their family and those of their neighbors to gather information regarding size of family, age distribution, divisions of labor, roles of and rules for family membership.

From the discipline of anthropology the children can conduct interviews with older family informants, to learn of family traditions, histories, origins, religious and ethnic holidays, etc. Cross-cultural study may encourage the in-depth comparison of an African or Asian family with a European family.

These themes require the "doing" of social science as the students become familiar with various methodologies. The study of human beings is not readily divisible by disciplines, nor should it be. Learning Centers developed and built around such problem areas and themes can be a powerful educational experience.

Below are other examples of themes, designed and developed using the Learning Center format. These centers were built by our undergraduate students and have been successfully used in elementary classrooms.

1. Moving Right Along—a Look at the Automobile Industry
2. The Individual—an Awareness and an Understanding
3. Our City—the Ugly and the Beautiful
4. Survival and Adaptation: Life in the Desert
5. The American Indian: Examining Stereotypes
6. The Early American Settler
7. Black Africa and Black America
8. Philadelphia: Man and the City
9. People's Republic of China
10. Cultural Change in Mexico
11. You Are What You Value
12. Pre-History and Early Man
13. Ethnic Groups and Immigration
14. Individuals and Groups
15. Race and Racism
16. Magic and Witchcraft
17. Your Civil Rights
18. Religions
19. Water Pollution
20. What Is a Family?
21. Cooperation and Conflict
22. Learning War—Teaching Peace

B. Theme Selection and Definitions of Learning Centers and Learning Stations. It is legitimate, especially initially, for themes to be selected by the teacher. They may focus on a topic suggested in the grade level curriculum guide, or they may relate to topics in which the teacher has special competence or interest. Teachers might select a theme or problem area out of concerns that they have heard articulated by the students. But, whatever the method of selection, it is the interrelationships among the variety of activities that help develop the intellectual depth of the concept. Without this standard against which each activity must be checked for appropriateness, the Learning Center could degenerate into a collection of fragmented activities.

A curricular interest of the teacher may be the interdependence of human beings in a metropolitan environment. This concept becomes the organizing theme for a Learning Center. One approach is to mount and display large aerial photographs of the region. The photographs should be of high quality so that children are able to clearly distinguish streets, houses, industrial and commercial areas, transportation facilities, etc. Some specific social studies topics for explicating human beings' interdependence in a metropolitan environment may be:

1. Work
2. Transportation
3. Housing Patterns
4. Pollution
5. Urban Blight
6. Government
7. Ethnic Groups
8. Schooling
9. The Changing Metropolitan Environment

These topics are developed in depth at the various learning stations within the Learning Centers. For example, the learning station on Work may contain pictures of typical work activities and working areas (outside and inside). A list of wage scales can be listed for various occupations using local labor department data. Reading materials on work should have specific task assignments for the children to gather more information. Some students could develop an interview questionnaire and contact different people regarding their work and record the interview, for playback in the station. All of the students could gather data from their parents regarding where they work, what they do at work, their likes and dislikes, length of time in this activity, wages, and working conditions. Mothers may be particularly qualified to speak to experiences of discrimination in seeking work.

By examining the world of work in one station the students could probe the relationships of work to housing patterns and metropolitan transportation systems. These topics will lead into the issues of pollution and the ecology of the region, government programs and structures, schools, and the ethnic makeup of the area.

C. *Mechanics of "Doing" Centers.* The teacher's purpose, curricular demands, and student abilities and interests will all help determine the nature of the center's themes and learning station topics. As a mechanism for directing student learning, the center can be creatively developed and utilized, to accomplish specific pedagogical objectives: these might include opportunities to develop cognitive skills, such as categorizing or identifying cause and effect; opportunities for concrete manipulative experiences; opportunities for fantasizing; opportunities for students to build habits of cooperation. These opportunities are limited only by the enthusiasm and creativity of the contributing teachers and students.

The pattern of student involvement in the Learning Center (individually or small groups) and the length of time necessary for study of the organizing theme and topics can be quite variable. Not all children need complete each station, nor does each child have to perform the same activities in the same order in the center. The Learning Center format necessitates considerable individualization, but one of its great strengths requires the continual "doing" of social science and communicating the findings of various investigations. Each station can be a complete study in itself, but collectively, the stations comprising the center become a more powerful source of learning.

The use of Learning Centers requires a wide range of curricular materials: books, photographs, recordings, tapes, films, questionnaires, games, and large quantities of art materials. A major advantage of this format is the necessity to draw on and incorporate the life experience and knowledge of the class as they are directly involved in gathering data, observing, making inferences, hypothesizing, and organizing information, both for use in a particular station or in the development of other stations.

D. Individual and Group Work. The Learning Center differs primarily from some units in that it is not a series of discussions and activities sequentially arranged in which every child, simultaneously, is doing the same thing as every other child. Rather, it is a variety of learning stations with activities and explorations that pursue different objectives, utilize different methodologies, incorporate different materials and ideas to initiate attacks on creating knowledge about the central concern. In getting started, the teacher should not "over-plan." The Learning Center can be an evolving, growing structure in which both the teacher and the students contribute to the planning as they pursue their interests. However, the teacher, as shaper of the environment, should initiate with the students at least two or three learning stations. These can function as springboards, to point out some of the issues and approaches that can be undertaken in the investigation of the organizing concern.

During the planning, certain principles should be kept in mind. Basically one of the strengths of the Learning Center is that it allows the learner to plan and choose. Implicit in the act of choosing is a view of the learner as a unique individual, capable of his own meaning-making, and the legitimation of his role and monitoring of his own work schedule. It is his responsibility to assess his own needs and interest, to decide how he works best and what he likes doing. While using a Learning Center the individual child shares the responsibility for deciding how much time and energy he must invest to gain closure on the tasks and to decide the continuity and sequence of tasks that would be meaningful to him. It is the individual student's responsibility, as well as the teacher's, to evaluate how well and how satisfactorily he gains knowledge and learns for himself.

The Learning Center should contain a variety of activities that reflect individual growth and cognitive learning styles. There should be stations in which different cognitive skills are utilized: categorizing vs. interpreting pictures vs. predicting and testing hypothesis. There should be activities that allow for the development of a range of reading skills and interpersonal competencies. There should be stations in which individuals will work alone or together in informal or formal groups.

Stations should be established so that the Learning Center as a whole has the potential for providing resources for involving the entire class at one time, if this is what the teacher desires. A mechanism may need to be designed by the teacher to facilitate easy access and movement through the center: a daily sign-up sheet or perhaps a board on which each child could put his name tag on one of the labeled activity hooks. This mechanism would (1) help monitor the use of the different learning stations, insuring that certain activities were not monopolized exclusively by certain students, and (2) help the students develop the attitudes and skills necessary to learn for themselves as individuals. Students need to learn how to choose an activity, how to be responsible for a task, how to work together in a small group. A Learning Center may be an excellent vehicle for individualizing part of the day or for slowly developing and testing techniques for a potential move into an open classroom structure.

III. Design and Construction of Learning Centers

Even if it is initially teacher planned, in no event should the Learning Center be teacher-built. This is not a project like a bulletin board that keeps a teacher after school five nights a week. Rather, each child, being partly responsible for his learning and sometimes teacher of his peers, should also have a hand in its construction—bringing in materials, writing the activities and directions for others to follow, designing and cutting cardboard and building the center and its stations.

Utilization of space in the classroom can be planned so as to include many surfaces within a minimal area. These surfaces can be used to display step-by-step directions to individual activities and to display the students' work. Structural designs might focus on how the students are grouped and the aesthetic warmth of the structure (see p. 50). Design A can be made from a large appliance box (washing machine size), is durable, and will provide surface area for four stations in one center. Design B provides a maximum amount of eight surface areas. Both A and B allow four groups of two or three children to attend to each station without disruption.

Design C is like a revolving book rack at a drugstore. With proper construction, this revolving center can be fairly permanent as panels for new stations can be suspended from hooks on the arms of the structure.

Another center design may resemble the bulletin board. This center is like a large mural with a number of stations set along a wall. The mural design should have the various activities positioned at eye level when the students are sitting at a chair or desk going through the center. This arrangement uses little space and yet allows a vast range of activities for the students. We have seen some classrooms where all of the walls are in use with learning centers.

One student built a four-sided house (Design D), allowing the use of the four inner and outer walls as stations. This center concerned the housing structures of various people around the world. It even came with different roofs designed to explicate different housing designs.

These few basic designs, with the suggestion that the teacher establish building, designing, and up-keep teams, should be quite useful to a teacher interested in using centers in his or her classroom.

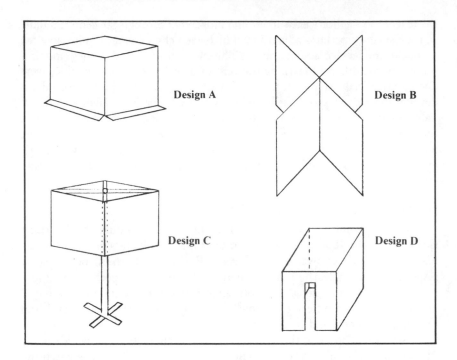

IV. Two Learning Centers

A. Primary Level Learning Center, Who Am I?: The Child Is the Curriculum. This primary level Learning Center is designed to encourage the child to begin the process of getting to know about himself or herself. The major concepts developed in the center will be the individual as a unique person, and the individual as similar to, but different than, other individuals in the classroom. The tension between these seemingly opposite constructs provides the impetus to know more about self and others throughout this Learning Center.

In the Learning Center we will describe various activities (as learning stations) that should enable the children to examine the question, Who Am I? The center will be built around two themes, *Exploring My Outside* and *Exploring My Inside.* This focus on self will encourage each child to gather data, perform tasks, organize information, develop charts and drawings, conduct interviews, and write stories, poems, or songs about their Outside and their Inside.

1. Exploring My Outside

Station I—What We See. A large photograph depicting great numbers of people, structures and activities. (A beach scene in summer, a crowded park or city street.) The photo should invite careful examination from the children as a great variety of objects are perceived. Suggested activities for this station are: (1) write on 5 × 8 cards questions that ask the children to write down three things they see in the photograph, (2) ask if they have ever been in a place like the one in the photograph, and (3) ask them to look again very carefully to find one more object in the photo.

Station II—The Mirror. Station II is a large mirror with activity cards that ask the child:

  (a) Look very carefully at your face and draw a picture of yourself.
  (b) Be sure to draw eyes, nose, hair, mouth, ears, chin, cheeks, eyebrows, eyelashes, etc.
  (c) In teams of two, the children should draw the face of another child in the room and give it to him or her. Each child should have two drawings of his face.

These two stations help build experiences in which children understand that people see things differently and these differences help to make us who we are. The teacher can have discussions, first in small groups and later as a class, that focus on the children's varied experiences that shape their perceptions, and the genetic inheritance that contributes to the development of each child's unique self.

Station III—My Body. Station III asks the children to draw their whole body. A roll of brown wrapping paper can be used, cut so each child's body outline, with shape and contours, from head to feet, will fit on the paper. Again the children can work in teams outlining each other. They can list their heights, and a scale will allow them to weigh themselves and list this also on the drawing.

Station IV—Getting To Know Me. The activities in Station IV require the child to weigh, measure, draw, and record as much about his or her body as possible. Again in teams of two or three the children can weigh and measure their heads, hands, feet, legs, arms, chest, waist, etc. All these data can be recorded on the large outline drawing of their bodies.

These four stations focus the child's attention on his or her "outside." The activities encourage teams of children working together to help each other construct their unique selves. Drawings of the various body parts can be attached as inserts around the larger drawing of the body outline. The activities for the theme *Exploring My Outside* should be done with care, and the children must have enough time to be able to learn to weigh and measure each other. The classroom display of these drawings is also encouraged, before they are taken home for hanging in the living room or bedroom.

The teacher's role throughout should facilitate the child's concentration on self. Care must be taken to be sensitive to questions that children ask regarding themselves: how they became who they are; why they look the way they do, etc. Class discussions will be necessary throughout these activities to allow time to consider questions. The teacher can list these for further examination as the children begin the *Exploring My Inside* segment of the Learning Center.

2. Exploring My Inside: The Child Is the Curriculum

Station I—Values. This station concerns the rank ordering of personal value preferences for children. The station should have photos, drawings, poems, or short stories that exemplify each value preference. On a mimeo sheet the child is to put a number from 1 to 8 beside the value preferences listed, from most to least valued.

Brave	Neat
Honest	Fair
Older	Obedient
Hardworking	Helpful

The photos, poems, etc. should be labeled with the value preference. After a group of four or five have completed the station, this group should discuss their preferences and attempt to establish consensus for the whole group. This activity aids the clarification process, encourages the children to publicly affirm their preferences and legitimates the diversity of personal values.

Station II—Different People. This station greatly individualizes the examination of the inside self. Each child is to collect and mount three pictures of people different from him/her, then list two or three of these differences for each picture, e.g., age, features, sex, race, role, dress.

After the pictures are mounted and differences noted, the teacher can ask the children to decide if they would like or not like this person as a friend, classmate, or neighbor and to discuss their reasons. A variation of this activity is to assemble a large number of pictures and ask the children to group these according to people they like and people they dislike. Either activity encourages reflective thinking and defensible choice as the child proceeds through the station.

Station III—Friends. This is a most popular topic for primary age children, and a very important one also. Station III attempts to help children distinguish kinds or types of friendships and encourages thought as to their distinguishing characteristics. The children can list attributes on three levels: Friend, Not a Friend, and Best Friend. Lead questions for this activity would concern when and how someone displays this behavior to the individual student. When is someone not a friend? When is someone a friend and when is someone a best friend? Appropriate stimuli for the center can be pictures of children in various situations or groupings.

An additional activity in this station would be to have the students write a poem about a friend of theirs, or their feelings when someone they love goes away. The students can "do" this station individually or in groups.

Station IV—Feeling Afraid. The musical *The King and I*, by Richard Rodgers and Oscar Hammerstein II, contains a song, "I Whistle a Happy Tune," suggesting the opposite of our intentions in this station.

After listening to the complete song on a record the class should discuss the issue of being afraid. When do we pretend that we are not afraid? When are we not able to pretend? Why do we fear letting others know about our being afraid of something or someone?

The teacher should read aloud to the class or tape a reading of a "scary" story. *Where the Wild Things Are*, *Hansel and Gretel*, or *Billy Goat's Gruff* will often have this effect on children. This controlled inducement of fear, and its examination and discussion by the children in a secure, trusting classroom, is a most powerful confrontation for children. Its importance lies in the fact that there are real fears in children's lives and our belief that open discussion and affective support and empathy are necessary if the students are to learn to deal with these conditions in their own lives. This indirect approach is much more effective than asking children why they are afraid, and then telling them not to be. A closing activity in Station IV may ask the students to write or tape a short story about some incident or object that makes them afraid.

Other appropriate topics that can help children examine their feelings are family roles and membership; being an older or younger brother or sister; and the issue of fairness—when we were fair and when we were not fair in our relations with others. These topics are the stuff of life, and, as such, the life of social study.

Station V—The Trust Walk. A well hidden side of the inside self of children is their interest in sometimes "tricking" others, and occasionally doing harmful and nasty things to others. When such conduct occurs in the primary classroom, the teacher usually is relegated to a quick judgment or adjudication, with some moralizing such as "We don't do that here," or "Stop that—go to the corner," or "Leave the room."

This station promotes activities that give children experience with developing trust and concern for others. By actually experiencing trust and concern, one is more able to give it to others. One of our favorite techniques is the affective strategy of a "Trust Walk." The station requires pairs of children and a cloth blindfold. Without being spoken to, one child is to lead and guide another by the hand on a walk over and around some "difficult" terrain, such as an area where, without sight, one would fall or walk into something. (Extreme care must be taken by the teacher so that serious danger is avoided.) After the walks of both children (about 10 minutes each), they might discuss the experience along the following topic headings:

(1) holding hands
(2) leading and following
(3) being blind
(4) levels of trust
(5) specific incidents experienced in the walk
(6) peeking under or over the blindfold
(7) occurrence of squeezing the hand when afraid or feeling threatened

These topics help the children organize the experience of trusting. When do we trust others? How and whom we trust can then be discussed with the whole class when everyone has had this experience. Are there times, without being blind, that we need to trust others? At home? In class? On the street? While swimming or participating in sports? In sharing secrets?

The station can have photographs of situations, poems, or stories that exemplify our interdependence and need to trust others as initiating stimuli.

The teacher should hold a general class discussion of the issue of trust. A clear description of the trust walk, the blindfold, and rules for the walk should be listed at the station.

Station VI—Life Lines. Like the trust walk, the life line theme is quite well known by now. We include a learning station description of it because it is such a powerful idea, and it very effectively summarizes the general Learning Center theme of Who Am I?

The Learning Center construction team should assemble these materials at the life line learning station: string, scissors, construction paper, magazine pictures, index cards, paste, stapler, magic markers, and tape. The instructions for constructing a life line are: build a life line using a piece of string to represent your lifetime. Any and all life events, past, present, and future are appropriate, as the child wishes. The materials can be used in any manner but the representation of the life events should be attached to the string.

Children can make these life lines individually or in groups of two or three. Ask them to reflect back over the various activities in the *Who Am I?* Learning Center. These activities can contribute to the students' gaining some closure as reflections of their individual self. Some children will label and display more events than others, and the sharing of these life lines will remind others about particular events that they forgot to include in their lines. We strongly suggest that additional time be provided for any changes in the life lines. In any event, symbolic construction of one's life and sharing of the stories and experiences inherent in the life line is the essence of the activity. This can be done in small groups at first and later in larger groups. The final activity can be the attachment of the life lines to the large drawn body outline from the *Exploring My Outside* segment of the Learning Center.

The central thrust of this Learning Center has been to afford the child the opportunity to examine issues of a personal nature. The classroom climate for these activities must be open and supportive to entertain the children's unique and sometimes similar presentation of their "outside self." Often in social studies education we ask children to empathize or "wear the shoes" of another person in cross-cultural studies. The activities in this center are designed to bring that task "home" to the classroom as teachers attempt to build mutual trust, respect and support among the children, so that they will be better able to accord to others, in different cultures, mutual respect for differences.

By "Exploring My Inside" we are encouraging the child to examine some often hidden and special themes concerning self: feelings, fears, hopes, beliefs, family and peer relationships. These areas of concern are often ignored in the classroom. We would maintain that a child's familiarity with self, and his willingness and ability to deal with some of these issues will greatly aid his understanding and appreciation of other people. Indeed, some of the "strangeness of others," often exhibited by children in primary level social study of other people, may be attributed to the child's paucity of experience in dealing with some of the hidden areas of self. There are numerous examples of our uniqueness as individuals, and numerous examples of our similarity to others of the human family. Efforts in social studies classes that help children learn more about themselves will help them learn more about others in less of a judgmental atmosphere, a classroom milieu based on trust and acceptance.

B. Intermediate Level Learning Center: North American Indians. A unit and Learning Center about North American Indian cultures would provide an important and provocative topic for students in the intermediate grades. Such studies could help correct the ignorance and stereotypes about "the" Indian that are perpetuated by T.V. Westerns and insensitive children's textbooks and trade books. The basic approach we propose is for students to engage in cross-cultural ethnographic studies about several very different Indian cultures. The cultures we selected were chosen because of (1) their different economies based on different environments, (2) the availability of sufficient information at the students' reading level, and (3) their significance for Indian and American history. We selected the Iroquois of the Northeast Woodlands, the Sioux of the Plains, and the Navaho of the Southwest, to illustrate this type of Learning Center:

Orientation and Purpose

It is the intent of this Learning Center that several themes be prominent.

Theme 1: There should be an ethnographic, ecologically-oriented approach to each culture. Questions to investigate would include:

A. Adaptation to the environment
How were available plants used?
How were the available animals utilized for food, clothing, tools?
B. Types of social groupings
What was the division of labor?
Who lived together and what family patterns were in evidence?
Who made the decisions for the group? Who were the leaders?
C. Transmission of the culture
What skills and knowledge were necessary for survival?
To whom and how were they taught?
D. Sensitivity to values, world view, cultural heritage
What customs and traditions were important to the people?
What types of ceremonies did they have and why?
What myths and legends did they tell? (Their world view was affected by their environment.)

Theme 2: Each student should be encouraged to learn more about himself by contrasting his culture and lifestyle to that of the Indians' cultures. For example, when he studies how the Iroquois utilized deer, he might contrast it with the utilization we make of animals in our daily lives.

There should also be contrast between the different Indian cultures. One way to do this might be the creation of a large brown paper retrieval chart

Figure 1

Culture	Iroquois	Sioux	Navaho
Description of Environment			
Use of Plants			
Use of Animals			
Settlement Patterns			
Transportation			
Division of Labor			
Life Cycle			
World View			

(Figure 1) in which the students enumerate and classify the data they have gathered in response to questions in the Learning Center. This type of chart could be developed by the students for organizing data so that contrasts are evident, and many questions about similarities and differences, patterns of effects and causation could be investigated.

Theme 3: A historical orientation is essential, for each Indian culture has changed through decades and has a history. Too often it is presumed that Africans, Indians, Eskimos and others, who have an oral tradition rather than a written one, have no history. A powerful way of challenging this stereotype is to approach North American Indian cultures from what Tabachnick, Fielder, and Clements perceive as the "There and Then" and the "There and Now" structural concept.[1] For example, questions that could be asked of the Indians in the There and Then might be: Where did this Indian culture come from? What was it like before the white men and women came? How do we know? What is its relationship with the non-Indian? What did the Indians of There and Then have to say about their culture? What did the non-Indians of There and Then have to say about the Indian's culture? This should be contrasted with Indian cultures of today. What are their varied lives like today? What does the Indian today have to say about his or her condition? What does the non-Indian have to say about the Indian? The implications and ramifications of significant cultural change and acculturation in both directions should be emphasized. How has the non-Indian affected the Indian? How has the Indian affected the non-Indian?

Theme 4: The final concurrent theme is to be conscious of how knowledge has been created about the Indian. How do we learn about the Indian? How and what can we learn about the Indian from artifacts, from photographs, television, movies and advertisements? What can we learn from paintings of Indians (both by Indians and non-Indians), and from textbooks and trade books, articles and speeches, legends and poetry? The students should be able to examine both primary and secondary sources and infer the advantages and disadvantages of both. They should be able to compare Indian and non-Indian accounts of the same event and discuss possible reasons for the similarities and differences.

This Learning Center is an extension of all four themes. Due to limitations of space, we will describe a few possible learning stations.

What We Have Learned About the Indian of There and Then

Station I—Perceptions of the Indians: Knowledge, Stereotypes, or Ignorance?

A. The students are to devise a short questionnaire (3-4 questions) with which to interview classmates and parents about their knowledge of the Indians and their beliefs about them. Sample questions might be:

1. What do you know or what have you heard about the North American Indians?
2. How are the Indians of long ago and the Indians of today different?
3. How do you feel about the Indians? How do you think others might feel about the Indians?
4. Where are the main sources that have shaped your learning about Indians?

B. The students select a sample of a population to be interviewed: classmates and parents, teachers, neighbors, and younger and older students.

C. After interviewing, they devise a chart on which to record and organize data.

D. They are to look for patterns in the data and make tentative generalizations about knowledge and beliefs about the North American Indians.

E. Students might develop their own pre- and post-test. After the unit and Learning Center, they might want to administer the questions again to their classmates, to see if attitudes, knowledge, and feelings had changed since the beginning of their study of Indians.

Station II—How We Learn about the Indian of the Nineteenth Century

A. We Can Learn from Scientists and Scholars: Several students would interview archeologists or anthropologists. The interview would be tape-recorded and placed in the Learning Center, so that other students could listen to a firsthand account of "a dig" and learn what artifacts were found, and what archeologists learn from these remains of people.

B. We Can Learn from Artifacts: The teacher and students can amass several artifacts (being careful at first to keep them in separate cultural traditions, i.e., no Navaho blanket with Woodland model canoe).

Genuine artifacts such as Navaho silver squash blossoms and arrowheads as well as authentic replicas of an Iroquois False Face Mask and photographs of artifacts can be ordered from museum catalogs.[2]

Directions to the students might include: Imagine you are an archeologist. What can you figure out about these things, the people who made them, and how they lived? Students usually will (or should be encouraged to) comment on what the thing is, how it was used, what materials it was made of, and what this may tell you about what was important to the people.

C. We Can Learn from Books: The Learning Center should include a multitude of books and articles about the North American Indians, with an appropriate range of reading levels. Especially useful are those about the Iroquois, Sioux, and Navaho. Reference materials should include, if possible, museum publications, articles by social scientists, textbooks, encyclopedias, trade books, fiction and non-fiction materials.

The student would be asked to find and list an article by an anthropologist, an account from a museum, a work by a children's author, and a work by an Indian. The student would be asked to distinguish between primary and secondary sources, and evaluate the accuracy of each.

D. We Can Learn from Paintings: Paintings such as those by George Catlin could be contrasted with illustrations and works of art by Indian artists. What types of information they give one about Indian culture, what each artist seems to view as being important, and how they make the students feel about the Indians can be organized as individual projects.

E. We Can Learn from Maps: Map studies could be done to locate the different Indian culture areas: the Arctic, Subarctic, Northwest Coast Indians, Plains Indians, Indians of the Southwest, and Woodland Indians. Accompanying pictures could be drawn of what the environment looked like when the Indians lived there. The eighteenth-century locations of specific Indian cultures to be studied should be outlined within the shaded culture areas: the Iroquois, the Navaho, the Sioux (or Dakota), the Cherokee, the Nez Percé. On a separate map, five Indian reservations of today could be outlined. The maps could be compared and similarities and differences accounted for. The students might elect to pursue the matter by researching why the Cherokees, an Eastern culture, are now found in Oklahoma; why some of the Eastern cultures, such as the ones that befriended the Jamestown settlers, are not indicated on today's reservations; and how the Navahos were relocated and then moved back to their original location.

Comparative Ecologically-based Ethnographic Studies

Designs for two learning stations, one to inquire into "How the different parts of the available animals were utilized" (Station IV, questions B.1 and 2 below), will be described for the Iroquois and the Sioux cultures, respectively. It is hoped, however, that the creative teacher, whether in a unit or Learning Center, will pursue the majority of the sequenced ethnographic questions for a complete study of at least one culture.

Station III—How Did the Iroquois Adapt to Their Environment Through Their Use of Plants?

A. Students should make data cards from which their classmates can learn about the environment of the Iroquois. Each data card would include a picture and an informational paragraph. Data cards might be made on (1) places where Iroquois lived (similarities and differences between then and now in upstate New York might be mentioned); (2) climate, with special emphasis on the different seasons; (3) plants in the area, (note should be made of which ones grew wild and which ones the Iroquois cultivated); (4) animals in the area (the territory and habits of the animals should be noted).

B. There are many activities and processes by which to study how the Iroquois adapted to their environment through the use of plants:

    1. Write down the names of *all* the plants you can find in your research that the Iroquois used, and list the ways that they used them.

    2. Using a roll of white shelf paper, draw an illustrated cartoon strip or documentary movie with a sentence at the bottom of each frame telling how the Iroquois made maple sugar, or about the "three sisters" of the Iroquois (corn, squash, and beans). A cardboard box could serve as the T.V. cabinet. Two dowel rods, attached to the paper, will allow the students to "show" the movie.

C. Make an illustrated poster, showing all the different uses of the different parts of the corn plant.

D. The Iroquois made many objects out of cornhusks—masks, moccasins, mats, cornhusk dolls. Bring in cornhusks or ears of dried corn and make cornhusk dolls or necklaces of corn kernels strung on rawhide or string.

E. Plant some corn, bean, and squash seeds. Write a short story telling all you had to know and what you had to do. Compare this to how the Iroquois planted corn, squash, and beans. How were your experiences the same and how were they different? Where did you get your supplies and tools? Where did you learn how to do this? How did the Iroquois learn how to do this?

F. Research how the Iroquois turned corn into cornmeal. Grind some corn into cornmeal and use this to make cornbread.

G. The utilization of the forest trees: build a diorama of an Iroquois settlement. Show how they used these logs to build loghouses and palisades. Why did they have palisades? How often did they move their settlement? Why?

Station IV—How Did the Sioux Adapt to Their Environment Through Their Use of Animals?

A. Students should make data cards or posters from which their classmates can learn about the environment of the Sioux (see Task A, Station III).

B. The buffalo.

    1. Make an illustrated poster of a buffalo. Show with arrows all the different uses of the different parts of the buffalo.

    2. Make a list of all the things you use during a day that involve the utilization of an animal. Compare lists with a list of Sioux contacts with animal products. What conclusions can be drawn?

    3. Make a model of articles made from the buffalo, i.e.; a tipi, warrior's shield, toys carved from buffalo horns.

4. Stage a play representing a festival or ceremony about the buffalo; include a Sioux legend or a Sioux chant. Explain why you were dressed and decorated the way you were, and the meaning of the ceremony after your presentation.

C. A discussion of the ritual surrounding the introduction of a new child to the world by the priests of the Omaha (Plains Indians) subclan could follow from a sensitive reading of this chant:

Ho! Ye Sun, Moon, Stars, all ye that move in the heavens,
  I bid you hear me!
Into your midst has come a new life.
  Consent ye, I implore!
Make its path smooth, that it may reach the brow of the first hill!
Ho! Ye Winds, Clouds, Rain, Mist, all ye that move in the air,
  I bid you hear me!
Into your midst has come a new life.
  Consent ye, I implore!
Make its path smooth, that it may reach the brow of the second hill!
Ho! Ye Hills, Valleys, Rivers, Lakes, Trees, Grasses, all ye of the earth,
  I bid you hear me!
Into your midst has come a new life.
  Consent ye, I implore!
Make its path smooth, that it may reach the brow of the third hill!
Ho! Ye Birds, great and small, that fly in the air,
Ho! Ye Animals, great and small, that dwell in the forest,
Ho! Ye Insects that creep among the grasses and burrow in the ground,
  I bid you hear me!
Into your midst has come a new life.
  Consent ye, I implore!
Make its path smooth, that it may reach the brow of the fourth hill!
Ho! All ye of the Heavens, all ye of the Air, all ye of the Earth,
  I bid you all to hear me!
Into your midst has come a new life.
  Consent ye, consent ye all, I implore!
Make its path smooth—then shall it travel beyond the four hills![3]

Comparisons could be made between their ceremonies and wishes for the new child and ours (survey of messages on birth announcements and greeting cards).

D. The use of Indian legends and folklore is encouraged.
  1. Legends could be used to encourage aesthetic sensitivity to the culture and could be a source of information for values discussions. Clues as to how the Indians felt and behaved towards their environment could be discovered.
  2. Folk tales could be examined for models of cultural heroes. What characteristics should a good Sioux or Navaho have? Why? (How might these be adaptive?) This could be contrasted with norms for the "good" American schoolboy or girl and the "good" American father or mother.

E. Learning stations on the Navaho should include activities involving weaving, and a documentary movie tracing the wool from the birth of a lamb to the finished blanket. Looms could be built and weaving done in the classroom.

F. Learning stations on the Navaho should include an activity in which the students do a Navaho sandpainting; research should be done on the gathering of supplies, the meaning of the symbols, why it was done, and by whom and on what occasions.

Station V—What Really Happened at the Battle at the Little Big Horn or the Battle of Wounded Knee?

There should be contrasting accounts of these battles. Perhaps an account by a government publication and an account from an anthropologist,[4] an account in a children's trade book[5] and an account from an Indian eye-witness.[6] Students would be asked to note (1) how the different accounts made them feel; (2) how they were similar; (3) how they were different; (4) why each account was different; (5) what they have learned from this experience about the "facts" of history.

Station VI—Indians have affected the lives of the non-Indian in the United States and the non-Indian has affected the lives of the Indian. Make a list of words, ideas and activities that we have borrowed from American Indians. Start by looking at maps of North America, your state and community. What states, bodies of water, cities and streets in your town bear Indian names?

Topics for additional activities on the history of North American Indians might include (a) origins of the Indians; (b) the story of the Indians and the early settlements of Jamestown and the Pilgrims; (c) the "Trail of Tears" (the removal of the Cherokee), and the "Ghost Dance Religion." Research might be done on famous Indians (and the question asked, "famous to whom?"). How might our list of famous Indians differ from an Indian's list? Candidates for study might include Sequoyah, Tecumseh, Hiawatha, Crazy Horse, Chief Joseph, or Ishi. Students may wish to do historical research about the origin of popular stereotypes about Indians, such as scalping.

In terms of acculturation, the Iroquois' trade and treaty arrangements with the early settlers and the governments of England and France can be studied. What happened to the famous Six Nations? How do these Indians live today?

The Sioux may be studied in terms of the impact of the horse on their culture. What was their life like prior to the introduction of the horse? Who introduced the horse? How did it change their means of procuring food, their style of settlement, their wars with neighboring cultures? The implications of the disappearance of the buffalo should also be studied. Why and how was the buffalo decimated? What happened to the Sioux as a result of the slaughter of buffalo?

The Navaho are an excellent example of the acculturation process. Their incorporation of herding sheep, weaving blankets, and becoming silversmiths could all be studied from this perspective.

Station VII—What do Indians today have to say about their way of life? Students can write letters to acquire issues of Indian newspapers.[7] Selections should be made to include in the sample a militant Indian newspaper, a newspaper specific to one culture (e.g., *The Navaho Times*), a newsletter put out by an Indian Mission. These could be compared to an issue of the students' local newspaper.

Station VIII—What do Indians and non-Indians today have to say about Indian problems? There should be a balanced selection of articles and poetry from both militant and non-militant, reservation and non-reservation Indians. Station VIII contains these three sources of information on Indian life and culture:

    A. The song "My Country 'Tis of Thy People You're Dying" by Buffy Sainte-Marie.

    B. "School and the Six Nations Museum" by John Fadden (Mohawk).[8]

    C. "Message from the President of the United States, March 6, 1968," by President Lyndon Johnson.[9]

Questions that might be discussed from each source are: What is important to the author? What problems of the Indian do they perceive? Are any answers proposed by the author?

The explication of the various themes concerning North American Indians has been designed to get students directly involved in the teaching/learning process. This sample of eight stations was presented to demonstrate both the possible range and depth of investigation inherent in the Learning Center approach to a complex and challenging topic.

Both the Who Am I? and the North American Indians Learning Centers stress activities designed to have students "do" social science. Affective and cognitive processes were integrated throughout a variety of learning stations, and the use of these Learning Centers requires an active engaged role for both students and teachers.

V. Evaluation of Learning Center Activities

Many of the activities in the Learning Center serve the function of helping the student to organize, synthesize, and evaluate the content and processes that he or she has acquired. Sometimes it is important for the student to have a concrete representation of what he has learned to be able to show and share with others. Examples of this might be his notebook on the Indians, data organized from questionnaires, poems and stories, face and body drawings, and other materials collected from the various learning stations. Prominent public display of student posters or student-created learning stations, photographs of role-playing, puppet shows, and presentations to the class are important. They give the student, his peers, and the teacher a chance to see, take pride in, and evaluate what has been learned.

The teacher may deliberately include in a learning station an activity designed to organize and order, sequentially or by comparison, much of the data many students have been collecting. Examples might be the ordering, in the hand-drawn "movie," of the sequence of subsistence activities of the Indians in the different seasons of the year, or of the important stages and ceremonies in the life of Sioux children.

The teacher and students are often astonished and pleased to see how much knowledge they have generated when they integrate and reflect upon their data in retrieval charts. One example is a chart that organizes all the data about the Sioux, Navaho, and Iroquois so that similarities and differences can be noted. The teacher might include as a final step in the station:

A. list five differences you notice among North American Indians;
B. list five patterns of life that you see as similar;
C. using one of your comparisons, write a sentence that explains why you think that there is this similarity or difference among the Indians.

A chart on the problems of the Indians of today might contain a column of problems, a column of ideal solutions, and a column containing information on what is currently being done to alleviate the problems. Many activities that result in concrete products or charts that order, synthesize, and require higher level abstract thinking skills can be included in the Learning Center; we maintain that such activities may be more powerful, more fun, and far more of an indicator of comprehension and cognitive growth than traditional objective tests.

Stations in the Learning Center can be devoted to the development of self-evaluation skills. One very simple technique is to have the students list three or four things they have learned in this learning station. These can then be displayed for others to read.

A station might be devoted to the creation and administration of pre- and post-tests by the students themselves. For example, the students might interview their classmates to ascertain the verified information, stereotypes, and ignorance held about a particular group of people prior to and after the development of a Learning Center.

Students who built projects or learning stations for use by their peers should explain the processes and decisions involved in developing the station. Students can attach to learning stations cards that explain the rational construction and use.

The entire class should also evaluate the Learning Center. The teacher may want to model how one evaluates by first using as an example a learning station she has created. She may ask for comments on the learning station's physical appearance, quality of the ideas presented, type of construction, and sources from which the information was obtained. She might seek suggestions as to how it might be improved or suggestions to show that there is not one right way to build a center.

Comments by peers about each other's work are powerful. Students see that opinions differ and different students prefer different activities for different reasons. Ultimately the Learning Center should be evaluated on a functional basis: "As we examine this activity, how well did it teach us and how well did we learn?"

Useful Resources for the *Who Am I? Learning Center*
de Regniers, M.M., *et al.* (eds.), *Poems Children Will Sit For*, New York: Scholastic Book Services, 1973.
Dewey, John, *How We Think*, New York: D.C. Heath and Co., 1933.

Freire, Paulo, *Pedagogy of the Oppressed*, New York: Herder and Herder, 1971.

Gibson, John S., *The Intergroup Relations Curriculum: A Program for Elementary School Education*, Vol. II, Medford, Mass: Lincoln Filene Center for Citizenship and Public Affairs, 1969.

Jones, Richard M., *Fantasy and Feeling in Education*, New York: Harper Colophone Books, 1970.

Peters, R. S., *Ethics and Education*, Atlanta: Scott, Foresman and Co., 1967.

——————— (ed.), *The Concept of Education*, New York: The Humanities Press, 1967.

Raths, Louis E., Harmin, Merrill, and Simon, Sidney B., *Values and Teaching*, Columbus: Charles Merrill Publishing Co., 1966.

Rogers, Vincent R. (ed.), *Teaching in the British Primary School*, Toronto: Macmillan, 1970.

Stanford, Gene and Roark, Albert E., *Human Interaction in Education*, Boston: Allyn and Bacon, Inc., 1974.

Wisniewski, Richard (ed.), *Teaching About Life in the City*, Washington, D.C.: National Council for the Social Studies, 1972.

Useful Resources for the *North American Indians Learning Center*

Bealer, Alex W., *Only the Names Remain: The Cherokees and the Trail of Tears*, Boston: Little, Brown and Company, 1972.

Bleeker, Sonia, *The Navajo: Herders, Weavers and Silversmiths*, New York: William Morrow and Company, 1958.

Glubok, Shirley, *The Art of the Southwest Indians*, New York: Macmillan, 1971.

Hirschfelder, Arlene, "Bibliography of Sources and Materials for Teaching About American Indians," *Social Education*, Vol. 36, No. 5, May 1972, pp. 488-493.

Jones, Charles (ed.), *Look to the Mountain Top: Our True Indian Heritage*, San Jose: Gousha Publications, 1972.

Josephy, Alvin, *The Patriot Chiefs*, New York: Viking Press, 1961.

Neihardt, John G., *Black Elk Speaks: Being the Life Story of a Holy Man of the Oglala Sioux*, Lincoln: The University of Nebraska Press, 1961.

North American Indians, text by Brown, Joseph Epes; photographs by Curtis, Edward S., Philadelphia: Philadelphia Museum of Art, 1972.

Willey, Gordon R., *An Introduction to American Archeology*, Vol. I, Englewood Cliffs: Prentice-Hall Inc., 1966.

Footnotes

[1] Millard H. Clements, William Fielder, and Robert Tabachnick, *Social Study: Inquiry in Elementary Classrooms*. New York: Bobbs-Merrill Co., 1966, pp. 25, 153.

[2] These authors purchased these artifacts and photographs of artifacts from the University Museum, University of Pennsylvania, 33rd & Spruce Streets, Philadelphia, Pa. 19104. Other museums and enrichment sources are suggested in *Social Education*, Vol. 36, No. 5, May, 1972, pp. 488-494.

[3] A.C. Fletcher and F. LaFlesche, *The Omaha Tribe*. Bureau of American Ethnology, Annual Report 27, 1911, pp. 115-116 as cited in E. Adamson Hoebel, *Man in the Primitive World*. New York: McGraw-Hill Book Co., 1958, pp. 375-376. Used with permission of McGraw-Hill.

[4] James Mooney, *The Ghost Dance Religion and the Sioux Outbreak of 1890*. Chicago: The University of Chicago Press, 1965.

[5] Sonia Bleaker, *The Sioux*. New York: William Morrow & Co., pp. 130-136 (Custer's Last Stand), pp. 145-150 (Battle of Wounded Knee).

[6] John Neihardt, *Black Elk Speaks*. Lincoln: University of Nebraska Press, 1961.

[7] Addresses will be found in "Current North American Indian Periodicals" by the Center for the Study of Man, Smithsonian Institution. *Social Education* Vol. 36, No. 5, May 1972, pp. 494-500.

[8] *Ibid.*, p. 507.

[9] *Ibid.*, p. 506.

A Framework for Utilizing the Community for Social Learning in Grades 4 to 6

David G. Armstrong and Tom V. Savage, Jr.

Local communities provide extraordinary opportunities for teachers to introduce tangible sorts of learning experiences into middle-grades social studies classes. From physical contact with elements of their own community, youngsters build understandings that enhance their acquisition of abstract concepts and higher level information-processing skills.

In essence, the community can be the *laboratory* the learner uses to study data, make decisions, and test decisions against other data. While this learning sequence may not differ markedly from what may be utilized in the classroom using more familiar materials, the "concreteness" and the "real worldliness" of features of the local community are likely to stimulate a higher degree of personal commitment and enthusiasm for social studies than can be anticipated when books, films, and other simulators of reality are used.

The social studies "community laboratory" has unique features that give it even more potential for promoting learning than more familiar laboratories in the sciences. In the community laboratory, learners are both participants and observers, not just observers alone. Generalizations and inferences developed in the community setting assist pupils to understand why they live as they do; and how citizens, working together, can improve the quality of life in their community.

Learning in the community can have profound personal implications. For middle-grades youngsters, learning in the community can put to rest the myth that "learning" occurs only within the walls of the school building and that it has marginal "real world" utility. By teachers encouraging the view

DAVID G. ARMSTRONG is Assistant Professor of Education at Texas A & M University, College Station. TOM V. SAVAGE, JR., is Chairperson of the Department of Education at Whitworth College, Spokane, Washington.

that learning occurs wherever learning opportunities are present, youngsters are encouraged to see learning as a personally meaningful lifelong experience that can serve them faithfully long after their school years have passed.

A successful community-focused social studies program for middle-grades pupils depends on (1) a careful identification and categorization of *stimulus experiences* and (2) a clear explication of categories of *anticipated pupil learnings.*

Stimulus experiences can be divided into three broad categories:

  a. historical residues
  b. present interactional processes
  c. likely future patterns

Anticipated pupil learnings can be divided into the areas of:

  a. ability to make grounded generalizations
  b. ability to examine values
  c. ability to make decisions

The next two sections will explore specific features of the *stimulus experience* component and the *anticipated pupil learnings* component of the well-planned community-focused middle-grades social studies program.

1. Stimulus Experiences

Historical residues. Historical residues are physical traces of the community's past. Drawing heavily on techniques from the discipline of history, pupils might be encouraged to look at old buildings, city records, diaries of early residents, and old maps. They could interview longtime residents or younger descendants of early settlers. Historical residues can serve as a mechanism for teaching pupils how to use the basic tools of historical research. Youngsters can learn how to make inferences from examinations of artifacts and other data and to write short historical accounts. An outstanding culminating activity might be a "history fair."

At the history fair, all the pictures, accounts, maps, and other moveable historical residues pupils had gathered could be arranged into individual exhibits. Certain youngsters might be assigned as "experts" on specific exhibits to provide background information to visitors. Special events might include demonstrations of early pioneer home activities (making yarn, butter, knives, etc.), demonstration of early social activities (traditional dances, corn-husking bees, etc.), or reënactments of important historical events (battles, treaties with Indians, etc.).

Present interactions. Present interactions involve a complex set of inter-dependencies found within all communities. There are, for example, inter-actions among people, interactions relating to geographic distributions, inter-changes involving goods and services, and a host of other dependencies involving rules, laws, traditions, and institutions. At the community level, the study of present interactions draws heavily upon insights from the disciplines of sociology, geography, economics, and political science.

Individuals use the community according to fairly regular patterns of interaction. To help youngsters determine the patterns of community use of their own families, they can keep detailed logs for one week in which they note every location in the community visited by a family member. At the end of the week, using his/her log book as a source of information, each class member can mark an "X" on a personal outline map of the community at each location visited by a family member. If there were multiple trips during the week to the same location, an "X" should be marked for each different day of the week someone in the family visited that location (for example, if the pupil attended school 5 days during the week, then 5 "Xs" should be placed on the map at the location of the school).

When these "family community use maps" have been completed, a master class map can be constructed. Each youngster should be asked to place "Xs" from his/her map on a large (preferably wall-sized) map of the community. When all the "Xs" from the class have been added, data are at hand for a good inquiry discussion: What places in the community do we use most? What goes on at those places? What places in the community were visited by only a few of us? What do you think the difference is between a place many of us visited and a place only a few of us visited?

Various social and economic functions in the community affect individuals. In order to help youngsters understand differing patterns of distribution of these functions, information sources including the city directory and the yellow pages of the telephone book can be used. Each youngster should be given these source materials and an outline map of the community. The teacher should assign each person in the class to plot the locations on the outline map he or she has been given of one social or economic service. For example, one youngster might map locations of all the schools, another all the doctors' offices, and still another all of the new and used car sales outlets.

When individual maps are completed, each youngster can mark on a large wall map the locations of the social or economic function he/she found and logged on his/her personal map. If a color code is used (for example, red "Xs" for fire stations, green "Xs" for doctors' offices, etc.), a master map including all community functions located by class members will result. A map of this type can serve as a stimulus for a productive inquiry session focusing on such questions as: Why are doctors' offices and jewelry stores distributed differently? What is the pattern of distribution of new and used car dealers? Which economic and service functions tend to have similar distribution patterns? Which ones have dissimilar patterns? How do you explain the patterns you see?

A given community interacts with other communities. One way to bring this reality home to youngsters involves the use of school records indicating where people moving into the school attendance area have come from and where people moving out have gone. Using this information, the class can develop two maps, one indicating where people have come from and one indicating where they have moved after leaving the area. The first of these might be constructed with the school as a hub with lines and arrows pointing to the school from locations representing former residences of newcomers. The second map might be similar in form with the exception that lines and arrows could be drawn pointing away from the school in the direction of locations to which former students and their families have moved. Taken together, these maps might stimulate youngsters to deal with such questions as: Where are our people moving? Where are new people coming from? Are people moving to the same areas that other people are coming from? Why do people seem to be moving to some areas and not to others?

Pupils who begin to develop an understanding of patterns of interaction as they occur at the level of the local community are likely to sense a greater affinity for people involved in similar processes in areas beyond the geographic environs the pupils think of as home. These community-based lessons can provide the bases for meaningful comparisons between and among communities: How are we the same? How are we different? What accounts for the similarities and the differences?

Likely future patterns. An examination of likely future patterns involves pupils in an analysis of community features that are in flux. A confrontation with change within the local community can serve as a basis for decision-making relating to the desirability or non-desirability of the change.

A symposium involving a cross-section of community leaders can provide youngsters with desirable background information as they attempt to identify likely future patterns. As participants, community figures, including city council and planning commission members, leaders of the local Bar Association, prominent figures in health services, educational leaders and others, might present their views about selected aspects of the community's future. The event might be organized as a special "Community Futures Day" with each participant directed to spend about ten minutes explaining the future as seen by members of his or her own service, professional, or other occupational group. Speakers ought to be asked to key their remarks to the level of the youngsters and to leave time for questions.

Using information from the "Community Futures Day" symposium as a starting point, youngsters can be divided into groups. Each group should be instructed to focus on possible future trends for a single community function. For example, one group might deal with health care, another group with government, another group with education, and still another group with transportation. A recorder should be designated for each group to write down findings and predictions for each group on a large sheet of butcher paper. At the conclusion of the activity, each youngster who served as a recorder can post the prediction sheet for his/her group. One by one, each group can be called upon to explain findings in its area of emphasis.

As a culminating activity, the class might design and construct a model of the community as it might look twenty-five or fifty years in the future. This model could be displayed at a parents' meeting and might be accompanied by several pupil guides. Two or three youngsters could be designated to provide general background information about the model to parents, explaining, for example, why the class decided the community would have the physical appearance depicted. Other youngsters, drawn from the special community functions groups described above, would be assigned to provide "expert testimony" on the future of medicine, government, education, transportation, and other areas.

Involvement in exercises centering on likely future patterns engages pupils in two concurrent learning experiences. First, using available evidence, they learn how to specify what is happening now and to infer future consequences of that "happening." Second, they learn how to determine their own personal value priorities as they make judgments about the qualitative effects of projected changes in the community. This two-step process involves youngsters in the kind of decision-making that is the essence of responsible citizenship.

2. Anticipated Pupil Learnings

Making grounded generalizations. Making grounded generalizations involves youngsters in cognitive processes requiring the manipulation of specific data from the local community. These data may be organized under each of the three categories of stimulus experiences (historical residues, present interactional processes, likely future patterns), and pupils can be asked to respond to questions about each. Some suggested questions are provided here under each heading:

(1) Historical residues
   —What has been left?
   —What do these residues tell us about what life used to be like here?
   —Why did you reach those conclusions?
   —How might we check the accuracy of those conclusions?
(2) Present interactional processes
   —What is made here and sent out? What is brought in?
   —Where do people live and where do they work in the community? How do they get back and forth? How do you know?
   —How do you account for any changes you see? How might we check the accuracy of your explanation?
(3) Likely future patterns
   —What is life here going to be like in ten years? In fifty years?
   —What specific things happening now lead you to predict what life will be like in the future?
   —What changes that have not yet been observed must take place before your predicted future can occur?

Examining values. Examining values in the local community involves a two-part process. On the one hand, pupils look at the community to identify values underlying decisions that have shaped the community. On the other hand, they test their own values for congruence against the wider values of the community. Some suggested questions designed to elicit information regarding both community values and personal values have been organized under the three stimulus experiences categories:

(1) Historical residues
—*community values*: What values of people who lived in this community in the past are suggested by remaining residues?
—*personal values*: How do you feel about life in the past in this community as it is suggested by remaining residues?
(2) Present interactional processes
—*community values*: What values, priorities are associated with present ways of life in this community?
—*personal values*: How do you feel about values, priorities reflected in present ways of life in this community?
(3) Likely future patterns
—*community values*: What values are reflected in the likely future of this community?
—*personal values*: How do you feel about values reflected in the likely future of this community?

Making decisions. Making decisions results from an interaction between available evidence and personal values. In the community setting, decision-making by pupils parallels the sorts of policy decisions that must be made by the reflective adult citizen. Some samples of the sorts of questions with which pupils might be asked to deal have been provided here under each of the three stimulus experiences categories:

(1) Historical residues
—What do you think life in the community was really like in the past? Why did you reach that conclusion?
—What features of life deriving from this community's past should continue to be emphasized? Why?
—Were there some things that happened in the past that set undesirable precedents for the present and for the future? Which ones, and why?
(2) Present interactional processes
—What aspects of present life in this community most appeal to you? Why?
—What aspects of present life in this community do you find most distressing? Why?
—What aspects of life in this community are most in need of change? Why?
—How might you begin working with others to bring about changes you desire?
(3) Likely future patterns
—What kind of a community would you like to live in? Why?
—What are the differences between the kind of a community you would like to live in and this community?
—How might you begin to work with others to bring about the type of community here you would most like to live in?

Figure 1: A Framework for Focus Questions in Community-Centered Middle-Grades Social Studies

	Historical Residues	As Stimulus Materials Pupils Look At — Present Interactional Processes	Likely Future Patterns
Make Grounded Generalizations	What has been left? What do residues tell us about what life used to be like here? How could we check on the accuracy of these conclusions?	What is made here and sent out? What is brought into the community? What is your evidence? Where do people live and where do they work in the community? How do they get back and forth? How do you know? How do you account for any changes you see? How might we check on the accuracy of your explanation?	What is life in the community going to be like in ten years? In fifty years? What specific things are happening now that lead you to predict what life will be like in the future? What changes that have not yet been observed must take place before your predicted future for the community can occur?
Examine Values	*Community values:* What values of people who lived in this community in the past are suggested by remaining residues? *Personal values:* How do you feel about life in the past in this community as it is suggested by remaining residues?	*Community values:* What values, priorities are associated with present ways of life in this community? *Personal values:* How do you feel about values, priorities reflected in present ways of life in this community?	*Community values:* What values are reflected in the likely future of this community? *Personal values:* How do you feel about values reflected in the likely future of this community?
Make Decisions	What do you think life in the community was really like in the past? Why did you reach that conclusion? What features of life deriving from this community's past should continue to be emphasized? Why? Were there some things that happened in the past that set undesirable precedents for the present and the future? Which ones, and why?	What aspects of present life in this community most appeal to you? Why? What aspects of present life in this community do you find most distressing? Why? What aspects of life in this community are most in need of change? Why? How might you begin working with others to bring about changes you desire?	What kind of a community would you like to live in? Why? What are the differences between the kind of community you would like to live in and this community? How might you begin to work with others to bring about the type of community here you would most like to live in?

3. A Framework for Community-Focused Social Studies

Utilizing the community to provide social learning for middle-grades youngsters involves a consideration of both appropriate stimulus experiences and anticipated pupil learnings. When a relationship between a specific stimulus experience and a specific anticipated pupil learning is made clear, planning for instruction is facilitated. A graphic representation of possible combinations of stimulus experiences and pupil learnings is presented in matrix form in the chart, Figure 1 (see p. 71). A conscientious effort to promote pupils' consideration of questions derived from each cell of the matrix will go a long way toward assuring a comprehensive program.

4. Conclusion

Direct, concrete sorts of experiences available in local communities can provide a solid conceptual base for youngsters to draw upon as they attempt to make generalizations relating to similarities and differences between themselves and other peoples and cultures. Time spent in the local community promotes the view that learners, as decision-makers, have the capacity to influence the conditions under which they live. There are possibilities for developing (1) a world view grounded in learners' solid understanding of their own place and time and (2) an attitude that human beings have the power to shape events, and these possibilities suggest that the local community affords a marvelous opportunity for social learning in the middle grades.

The Use of Modules
in Teacher Education

Michael L. Hawkins

The social studies methods sequence at the University of Georgia is based on two assumptions: there is a certain body of knowledge about method which a prospective elementary teacher should acquire, and the degree of this acquisition can be observed as the prospective teacher works with pupils. These assumptions are an outgrowth of the Georgia Education Model for the Preparation of Elementary Teachers[1] and the Feasibility Study[2] which tested the cost effectiveness of a model teacher education program. The prime instructional tool used throughout the program is the proficiency module, as described in this article.

Background for Module Development

The key terms *modular instruction* and *instructional models* have distinct meanings. As defined in the Georgia Education Model, modular instruction is a system incorporating objectives, pre-assessment, learning activities, and post-assessment.[3] Instructional modules are self-instructional devices which enable preservice teachers to move through the instructional system at their own rate. They are self-contained, inexpensive, and focus on methodological content which the designers of the Georgia Education Model regarded as basic to effective elementary teaching.

Preliminary data gleaned from studies conducted at the University of Georgia indicated that the original social studies and science modules did not function in a totally satisfactory manner when used at the preservice level.[4] These modules included matched listings of objectives and texts, films, tapes, and other commercially produced materials from which the reader chose to

MICHAEL L. HAWKINS is Associate Professor of Education at the University of Georgia, Athens.

read, listen to, or watch as information input. The revised modules include structured sequences of information and activities which facilitate the acquisition of information at each step in the module.

Findings of other studies on module instruction, though limited, are encouraging. For example, Merwin and Schneider found that self-instructional modules resulted in significantly higher achievement test scores and student teacher performance ratings by secondary school social studies preservice teachers than traditional instruction; further, these writers state that they ". . . anticipate a generally favorable student reaction to future utilization of self-instructional modules."[5] The positive findings of an extensive review of the literature by Merwin,[6] coupled with the author's broad personal experience with modular instruction, support the contention that modules are a viable mode for instructing prospective teachers.

Module Construction

An integral part of a performance-based program is the identification and description of the tasks needed by a teacher in the classroom. In order to specify tasks, objectives need to be determined. In the Georgia program, objectives were drawn from the original Model program, from public school teachers' opinion, and from professors' judgments. Selected objectives then directed the specification of competencies. These competencies were grouped into the three major areas of concept development, value analysis, and skill development. Next, they were published and distributed to preservice teachers enrolled in social studies methods courses, and to their public school teacher-supervisors. The competency statements follow:

Competency Statements: Social Studies

1. *Concept Development.* While using a self-written learning plan designed according to an accepted strategy for teaching a concept, the preservice teacher will teach an appropriate social science concept to a small group or entire class of elementary school pupils at a grade level of choice. Performance will be judged according to the following criteria:
   a. The teaching strategy follows a model strategy or is an acceptable modification of it.
   b. The concept is appropriate for the given age level.
   c. The examples include necessary attributes and exclude extraneous detail.
   d. Appropriate verbal behavior is used during the various steps of the teaching strategy.
2. *Value Analysis.* While using a self-written learning plan designed according to an accepted value analysis strategy, the preservice teacher will conduct a value analysis lesson with a small group or entire class of elementary school pupils at a grade level of choice.[7]
3. *Skill Development.* While using a self-written learning plan designed according to an accepted skill development strategy for teaching a skill,

the preservice teacher will conduct a skills lesson with a small group or entire class of elementary school pupils at a grade level of choice. The titles of the modules are:

- *Organizing Knowledge for Instruction*
- *Harmonizing Questions and Activities Used by Teachers with the Level of Cognitive Behavior Expected of Pupils*
- *Concept Formation— Concept Teaching*
- *Interpreting Data*
- *Values and the Valuing Process*
- *Simulation Games and Role Playing*
- *Intercultural Understanding—The Problem and a Process*
- *Skill Development—Maps and Globes*

The eight modules were designed and written by a team of elementary school social studies specialists at the University of Georgia, and first tested in the Spring of 1972. The production of each module followed this sequence.

1. Based on the performance needs of the elementary teacher, a social studies content topic was selected by the writing team.
2. The module included a rationale and an overview of the tasks to be accomplished.
3. Both terminal and enabling objectives specified the performance necessary to complete the module.
4. Supportive information was provided for each enabling objective, examples of the enabling task were shown, and finally an enabling activity was presented that was to be completed by the reader.
5. A terminal activity was selected. Usually the terminal activity required the reader to write an appropriate lesson plan for pupils in the classroom.

Description of a Module

The *Concept Formation* module is presented here in detail to illustrate the instructional sequence of the module.

Concept Formation—Concept Teaching

INTRODUCTION

This section presents a rationale for the content of the module, and an overview of the tasks to be performed. *Terminal objective:* "While using a unit of instruction in an elementary school social studies textbook at a grade level of choice, the reader will be able to identify two or more key concepts in the unit, and write a lesson plan describing the methods and materials to be used in teaching one of these concepts." *Enabling objectives:* "Given a list of concepts, the reader will be able to write four attributes based on his understanding of each concept." "Given a specific social studies concept, the reader will demonstrate his understanding of the Gagné model for teaching a concept by writing examples and non-examples for the given concept, and by placing these along with teacher statements in correct order."

PART 1—*Concepts and Their Attributes*

This section defines concepts and their attributes. It includes such examples as "RIVER: water, flowing, channelized, carries sediments." An enabling activity follows which presents abstract and concrete concepts: "lake," "man," "change," "transportation," etc. The reader then identifies attributes of these concepts.

PART 2—*Concept Formation*

This section describes how conceptualization takes place in a child. Stress is placed upon experience in the process of conceptualizing. Concrete concepts are used as examples.

PART 3—*Why Teach Concepts*

The function of concepts as part of a person's mental data-processing system is discussed with an emphasis on concepts as organizers of information. A rationale for a conceptually-based social studies curriculum is presented as a process resembling the mental activity of people. Abstract concepts are used as illustrations.

PART 4—*Teaching Concepts*

This section introduces Gagné's model for teaching a concept.[8] The reader is shown an example using a fictitious concept to illustrate the progression of examples and non-examples specified by the model. Teacher statements illustrate what is said to pupils as the teacher moves through the presentation. The fictitious concept consists of geometric figures: rectangle, square, and circle. The figures and specific placement of the figures are the key attributes. Then, using a real concept, "water transportation," the reader completes a lesson plan by writing or drawing examples of water transportation (barge, tanker, etc.), listing non-examples (automobile, airplane, etc.), and writing probable teacher statements ("This is an example of . . ."), to teach the concept.

PART 5—*Writing Lesson Plans for Teaching a Concept*

A form for a lesson plan is introduced that serves throughout the remainder of the series. The example of the concept "roles" is presented.

Upon completion of the enabling activities, the reader is given a restatement of the terminal objective and a blank lesson plan form. The reader is directed to use his accumulated knowledge of concept formation in selecting four concepts from a child's textbook, and in writing a lesson plan employing the Gagné Model to teach one of the concepts.

The Instructional Sequence

Regardless of the sophistication of the textbook, module, or other device used to transmit information to the student, the philosophy of the program supports a close relationship between the methods' professor and preservice teachers and between the preservice teacher and his or her peers. During the academic quarter, preservice teachers spend approximately ten two-hour sessions on campus in the social studies methods class. Simultaneously they receive on-campus instruction in general methodology and special methods in language arts, science, and reading.

At the beginning of the concept segment of the social studies sequence, preservice teachers receive copies of the competency statement and performance criteria. Then they are required to complete the concept formation module outside of class. The professor and the class of prospective teachers work through the content of the module. Next, the professor gives several demonstrations of the model; afterward, the preservice teachers practice the strategy in pairs or in small groups. Two other concept teaching models are covered in the same fashion, except that these are not part of the module series.[9] At this point, the preservice teachers are able to complete the module outside of class. Upon completion of this instructional sequence, the neophyte has three concept development models to choose from to complete the teaching requirement of the competency.

With the help of the classroom teacher, the preservice teacher selects a concept that fits into the program of the classroom. While following the instructions of the module, he or she writes a lesson plan which is formally evaluated by the college instructor. A typical lesson plan is on p. 78.

Preservice Teacher Activity in the Public School

Since the on-campus phase of the instructional program in the methods course is conducted in the afternoons, preservice teachers spend entire mornings, Monday through Thursday, or a total of twelve hours per week, in a nearby elementary school.

Upon completion of the on-campus instructional module in concept development, the methods professor makes an appointment with the preservice teacher to observe the use of the approved lesson plan with either a small group or an entire class of children. During the observation the professor completes a rating form which includes the following items:

Strategy
   Follows proper sequencing of the strategy steps.
   Good pacing from step to step.
Materials used
   Neat and precise.
   Large enough for all to see.
   Correct in content.
Intern verbal behavior
   Questions or statements used were appropriate for the strategy steps.
   Reinforcing and non-threatening.
Pupil involvement
   Degree to which pupils participated verbally or actively in the lesson.
Appropriateness of concept
   Degree to which the content taught is appropriate to the age level of the pupil.

Concept Teaching Lesson Plan

Name_____ *John or Jane Doe* _____ Grade_____ *First* _____

Date_____ *October 6* _____Time required_____ *30 minutes* _____

Behavioral Objective: Given photographs of different types of shelter, the pupil can identify those that are not shelter.

Materials: Families and Their Needs, Silver Burdett, 1972. Denoyer-Geppert Study Prints.

Procedure: (Preservice Teacher fills in procedure)

Steps	Activities or Examples	Statements or Questions
1.	Show examples of shelter: Rural house in winter, p. 36 Thatched roof house, p. 37 Farm house, pp. 38–39	This is a picture of one kind of shelter. This is an example of shelter. This is a shelter. Define shelter as a place for protection.
2.	Show more examples of shelter: Row house, pp. 38–39 Camper, p. 40 Oriental houseboat, p. 41	This is shelter in a city. What is this family doing? What is their shelter in the woods? This is a different kind of shelter.
3.	Show non-examples: Woman shopping, p. 9 Eskimos playing with dog, p. 10 Man and children in canoe, p. 15	This is not a shelter. Neither is this. What is happening in this picture? This is not a shelter.
4.	Show examples and non-examples: Log house in Arctic, p. 48 Log cabin, p. 108 Housing project apartments, p. 131. Tent on mountain, p. 137 Policeman directing traffic, p. 38 Road construction, p. 144 Agricultural workers, p. 145 Family swimming, p. 153	These are examples of different kinds of shelters. These pictures are not shelters.
5.	Evaluation step: Show 5 examples of shelter and 5 non-examples from Denoyer-Geppert study prints.	Distribute everybody-show cards. "If I show a picture of shelter, you hold up card marked YES when I say SHOW. If I show a picture that is not shelter, hold up the card marked NO.

Following the lesson, with added suggestions by the classroom teacher, the professor assists the neophyte to identify strengths and weaknesses of the lesson. When the performance task is completed satisfactorily, the preservice teacher moves into the cycle again to begin work on another competency. When the preservice teacher has an unsatisfactory lesson, she or he is helped during the post-observation conference to rethink the original lesson in order to identify difficulties. The preservice teacher is observed again as she or he reteaches the concept to another group of pupils or teaches another concept to the same group.

Advantages and Disadvantages

The module program has advantages and disadvantages for preservice teachers and methods professors. For preservice teachers, one prime advantage is the absence of guesswork about course requirements; they know what they must do and the level which they must achieve. Further, they develop confidence in their ability to instruct children. Also, their training in a performance-based teacher education program makes them more employable than graduates of traditional programs.

The chief disadvantage for the preservice teacher is the numerous hours spent in preparing for on-campus classes as well as for their work in the elementary school. A typical day begins with children early in the morning and ends with on-campus classes in the late afternoon. This intensive experience could also be an advantage because it accurately represents a typical day for a teacher.

Within this modular program, the classic instructor-dominated college classroom is supplanted by student-centered activity based on skills needed in elementary social studies instruction. The college instructor benefits by having intensive contact with preservice teachers, children, teachers, and administrators; exposure to the public schools gets college instructors out of the ivory tower and keeps them abreast of current developments in the schools.

Summary

This article describes a modification of the Georgia Education Model for the Preparation of Elementary Teachers. The prime instructional tool in this model is the self-instructional module. The modules benefit preservice teachers, who learn specific performance competencies and practice them with children in a nearby elementary school. Benefits accrue to public elementary classroom teachers as they monitor preservice teachers' instruction in foundational skills in the social studies; also, the preservice teachers provide valuable assistance in the classroom. These mutual benefits seem to underscore a propitious arrangement that is consistent with the function of a teacher-training institution.

Footnotes

[1] Charles E. Johnson, Gilbert F. Shearron, and A. John Stauffer, *Final Report: Georgia Education Model Specifications for the Preparation of Elementary Teachers* (Washington, D.C.: Bureau of Research, Office of Education, U.S. Department of HEW, October, 1968).

[2] Charles E. Johnson and Gilbert F. Shearron (Editors), *The Feasibility of the Georgia Educational Model for Teacher Preparation—Elementary* (Washington, D.C.: Bureau of Research, Office of Education, U.S. Department of HEW, January, 1970).

[3] Gilbert F. Shearron and Charles E. Johnson, "A CBTE Program in Action: University of Georgia," *Journal of Teacher Education* 24 (Fall, 1973): 189-190.

[4] James E. Akenson and Michael L. Hawkins, *Reactions of College Students to a Social Science Education Proficiency Module,* GEM Bulletin 69-10 (Athens, Georgia: College of Education, University of Georgia, 1969). Kenneth S. Ricker and Michael L. Hawkins, *Reactions of College Students to a Science Education Proficiency Module,* GEM Bulletin 69-8 (Athens, Georgia: College of Education, University of Georgia, 1969). Kenneth S. Ricker and Michael L. Hawkins, *Testing a Science Education Proficiency Module with College Students,* GEM Bulletin 69-12 (Athens, Georgia: College of Education, University of Georgia, 1969).

[5] William C. Merwin and Donald O. Schneider, "The Use of Self-Instructional Modules in the Training of Social Studies Teachers to Employ Higher Cognitive Level Questioning Strategies," *Journal of Educational Research* 67 (September 1973): 18.

[6] William C. Merwin, "The Effectiveness of Self-Instructional Modules in Preparing Secondary School Social Studies Teacher-Trainees to Plan, Question, and Test for Higher Cognitive Processes" (unpublished Ed.D. dissertation, University of Georgia, 1972), pp. 15-49.

[7] Performance criteria for value analysis and skill development are essentially the same as for concept development.

[8] The concept development model used throughout this module was developed by Robert Gagné and is presented in "The Learning of Concepts," *The School Review* 73 (Autumn 1965): 191.

[9] See Hilda Taba and James Hills, *Teacher Handbook for Contra Costa Social Studies* (Contra Costa County, California: Contra Costa County Schools, 1966), p. 85; also, Rita Watrin and Elmer D. Williams, *Social Science for the Contemporary Classroom* (Morristown, N.J.: Silver Burdett, 1973), p. 22.

Microteaching/Videotaping Experiences in the Methods Course

Mario D. Rabozzi

Microteaching is defined as a scaled-down teaching encounter with a small group of pupils; the lesson is often recorded on video-tape for analysis by the teacher.[1] Peck and Tucker describe microteaching as "a conceptual system for identifying specified teaching skills with the use of videotape feedback to facilitate growth in teaching skills."[2] Typically, the procedure in preservice education consists of the instructor teaching a skill, reviewing the neophyte's written plan to teach the skill, videotaping the actual lesson with children, and conferring with the prospective teacher as the videotape is viewed.

Microteaching began in the early 1960s at Stanford University. It has served as a training technique for preservice and inservice teachers, and also as a research tool to assess training effects under controlled conditions. This article describes the use of microteaching/videotaping experiences with undergraduate students enrolled in the elementary school social methods course at State University of New York, Oswego.

The Literature

An examination of the literature indicates, as expected, that a large majority of articles described the use of microteaching, while relatively few research studies tested its effectiveness as a teacher-training technique. Nevertheless, more studies have been reported on microteaching than on most of the other innovative teaching methods described in this section on preservice training of teachers.

Allen and Fortune reported that after an eight-week microteaching program consisting of about ten hours per week, secondary school interns

MARIO D. RABOZZI is Professor of Education at the State University of New York, College of Arts and Science, at Oswego.

performed at a higher level of teaching competence than a comparable group of student teachers who spent 20-25 hours a week receiving traditional instruction with a related experience as teacher aides.[3] In a replication of Allen and Fortune's study, Kallenbach and Gall reported that the ratings of elementary school interns' teaching effectiveness were not significantly higher than ratings of interns who did not engage in microteaching.[4]

In an investigation designed to improve teachers' abilities to ask analytical questions, Koran found that videotape feedback was more effective than written feedback.[5] Emmer and Millett used microteaching and assessed terminal performance in a teaching laboratory. Their findings revealed that in the dimensions of determining readiness, motivating students, and evaluating student response, secondary education students in the experimental group performed significantly better than the control group.[6] In a comprehensive treatment of microteaching instruction involving minicourses, preservice teachers made impressive improvements in the skills of some courses; maintenance of some skills existed four months after the study.[7]

At best, three conclusions can be drawn from a perusal of these and other investigations. First, the results of studies concerned with the effectiveness of microteaching/videotaping experiences in teacher education have been mixed. Second, those who have used the technique have nearly always verified its utility in the instruction of basic skills. Finally, a count of the articles listed in *The Education Index* in the past five years indicates little change in the number of published articles on the subject.

Videotaping Promotes an Objective Analysis of the Lesson

All of us find it difficult to remember what we have seen in a classroom or on a street. The problem of observational reliability is exemplified in court cases in which several sincere witnesses to a bank robbery vary widely in their descriptions of the robbers and in their versions of the event. Often they cannot even agree on the number of bank robbers!

After observing a specific lesson taught in an elementary classroom, the college supervisor often has difficulty in recalling accurately what really occurred so that he or she can aid or support the prospective teacher during the post-teaching conference. The prospective teacher has even more of a problem in remembering what happened during instruction. While teaching, he or she had to cope with the condition of being observed and evaluated by the college supervisor while at the same time he or she was inextricably involved with the teaching-learning process.

The videotaped lesson shows it as it was. All one has to do is to view the tape to see what happened during the lesson. It promotes an objective analysis of the lesson. Important segments of instruction can be replayed and viewed as often as necessary.

The following sections describe the sequence of using microteaching/videotaping as a teaching technique in the social studies methods course at State University of New York, Oswego.

The Professional Semester

A team of four professors is responsible for teaching a class of approximately seventy-five preservice teachers the methods associated with language arts, mathematics, science, and social studies. During the semester, instruction in the college classroom is twice alternated with practicum experiences with children in the Swetman Learning Center, the campus laboratory school: the sequence entails five weeks in the college classroom, three weeks of practicum experiences, four weeks in the college classroom, and three weeks of practicum experiences.

In the elementary school social studies course, students receive instruction in basic skills appropriate for brief microteaching lessons, as well as in other strategies which typically entail longer periods of time. Each preservice teacher is required to teach a microteaching lesson which is videotaped during either the first or second practicum experience in the laboratory school.

Some of the skills taught by the instructor that have been popular selections by students for microteaching lessons include:

1. Directing the class toward a goal, content, activity, or procedure.
2. Negotiating with the class toward a goal, content, activity, or procedure.
3. Cooperative teacher-pupil planning of goals, procedures, activities, or content selection and study.
4. Picture examination: describing, inferring, or valuing.
5. Teaching a concept.
6. Conducting a discussion.
7. Using questioning strategies.

Planning and Taping the Lesson

The planning conference with the student is an attempt to insure that a microteaching lesson will be a personally beneficial experience. Much attention is centered on reducing the student's anxiety concerning the taping; for instance, the instructors stress that the purpose of the videotaping is self-diagnostic, rather than a form of evaluation imposed by the instructor. Also, assurance is given that only the student and the instructor will view the tape during the critique session, that no one will have access to it without the student's permission, and that the tape will be erased when its use has been served.

Moreover, the student's lesson plan is reviewed, discussed, and frequently altered to insure a better lesson. This lesson review permits the instructor to become acquainted with the ingredients of the lesson—movement by the student, visuals to be used, work session of pupils—which will assist him or her with the technical aspects of videotaping. At this point, students are advised not to teach to the camera.

On the appointed day and time, the lesson is videotaped by the instructor. The equipment consists of a compact, portable unit that accommodates a half-inch tape and natural lighting. At the beginning of the session, preservice teachers seem to be aware of the camera, but many later report that after a few minutes the teaching lesson itself pushes the idea of the camera into the subconscious. Generally, eight to twelve minutes of videotaping yield sufficient data about significant elements for discussion during the critique session.

Viewing and Critiquing the Tape

So that student concerns and anxieties have little chance to build up, the post-teaching conference is usually conducted immediately after the lesson. Since the purpose of the conference is to focus on self-analysis of one's teaching act, the student is assigned the task of identifying a few significant strengths and weaknesses. As the tape is viewed, the instructor jots down substantive statements made by the student for later examination.

Frequent stops are necessary to allow the student the opportunity to decipher and to evaluate the events and elements of the teaching behavior. At these points in the tape, many students seek praise, support, corroboration, encouragement, and direct assistance from the instructor in interpreting reasons for their or the pupils' behaviors.

When the student is urged to make judgments about his teaching behavior, he acts on the basis of his own personal experiences, rather than to feedback provided by the instructor or peers, which is often the case with non-videotape critiques. To facilitate this student-centered conference, it is essential for the instructor to assume an indirect posture that accepts student ideas and feelings, provides praise and encouragement, and asks non-threatening questions.

This private viewing of the tape—as opposed to peer viewing—helps a student to criticize himself in a supportive climate and to speculate about improvements. Some of the facets of a lesson to which students are requested to react are motivation, verbal and nonverbal behavior of the teacher and pupils, teacher-pupil interaction, interest of children, voice, clearness of directions, individual differences, and organization and execution of the lesson. Frequently, content load emerges as a concern when the student realizes that she or he attempted to cover too much ground in too brief a time, or that insufficient content impeded a discussion.

Often the instructor asks the student to rephrase key questions to achieve clarity, or to suggest another way to organize content. The following sample was audiotaped during a critique session:

> JOE: Look at me. I'm lecturing. Boy, is that deadly. I sound like some of my teachers.
> TEACHER: Thanks a lot.
> JOE: Not you. I mean when I was in high school. Why am I doing that? I thought I had my plans worked out and there I go telling them about the Constitution. Turn it off.
> TEACHER: How would you change it?
> JOE: I wouldn't lecture.
> TEACHER: Suggest a change.

JOE: I could put some of this on a ditto.

TEACHER: What else?

JOE: All those words. I should have written them on the board. Better still, I could have put them on colored strips and created a chart as I introduced each one. We talked about that in class.

TEACHER: Would you like to teach it again with the other fifth grade?

JOE: If you think I should . . .

TEACHER: Do you think you want to?

JOE: Yes. But I'll need time to plan it and make my visuals.[8]

In this instance the lesson was retaught to another group of children with marked success.

At the conclusion of the post-teaching conference, significant student statements that were jotted down by the college instructor during the viewing are read aloud to ensure that they are understood by both parties, and to underscore the strengths and needs of the student. This self-assessment process has often led to improved commitment by the student in his or her professional program, and to students' requests for specific topics to be treated in the course.

Benefits and Limitations

Microteaching/videotaping programs reduce the gap between what goes on in a college classroom and the teaching skills used with young children. In this regard, microteaching concentrates on a few, selected, significant elements of teaching rather than on a wide range of teacher behaviors. Also, the feedback provided by the videotape is objective; this reinforces positive student behaviors and encourages a student to recognize negative behaviors, and to alter them if he or she desires to teach a second taped lesson.

It has always been difficult for an instructor to express constructive criticism without impairing interpersonal relationships with the student. The videotape allows self-evaluation and fosters inner-directed efforts toward the goal of becoming a competent teacher. Additional benefits that might accrue to the student are internal (processes within the teacher; e.g., insights and confidence; also, the peculiarities of the teaching situation) and external (realities of the training system), which Parsons identified in his work on guided self-analysis.[9]

Although the author believes that the benefits of micro-teaching/videotaping far outweigh their limitations, he recognizes that videotaping does involve a sizeable expenditure of time and energy for pre- and post-teaching conferences and for taping lessons. But to provide solid training in any professional field, the instructor must spend a generous amount of time with the student.

Some critics have been concerned with the cost of the videotape equipment. Today, such equipment can be purchased for about $2000, a reasonable sum when compared with the cost of similar equipment purchased fifteen years ago. As with the factor of time, good education has always cost more than inferior education; in the author's opinion, the purchase of videotaping apparatus is certainly a justifiable expenditure of funds.

Other weaknesses of the program include the limited number of videotapings (only one or two tapings per student), the small group of children involved in the lessons, the brevity of lessons, and the artificial learning environment of microteaching. These limitations can be placed in perspective, however, when it is recognized that microteaching/videotaping is an advance over traditional forms of teacher training; and, indeed, may lead to even better training arrangements in the future.

Conclusion

For a long time it has been recognized that effective training of professionals consists of a balance between formal studies and on-the-job experiences. The microteaching/videotaping program described above combines instruction in skills in a college classroom with the practice of these skills with children. Used during the methods course, the videotape provides strong, objective feedback to preservice teachers during their formative education. It has been appropriately employed with student teachers too. As a compact, light, easily operated, and relatively inexpensive tool, the videotape apparatus offers much potential for improving teacher education programs.

Footnotes

[1] Carter V. Good (Editor), *Dictionary of Education* (New York: McGraw-Hill, 1973), p. 366.

[2] Robert F. Peck and James A. Tucker, "Research on Teacher Education," in *Second Handbook of Research on Teaching,* Robert M. W. Travers, Editor (Chicago: Rand McNally, 1973), Ch. 30, p. 951.

[3] D. W. Allen and J. C. Fortune, "An Analysis of Micro-Teaching: A New Procedure in Teacher Education," in *Micro-Teaching: A Description* (Stanford, Calif.: School of Education, Stanford University, 1967), Section III, pp. 1-11.

[4] W. W. Kallenbach and M. D. Call, "Micro-teaching versus Conventional Methods in Training Elementary Intern Teachers." *Journal of Educational Research* 63 (November 1969): 136-141.

[5] Mil Koran, R. E. Snow, and F. J. McDonald, "Teacher Aptitude and Observational Learning of a Teaching Skill," *Journal of Educational Psychology* 62 (June 1971) 219-228.

[6] E. T. Emmer and C. B. Millett, *An Assessment of Terminal Performance in a Teaching Laboratory: A Pilot Study* (Austin, Texas: University of Texas, Research and Development Center for Teacher Education, 1968). (mimeographed)

[7] W. R. Borg, M. L. Kelly, P. Langer, and M. Gall, *The Minicourse: A Microteaching Approach to Teacher Education* (Beverly Hills, Calif.: Macmillan Educational Services, 1970).

[8] Used with permission of student and teacher.

[9] Theodore W. Parsons, *Guided Self-Analysis System for Professional Development* (Berkeley, Calif.: University of California, 1968).

Performance Competencies: Lessons Using a Prototype, Simulation, and Protocol Materials

Wayne L. Herman, Jr.

"What can preservice teachers *do* after taking your course?" "What performance criteria are used to evaluate students in your social studies methods course?" Increasingly, questions focusing on observable behavioral outcomes of college courses are being leveled at professors across the nation by college students and administrators, state departments of education, and accrediting agencies. Without a doubt, the current thrust in teacher education emphasizes performance. Some professors have already made a move in this direction, but for many professors the heat is on.

It is well known that a research basis for performance competencies does not exist. Peck and Tucker state that very little research at the present time establishes a measurable effect of teachers on learner outcomes.[1] After reviewing the research on teacher education, Heath and Nielson drew a similar conclusion, and predicted: "Given the well documented, strong association between student achievement and variables such as socioeconomic status and ethnic status, the effects of techniques of teaching on achievement are likely to be inherently trivial."[2]

Nevertheless, it is likely that the newer techniques described in these articles on preservice education will spawn research at both the college and public school levels as increasing numbers of college instructors begin to add a performance component to their methods courses. There is some evidence (cited in these articles) that these techniques have been used successfully with preservice and inservice teachers.

WAYNE L. HERMAN, JR., is Associate Professor of Education at the University of Maryland, College Park.

Placing Performance Competencies in Perspective

Although a reasonable expectation of a methods course is that the students learn several critical teaching tasks, it is important as well that other dimensions of a teacher's development be stressed. One of these dimensions includes *knowledge* of teaching strategies, materials, and developmental characteristics of children. Another parameter, although difficult to assess, is the preservice teacher's *attitude* or interest in the social studies. Additional components of the methods course include social studies *research* information which provides a basis for various teacher behaviors, as well as *learning theory* which directs instructional practice. The last, but the most important and difficult component, is the amalgamation of all of the aforementioned parameters; collectively they should produce a sensitive, flexible, and objective *decision maker*.

The purpose of this article is to describe only the performance competency dimension of the author's methods course in elementary school social studies. The article centers on the selection of performance competencies; the teaching of three competencies in lessons using a prototype, a simulation, and protocol materials; and preservice teachers' practice of the performance skills with children.

Selecting and Planning the Competencies

The selection of critical teaching tasks or performance competencies is the first step. Critical teaching tasks can be defined as those teaching strategies which are used by most teachers for significant amounts of time in their instruction of the social studies. Some criteria that are helpful in choosing critical teaching tasks include:

1. The competency is a significant foundational and recurring topic in the educational literature. It is not a trivial or shallow skill.
2. The competency must possess utility; i.e., it is used or should be used frequently by teachers for significant amounts of time in their instruction of the social studies.
3. The competency has a research basis; i.e., evidence exists that the skill is needed or that the strategy will accomplish important, specified objectives.
4. The competency is valued highly by the professor.

To be sure, subjectivity exists in the selection process. Moreover, it is sometimes difficult to satisfy all of the above criteria for the selection of a particular performance competency. For instance, research evidence does not support the contention that the strategy of inquiry is related to higher learner achievement than traditional methods are; however, in one study 4,000 educators and non-educators of the United States and Canada ranked inquiry (intellectual curiosity) as the second highest goal of the schools, while the ability to think critically was ranked as the fourth highest goal.[3] The four criteria tend to limit the number of critical teaching tasks, thus making it possible for the instructor to teach intensively those which are chosen.

After a performance competency has been selected, the next step is to choose an instructional technique and plan for its use with preservice teachers. Some of the newer teaching techniques that support the thrust for reform in teacher education include modules, protocol materials, simulation, prototype lessons, curriculum materials analysis systems, classroom interaction analysis systems, and micro-teaching.[4] Different techniques can be used to accomplish the same teaching objective, but usually the nature of the instructional objective suggests an appropriate technique for either a competency or non-competency oriented lesson.

Performance Competencies	Teaching Techniques Used by College Instructor
1. Use readiness activities (motivate, tap children's background of experiences, teach concepts, set up purposes for reading) for a directed reading lesson.	Prototype
2. Direct a discussion on a controversial issue.	Simulation
3. Teach a current events lesson.	Simulation
4. Conduct a lesson using creativity: role-playing, construction, painting, writing, music or dance.	Simulation
5. Use an inquiry strategy: (1) Main problems approach, or (2) Comparison of two variables in a single dimension.	Prototype
6. Use all categories of Flander's Interaction Analysis in a discussion.	Protocol
7. Use a technique with children for backing up value positions with facts.	Prototype
8. Teach direction, map symbols, scale, grid, or legend.	Inquiry and Lecture
9. Use strategies which involve higher levels of thinking: (1) Classification, (2) Deduction, or (3) Induction.	Prototype
10. Ask higher level questions during a discussion.	Lecture and Simulation
11. Write and use with children evaluative items: true-false, matching, completion, multiple-choice, 2 and 3 word relationships, word analogy, or essay.	Lecture and Simulation

The performance competencies with their selected teaching techniques (see chart above) are emphasized in the author's social studies course.

Teaching Performance Competencies

The following lessons which employ prototype, simulation, and protocol materials illustrate the different teaching techniques used with preservice teachers. Since these teaching techniques are essentially student-centered and require active participation, after building a background on the topic (usually with a demonstration) the instructor spends a major portion of class time circulating among the students to observe them at work and to assist them with difficulties.

A Prototype Lesson

A prototype is defined as a commendable pattern, model, or exemplar which is offered as a sample lesson to be imitated with children. In this lesson a prototype is used for teaching the thinking strategy of concept formation[5] developed by Taba and her associates.[6] This is how it is taught to preservice teachers.

> The instructor informs the class that they are to pretend that they are second grade children who have been studying shelters and the materials of which they are constructed. The instructor continues, "Now, boys and girls, we have studied the many materials of which houses are made. I should like you to help me to LIST those materials." As the preservice teachers call out items, they are written on the blackboard: wood, nails, shingles, glass, wire, pipes, cement, etc. The instructor further directs, "Let's GROUP those items that go together for some reason." A student says that wood, shingles, and glass go together because they are used on the outside of houses; another suggests that wooden floor, room partitions, ceiling joists, rafters, and steps compose a group because the items are all wood. These groups are formed on the blackboard and the instructor asks, "Can you think of a LABEL or name for each group?" Some labels offered include *Exterior Building Materials* and *Wood Products.*

After using this prototype, students working in pairs selected any social studies topic on which to practice again the LIST, GROUP, LABEL steps of classification. After about five minutes, several students share their examples with the class.

A Simulation Lesson

A simulation is an enactment of an actual situation in which the participants assume specified roles. In this lesson the technique of simulation is employed to teach preservice teachers the method of informal dramatic play.[7] After the parts of informal play are explained by the instructor, topics for the play are selected from a typical unit on Mexico, and three groups of undergraduates are formed. Since time is a limiting factor, the sequence of informal dramatic play is telescoped. The three committees in their designated areas of the classroom are observed planning briefly the various topics of the play which entails assigning roles, constructing crude props, and choosing a plan for the enactment of the topic.

Then, without an audience, the committees simultaneously commence the play. One group pretends that, as Aztecs, they are building islands for homesites in the marshlands by cutting trees and transporting them by canoe to the building site, by standing them upright around the marshland and lashing them together, and by procuring and dumping dirt in the enclosures. The members of another group have placed a coed horizontally on a table and are skipping and chanting around her as they portray the Aztec religious ceremony of the human sacrifice of a maiden to the gods. Cortez and his conquest of Montezuma and the Aztec Empire are imitated by the third group, which is engaged in a fight in an open part of the classroom.

After each group has had a chance to play out all of the topics, the undergraduate class comes together to evaluate the drama as an elementary school class would. The headings *Things We Did Right* and *Things We Need To Improve* are placed on the blackboard, and items are listed as class members mention them in the ensuing discussion.

A Lesson Using Protocol Materials

A protocol is a record of behavior which is appropriate to the concerns of teachers. As Patrick points out, the record may be visual, auditory, or printed.[8] Babick and Gliessman state that the purpose of protocol materials is to provide data which may be studied by teachers in a controlled and systematic way.[9] Although the development and use of protocol materials seem to be one of the stronger thrusts in the reform of teacher education, Cooper writes that no attempt has yet been made to establish the influence of protocols in teacher education on the behavior of pupils; notwithstanding, Cooper cites evidence that protocols have been used successfully to teach concepts to preservice and in-service teachers alike.[10]

A printed protocol material is used in this lesson to acquaint preservice teachers with Interaction Analysis, a coding system for the verbal behavior of the teacher and pupils engaged in a discussion.[11] While using mimeographed materials, the students undergo a training program in which initially they are able to distinguish the different kinds of teacher and pupil talk; at the conclusion, they are able to use verbally the seven types of teacher-talk.

Two protocols representing two actual fifth-grade classroom discussions – one by Ms. Sourball and the other by Ms. Etiquette—are presented in the middle of the training program for coding and analysis. The purpose of the two lessons is the same: both Ms. Sourball and Ms. Etiquette attempt to relate the weaknesses of the Jamestown Colony to some poor interpersonal relationships during class project work. Only the protocol for Ms. Sourball is presented here (see pp. 92–93).

Since studies have shown that teachers interact verbally with pupils for large amounts of time,[13] this protocol appropriately entails significant concerns of teachers. Moreover, the protocol presents data which may be analyzed in a systematic way to provide information on teacher influence of classroom climate, which Flanders reported is related to pupils' school achievement and attitudes.[14]

Practicing the Tasks with Children

The teacher education program for elementary school majors at the

---

Ms. Sourball's Discussion

Category[12]

6	Teacher:	Today we are going to review what you were supposed to read last night about the colonization of our
5		country. Do you know what colonization means? It means people are going to come from England or another foreign country to the New World and live here. The country they come from will have control
4		over them. Where do you suppose was the first English settlement?
8	Jim:	Chicago, or Jamestown. I forget which one.
7	Teacher:	Chicago? That's a ridiculous answer. Do you know
6		where Chicago is? Look on the map here. It's way
5		out here. Mary, do you think the colonists would
4		start a settlement in Chicago, or some place else?
———	Mary:	Probably somewhere close to the coast of the Atlantic Ocean.
———	Teacher:	Yes, that's right. As Mary said, the first settlement
———		was close to the water, near the place where they got
———		off their ships. Pay attention, Ronald, and sit up
———		straight. How many times do I have to tell you? Did
———		you ever hear of Jamestown, class?
———	Ted:	We went down to Jamestown last summer. There are some ships down there that we went on. It was great. The ships are . . .
———	Teacher:	Maybe you can tell us about your trip at another time,
===		Ted. Where is Jamestown, class? (No response) Look
———		here on the map. Here it is. It's on the James River,
———		near Richmond. Who was the leader of the group? (No
———		response) Well I think you had better get your text-
———		books out and turn to page 73. I can tell you didn't
		do your homework last night.

University of Maryland provides for a professional semester during the junior or senior year of study. The professional semester is characterized by the team concept; that is, about twenty preservice teachers are taught the five methods courses on Monday and Wednesday by five professors; during the same semester on Tuesday and Thursday, the preservice teachers are engaged in teacher-aide duties and microteaching lessons in a nearby elementary school.

From the eleven critical teaching competencies taught by the instructor and practiced by the preservice teachers in the campus classroom, the under-graduates select, after consultation with their assigned classroom teachers, five competencies which they will plan and execute with children in micro-teaching lessons. Some of these lessons are observed by the college instructor who is assigned during the semester for about five whole days in the ele-mentary school to supervise the preservice teachers.

———— Jane: The leader was Captain John Smith.
———— Teacher: Yes, that's right.
———— Pete: I know something about that, Miss Sourball. My father
told me the Indians taught the settlers how to
plant corn—to place a dead fish in the hole with the
kernel of corn.
———— Teacher: Not at Jamestown they didn't. The Indians fought the
═══════ settlers. Now, let's continue what we were talking
———— about. Do you think the settlement was a success?
———— Marilyn: They sent tobacco back to England.
———— Teacher: You misunderstood me, Marilyn. Did the settlers get
———— along with each other? Did everybody live?
———— Mike: The book said they argued and couldn't agree on things.
Many of them died from starvation and disease.
———— Teacher: They acted just like you do when you work on projects.
You people have to learn to get along with each other
or you will be a failure, just like Jamestown was. Do
———— you remember which year the settlement began?
———— Carolyn: About a hundred years ago.
———— Teacher: Gracious, do you think it was that short a time ago? Jim?
———— Jim: I remember; it was in 1607, about the time of the
Italian Renaissance, when Michaelangelo was sculpting
and painting.
———— Teacher: Good, it was in 1607. Now I want you to re-read pages
———— 75 to 78—about the Pilgrim and Puritans—which we
———— won't discuss now because you did so poorly with the
———— Jamestown settlement. And tomorrow I hope you are
better prepared than you were today. I'm going to
———— watch you the next time project work is done. And if
———— you argue and fool around, I'm going to embarrass you
and call you a Jamestown settler.

Assessment of Performance

Although several evaluative modes are employed, assessment of the level of performance of the critical teaching competencies is very difficult. The following assessments are used during the semester:

On-campus practice of competencies. A subjective measure which includes instructor observation of simulations, class and individual coding of the protocol, and paired preservice teachers' practice of the prototypes.

Rating of lesson with children. A subjective measure used when observing preservice teachers' microteaching lessons.

Written critiques of lessons. Students submit critiques of five microteaching lessons.

Written tests and examinations. Parts of the objective instrument are related to competencies and include items of true-false, multiple-choice, and three word relationships. The subjective instruments direct preservice teachers to describe in writing specified competencies based on the content of a feature article of *Weekly Reader* and their constructed teaching units.

Problems of the Field Experiences

A serious problem of the field experiences vis-à-vis social studies is the difficulty of ensuring that all students have developed an adequate understanding of and proficiency in the critical teaching tasks while learning them in the college classroom and also while using them on the firing line with children. The element of time makes it practically impossible for the instructor to verify that each of twenty preservice teachers has a firm grasp of the eleven performance competencies or even of the five competencies selected for microteaching lessons. On-campus tests and examinations, however, do establish a reliable paper-and-pencil assessment. Also, the written critiques of lessons turned in to the instructor provide additional assessment data.

The scheduling of microteaching lessons in which the performance competencies are used with children presents several problems. One is the difficulty of blending a specific performance competency—that is, an inquiry strategy—with the ongoing curricular program of the school; some microteaching lessons, therefore, are totally unrelated to the social studies unit being studied. In addition, conducting a microteaching lesson in social studies when another school subject—for instance, mathematics—is being taught by the classroom teacher works a hardship on children who are required to play catch-up with classwork that was missed.

Also, some of the critical performance tasks in the social studies (e.g., the inductive strategy) entail plural sessions to complete; and because of time limitations, these lessons are telescoped and consequently suffer from an inadequate and sometimes incomplete treatment. Scheduling social studies microteaching lessons for those days when the college instructor of social studies will be at the school is yet another bothersome problem. When the instructor is at the elementary school, the role of counseling preservice teachers with their personal or teaching problems often supplants the role of observation.

Conclusion

The innovations described in this article create their own unique set of problems. The important question is whether or not prototypes, simulations, and protocol materials are in fact improving teacher education programs. Since the professional literature proliferates with articles describing the use of these newer techniques in teacher education, it would appear that the hard data should start coming in soon.

At the present time, from the author's experience and from limited research evidence, it can be stated that the above teaching techniques have been used successfully to teach concepts and performance competencies to preservice teachers, and that preservice teachers have strongly endorsed these instructional techniques. On these bases, the innovations appear to hold much promise for teacher education.

Footnotes

[1] Robert F. Peck and James A. Tucker, "Research on Teacher Education," in *Second Handbook of Research on Teaching*, N. L. Gage, Editor (New York: Rand McNally, 1973), Ch. 30, p. 943.

[2] Robert W. Heath and Mark A. Nielson, "The Research Basis for Performance-Based Teacher Education," *Review of Educational Research* 44 (Fall 1974): 463-484.

[3] Allen T. Slagle, "What Is the Task of Our Schools?", *Elementary School Journal* 60 (December 1959): 140-145.

[4] For an explanation of these techniques, see John J. Patrick, *Reforming the Social Studies Methods Course*, Publication #155 (Boulder, Colorado: Social Science Education Consortium, 1973).

[5] This strategy is more properly called "classification."

[6] Hilda Taba et al., *Thinking in Elementary School Children*, United States Office of Education Cooperative Research Project 1574 (California: San Francisco State College, 1964).

[7] An impressive number of research findings support the use of dramatic play with children of various ages. For studies that support cognitive development, see T. K. Bost and C. Martin, "The Role of Dramatic Play in the Young Child's Clarification of Reality," *Elementary School Journal* 57 (February 1957): 276-280; Laurence M. Conner, "An Investigation of the Effects of Selected Educational Dramatics Techniques on General Cognitive Abilities," *Dissertation Abstracts International*, 34 (March 1974): 6162-A; Edwina Hartshorne and John C. Brantley, "Effects of Dramatic Play on Classroom Problem-Solving Ability," *Journal of Educational Research* 66 (February 1973): 243-246; Phoebe H. Lewis, "The Relationship of Sociodramatic Play to Various Cognitive Abilities in Kindergarten Children," *Dissertation Abstracts International* 33 (May 1973): 6179-A; Sara Smilansky, *The Effects of Sociodrama Play on Disadvantaged Pre-school Children* (New York: Wiley, 1968), pp. 98, 136. For studies that support social development, see William E. Blank, "The Effectiveness of Creative Dramatics in Developing Voice, Vocabulary, and Personality in the Primary Grades," *Speech Monographs* 21 (August 1954): 190; Muriel R. I. Vogel, "The Effect of a Program of Creative Dramatics on Young Children with Specific Learning Disabilities," *Dissertation Abstracts International* 36 (September 1975): 1441-A. For studies that support subject achievement and behavior, see J. D. McKinney and Loretta Golden, "Social Studies Dramatic Play with Elementary School Children," *Journal of Educational Research* 67 (December 1973): 172-176; R. Harth, "Changing Attitudes Toward School, Classroom Behavior, and Reaction to Frustration of Emotionally Disturbed Children Through Role Playing," *Exceptional Children* 33 (October 1966): 119-120. For a study that supports moral growth, see O. P. Traviss, "The Growth of Moral Judgment of Fifth Grade Children Through Role-Playing," *Dissertation Abstracts International* 35 (December 1974): 3581-A-3582-A.

[8] Patrick, *Reforming the Social Studies Methods Course*, p. 13.

[9] Arthur Babick and David Gliessman, "Nature and Systematic Use of Protocol Materials in Teacher Education," in *Viewpoints: Bulletin of the School of Education, Indiana University* 46 (November 1970): 129-139.

[10] John E. Cooper, "A Survey of Protocol Materials Evaluation," *Journal of Teacher Education* 26 (Spring 1975) 69-77; the reader is referred to a thematic section on protocols in the *Journal of Teacher Education*, Vol. 25, Winter 1974; *Protocol Catalog: Materials for Teacher Education*, 4th edition (Tallahassee, Florida: Department of Education, December 1974), 38 p. mimeographed; and B. Othanel Smith, Donald E. Orlosky, and Jean Borg, *Handbook of the Development and Use of Protocol Materials for Teacher Education* (Chipley, Florida: Panhandle Area Educational Cooperative, 1973).

[11] Edmund Amidon and Ned A. Flanders, *The Role of the Teacher in the Classroom*, rev. ed. (Minneapolis: Association for Productive Teaching, 1967). By number, the teacher categories are: (1) Accepts feeling, (2) Praises, (3) Accepts ideas, (4) Asks questions, (5) Lectures, (6) Directs, (7) Criticizes. The pupil categories are: (8) Teacher-solicited pupil talk, (9) Pupil-initiated talk, and (10) Silence or confusion.

[12] At this level of training, instead of coding every three seconds the category in use, the student codes only each change of category.

[13] Flanders enunciated (and other researchers corroborated) the 2/3 Rule; i.e., two-thirds of the time in a typical classroom somebody is talking; two thirds of this time it is the teacher; and two-thirds of the teacher's talk is autocratic. See Ned A. Flanders, *Teacher Influence, Pupil Attitudes, and Achievement*, Cooperative Research Monograph No. 12, U.S.O.E. (Washington, D.C.: Government Printing Office, 1965). Three-quarters of the time during sixty observation hours in fourteen fifth-grade social studies classrooms was spent in discussion as reported in Wayne L. Herman, Jr., "The Use of Language Arts in Social Studies Lessons," *American Educational Research Journal* 4 (March 1967): 117-124.

[14] Flanders, *Teacher Influence, Pupil Attitudes, and Achievement*.

SECTION II
Instructional Topics, Programs of Study, and Textbooks

This section centers on curricular decisions affecting the social studies. The articles speak to a prevailing as well as frequently frustrating characteristic of social studies education: the diversity of topics and programs that must be considered for possible implementation. New topics arise to compete with old ones that are sometimes refurbished, frequently reflecting such current or persistent societal concerns as career education, ethnic studies, moral education, and global education. At times the topics and themes are translated into such sets of specific instructional strategies and materials as *Man: A Course of Study*; these in turn, have become foci for discussion, debate—and even controversy.

The crucial problem is to decide which among the competing topics, ideologies, and programs is to be awarded the relatively few moments of instructional time the schools have traditionally given to the social studies in the elementary grades. Too often curricular content is selected in response to community pressures, opinions of "experts," teacher autonomy, and perceived needs of students. Proponents of each of the topics and programs presented in this section advance excellent reasons why their particular interests deserve to be showcased in whatever time and space are allocated to social studies instruction. The impossibility of responding to everyone's reasoning is one of the themes mirrored in the article on career education by Hansen and Tennyson. (Of course, inherent in the problem of choosing from among the many competing social studies instructional alternatives is the advantage of finding ourselves with a spectrum of changing and viable options from which to select—a situation that is sometimes nonexistent in other curricular areas.)

The relationships between these articles and topics and themes presented in other parts of this book might also be pursued. For example, some criticism has been leveled at spokespersons for values-clarification procedures for advocating a neutral, non-judgmental posture toward the values positions elicited during the suggested student activities. By contrast, Kohlberg posits that moral thinking occurs in developmental stages and that a legitimate function of schools is to help students ascend the levels identified in his hierarchical scheme. Similarly, the reader might consider the possible integration of Kohlberg's scheme with Gallagher's proposals regarding the study of rules, laws, and directives in the elementary grades.

Although programs and ideologies shift within the collective thinking and activity of social studies educators, the use of textbooks to implement what is "current" continues to dominate the instructional scenery. Thus, the proposals of Nichols and Ochoa for a systematic evaluation of textbooks remain pertinent.

97

The Role of Moral Education in the Public Elementary School

Richard K. Jantz and Trudi A. Fulda

In keeping with the doctrine of separation of church and state, moral education *per se* has been generally excluded from the public school curriculum. Recent symptoms in our society, however, have compelled educators to re-examine this state of affairs. Several factors have focused renewed interest on the role of moral education in the school curriculum: (1) Recent headlines and television news specials have highlighted the concerns of some people that a condition of moral anomie or breakdown exists in our society. Older people, pointing at the sexual promiscuity, drugs, and violence sometimes associated with youth, are blaming the younger generation for its lack of "moral responsibility." Younger people, pointing at corruption in labor unions, business, and government, are rejecting the moral values echoed by adults. (2) Education in the affective domain is again receiving much attention, brought about in part as a consequence of the accountability movement. Such educators as Combs, Greenberg, and Torrance are urging us to consider compassion as a worthy goal of education in addition to competencies. (3) The developmental psychologists have augmented the interest in moral education through their research in the area.

Moral Education and Moral Development Defined

Moral education has been defined as "either formal or incidental instruction in morals or rules of conduct."[1] Moral education then can either be conducted on a situational basis as circumstances present themselves or as a planned, systematic part of the school curriculum. Moral development can be

RICHARD K. JANTZ is Associate Professor of Elementary Education at the University of Maryland, College Park. When TRUDI A. FULDA co-authored this article, she was a doctoral student in elementary education at Ball State University, Muncie, Indiana.

considered as "the process of individual experience and growth by which the capacity to distinguish between standards of right and wrong is gradually achieved and becomes progressively influential in the individual's social behavior."[2]

Accepting these definitions the content of moral education then becomes that which brings about the development within an individual of a set of concepts based upon the capacity to distinguish between right and wrong. The question then becomes "whose right and whose wrong?" In a public school system, what right has one person to decide the answer to that question for his students? Kohlberg contends that moral education can legitimately occupy a place in the public schools. Moreover, Kohlberg believes that teachers need not be concerned with indoctrination or forcing value systems upon their pupils as long as primary concern is given to promoting values "which in themselves prohibit the imposition of beliefs of one group upon another."[3]

Both Piaget and Kohlberg contend that moral thinking cannot be separated from intellectual development. Since we do not expect a six-year-old to make the same intellectual decisions as an adult, we ought not expect him to be making the same kinds of moral decisions. Often we fail to consider this relationship of intellectual development and moral thinking when we ask a child to justify his moral action. There is a tendency to impose adult standards on moral thinking but not upon intellectual thinking.

The work of developmental psychologists would appear to be a good beginning place for any re-examination of the role of moral education in the public school system. A study of "stage" theory of moral development put forth by some developmental psychologists might well serve as a background for citizens and educators working to determine what role the school should play. The remainder of this article will attempt to compare and synthesize the stages of moral growth described by two developmental theorists, Jean Piaget and Lawrence Kohlberg, and set forth some possible implications of these theories for elementary schools

Piaget

Piaget identifies two major levels of moral thinking found in elementary school children. These levels or stages may "co-exist at the same age and even in the same child but the second gradually succeeds in dominating the first."[4] Piaget identifies these stages as a "morality of constraint" and a "morality of cooperation." Blind, unquestioning following of rules imposed by someone in authority characterizes the morality of constraint. Following the rules because of a conscious knowledge of the need for cooperation and the reasons behind the rules characterizes the morality of cooperation.[5]

Piaget calls the first major level of moral thinking the morality of constraint. This stage is characteristic of most students in the primary grades. During this period children view teachers as authority figures who are to be obeyed to the point where "tattling" may occur. During this stage, teachers need to consider the "constraints" they place upon children. Children need some guidance during this period, and it would be unfair to them if teachers did not set down some guidelines for children to follow. However, if the teacher totally restrains her pupils by making and dictating all of the moral decisions, her class may be slower in moving towards the next stage, a morality of cooperation.

According to Piaget, in a normally developing child, the morality of constraint is replaced with a morality of cooperation. The change occurs as the child gains many experiences of reciprocal respect and sympathy with peers. Children in upper elementary school classrooms (grades 4-6) normally make moral judgments that are typical of the morality of cooperation. The shift to this second level of moral thinking in Piaget's views can be exemplified by children's concepts of control, justice, and responsibility.

Control. A child's concept of *control* within a morality of constraint views duty as essentially obeying authorities. An act that shows obedience to a rule or even to an adult, regardless of what is commanded, is good. A rule is given to children ready-made and is not judged or analyzed by them. The rule is regarded by children as being revealed and imposed by adults. For example, the classroom rule is that you walk in a straight line and don't talk while going to the library. When Sally, a seven-year-old, was asked if she were a good girl in school, she replied, "No, good girls walk in a straight line and I walked beside Annette and talked to her."

In the second level of moral thinking the perception of *control* or authority changes from that imposed by adults or superiors to an authority of equals. In this stage authority is either mutually agreed upon with one's peers or rationally agreed upon with an adult. At the level of morality of cooperation individuals become concerned with the question of mutual control and the modifiability of rules. Rules no longer are sacred and can be changed by mutual agreement. For example, in the game of basketball, there is never one single way of playing the game among children of a given generation in a given locality. Within the "same" game there are variations depending upon when, where, and who plays. For example, children operating at the level of morality of cooperation can readily see the need to modify the rules as the number of players changes from six to ten and then have use of the full court and both baskets instead of half court and one basket.

Justice. A child's concept of *justice* within a morality of constraint requires that the letter rather than the spirit of the law be followed. According to Piaget, violations of the law are viewed as serious transgressions by children. Only the final outcome is taken into account in passing judgment on the actions of others and not another child's intentions. Mark, a first grader, was asked, "What should happen if you break the rules while playing basketball?" He replied, "You're kicked out of the game, and miss your recess for a week!"

Young children of three or four can readily identify their own unintentional violations of rules. They can rationalize in their own minds the position of "I didn't do it on purpose" or "I didn't mean to do it." Children use their intellectual skills to determine unintentional versus intentional behavior and can readily translate this into moral action. Because of their egocentrism children often have difficulty in applying this same principle to the actions of others. They have problems in recognizing other children's points of view and consequently judge their actions by the results rather than the intentions.

Piaget asked young children to provide examples of what they considered to be unfair acts. Their response fell into four categories:

(1) Forbidden—behavior that goes against commands.
(2) Games—behavior that goes against the rules of the game.
(3) Inequality—inequalities in punishment or treatment.
(4) Social injustice—acts of injustice connected with adult society.

Approximately 75 percent of the responses of those children in the primary grades were characteristic of the forbidden or game categories (morality of constraint). Children in the upper elementary grades had over three-fourths of their responses falling in the categories of inequalities or social injustice (morality of cooperation.)[6]

As a child moves from a morality of constraint to a morality of cooperation, his or her concept of justice shifts from a punitive view to one of restitution. When a fifth-grader was asked what happens if you break the rules while playing basketball, he replied, "You take the penalties. The other team will get the ball or you take a foul shot or something. I know the rules, certain rules have certain penalties." Instead of severely punishing the player in violation of a rule, an attempt is made to restore the scoring opportunity for the other team.

Responsibility. A child's concept of *responsibility* within a morality of constraint requires what Piaget calls an "objective conception" of responsibility. Acts are evaluated in terms of their exact conformity with established rules. Motives are not considered. The actions of Mike and Henry are characteristic of children's concepts of an objective view of responsibility.

It is a bright, sunny spring day and Mike and Henry are faced with the choice of selling magazines or playing marbles with their friend, Jim. Tomorrow is the last day of the magazine sale and if they can sell four new subscriptions their room has a good chance of winning a prize. Mike chooses to play marbles with Jim while Henry elects to sell magazines. Henry sells only two new subscriptions and their room does not win a prize. Henry blames Mike and states that if he had made the "right choice" their room would have won. Mike replies that he "didn't mean for their room to lose" but his response is not accepted. When Mike made the choice to play marbles *he did not intend* for his room to lose the contest. He was more concerned with the immediate action of his choice: mainly, the pleasure of playing marbles with Jim. Henry, in blaming Mike, could not include Mike's intention but only the *consequence of the action*, in forming his moral judgment of Mike. Only gradually does the child develop both the logical and moral principles needed to accept the right of others to their opinion, and to make moral judgments concerning others by examining their intentions as well as their actions.

This concept of responsibility changes as the child moves to a more cooperative level of moral development. He becomes more subjective in his moral judgments, and begins to consider the motives behind an act as well as the consequences of an action. This shift can be seen in children's responses to paired stories in experiments conducted by Piaget.[7]

Paired Story

A. A little boy (or a little girl) goes for a walk in the street and meets a big dog who frightens him very much. So then he goes home and tells his mother he has seen a dog that was as big as a cow.

B. A child comes home from school and tells his mother that the teacher had given him good marks, but it was not true; the teacher had given him no marks at all, either good or bad. Then his mother was very pleased and rewarded him.

When young children were asked which child was the naughtiest, FEL, age 6, replied, "The one with the dog because he told the worst lies." Her response was typical of a child operating at the level of a morality of constraint. DEP, age 9, answered the same question as "The lie about the teacher—because the story about the dog is nothing." Her comments were typical of those operating at the level of morality of cooperation.[8]

Kohlberg

Kohlbert (1970) also suggests that moral thinking occurs in developmental stages. He analyzed moral growth by means of theoretical constructs called moral structures or stages. The stage concept implies sequence, and Kohlberg has indicated that children go through these stages of moral development without skipping any stages, and that some individuals might remain in the lower stages of moral development throughout their lives.

These levels of moral thinking are characterized by statements such as: (1) "Moral value resides in external, quasi-physical happenings, in bad acts, or in quasi-physical needs rather than in persons and standards; (2) moral value resides in performing good or right roles, in maintaining the conventional order and the expectancies of others; and (3) moral value resides in conformity by the self to shared or shareable standards, rights, or duties."[9] Two different stages are identified by Kohlberg within each of these three levels. The characteristics of these stages can be examined by children's perceptions of rights and their motivations for action. The stages are:

Level 1 Stage 1:   Obedience and punishment orientation
        Stage 2:   Naively egoistic orientation
Level 2 Stage 3:   Good-boy or good-girl orientation

          Stage 4:   Authority and social order maintaining orientation
Level 3 Stage 5:   Contractual legalistic orientation
          Stage 6:   Conscience or principle orientation

Level 1. Moral thinking could be considered at a premoral level. Children's impulses to satisfy their personal or selfish needs are modified by punishments and rewards. In the obedience and punishment orientation stage, motivation for a child's actions is basically to avoid punishment or the threat of punishment. In this stage, children have no real concept of a right.

Stage 2 is illustrated by behaviors that bring rewards to a child and consequently result in his personal pleasure. In the second stage a child's behavior is motivated by actions that will produce personal pleasure regardless of whether these actions conflict with the rights of others.

Level 2. This level of moral development is characterized by customary role conformity, where an individual's behavior is influenced by social praise or blame. Characteristic of the good-boy or good-girl orientation stage is an individual's attempts to obtain social approval and good relationships with others. The concept of right is expanded to include the idea that no one has the right to do evil. Motivation is becoming internalized and actions are prompted to avoid disapproval by others.

An authority maintaining morality portrays Stage 4. Motivation is to escape feelings of guilt or blame by actions that might be disapproved by recognized authorities. A right becomes an earned privilege or payment from others.

Level 3. This level of moral development is based upon self-acceptance of moral principles controlling one's action. Recognition and acceptance of democratic laws govern the actions of individuals in Stage 5. Motivation is sparked by the approval or disapproval of actions by the greater community. The legality of community contracts that appear as laws is recognized. The concept of rights is tied to an individual's position in the community, but there begins to emerge the concept of unearned universal rights for mankind.

In Stage 6 a morality based upon universal principles for the dignity of man emerges. Feeling good about one's self and one's involvements becomes the motivation for moral action. Rights take on the broad meaning of a genuine concern for individual life and a respect for human dignity.

Summary and Implications

Characteristics of the developmental stages described by Kohlberg and Piaget can be combined to provide a description of two levels of moral thinking found in elementary school children. These levels might be labeled a morality of restraint, characterized by the egocentric nature of the child, and a morality of participation, exemplified by an increasing respect and sympathy with one's peers. The concepts of control, justice, and responsibility described by Piaget, and the concepts of motivation and rights described by Kohlberg are reflected in these two levels of moral thinking. Table 1 elaborates these concepts (see p. 104).

Table 1. Summary Characteristics of Levels of Moral Thinking

Concept	Morality of Restraint	Morality of Participation
Control	Duty Is Obeying Authorities *Good defined by obedience to rules* *Rules or laws not analyzed*	Mutual Agreement *Lessening of adult constraint* *Rules can be modified*
Justice	Letter of the Law *Anxiety over forbidden behavior* *Concern for violation of game rules* *Punitive justice* *Any transgression is serious*	Restitutive Justice *Concern for inequalities* *Concern for social injustices* *Spirit of law considered*
Responsibility	Objective View *Intentions not considered* *Egocentric position* *Judgments in relation to conformity to law*	Subjective View *Motives considered* *Rights of others to their opinions respected* *Judgments by situation*
Motivation	External Motivation *Punishment by another* *Rewards by another*	Internal Motivation *Disapproval by others* *Censure by legitimate authorities followed by guilt feelings* *Community respect and disrespect* *Self-condemnation*
Rights	Selfish Rights *No real concept of right* *Rights are factual ownership*	Rights of Others *No one has right to do evil* *A right is an earned claim on the actions of others* *Concept of unearned, universal rights* *Respect for individual life and personality of others*

The task of clarifying goals for moral education in the elementary school becomes easier if the developmental approach to moral growth is considered. Recognition of the levels of moral thinking should result in clearer statements of objectives for the elementary grades. This recognition can aid the teacher in helping her pupils move from one stage level to the next. The principal objective of moral education in the schools then becomes the attainment of the next higher level of moral development. To accomplish this, students must be provided with opportunities to make moral decisions that are within realistic expectations of their level of moral thinking.

Kohlberg suggests that a proper match exists between a child's level of moral thinking and his responses to moral dilemmas. Punishment is often used to resolve moral dilemmas by children operating at the obedience and punishment stages of moral thinking. Andrew didn't want Kim to play in the sandbox. When forced to let her play, he threw sand in her face.

To advance the level of moral thinking of such children as Andrew, Kohlberg advocates the use of the "match plus one" concept. Dissonance begins to build in a Stage 1 type child who is presented with a dilemma where actions typical of Stage 1 are not adequate to resolve the dilemma. Actions typical of Stage 2 moral thinking may help the child to reduce this inner-conflict. This child, faced with similar moral dilemmas over a period of time, will internalize those actions typical of Stage 2 type responses and begin to make moral judgments at that next higher level. For example, Kathy and other children suggested over a period of time to Andrew that sharing the sandbox with Kim and other kids could be fun. Andrew began feeling that sharing was fun (a type of reward), and his level of moral thinking moved from actions motivated by fear of punishment to actions motivated by promises of reward (Stage 1 to Stage 2).

In planning strategies for moral growth teachers need to consider the types of moral judgments they are asking children to make. These moral judgments ought to be consistent with their level of moral thinking. Just as children are not expected to make the same intellectual judgments as most adults because they do not have fully developed information-processing skills, children ought not to be required to make the same kinds of moral decisions adults are called on to make.

If the role of moral education is to be stressed in public education, then knowledge on the part of educators as to the moral growth of children is essential. The work of the developmental psychologists can provide us with some insight into this growth, but moral education can only become effective when teachers test these principles and apply the most pertinent of them in the classroom.

Footnotes

[1] Carter V. Good (ed.), *Dictionary of Education,* 2nd Edition (New York: McGraw-Hill Company, 1959), p. 352.

[2] *Ibid.,* p. 167.

[3] Lawrence Kohlberg, "Education for Justice," in J. Gustafson, et al., *Moral Education* (Cambridge, Massachusetts: Harvard University Press, 1970), p. 67.

[4] Jean Piaget, *The Moral Judgment of the Child* (New York: Free Press, 1965), p. 133.

[5] *Ibid.,* p. 395.

[6] *Ibid.,* p. 57.

[7] *Ibid.,* p. 144.

[8] *Ibid.,* pp. 153-154. FEL and DEP are the French names of two of Piaget's subjects.

[9] Kohlberg, *op. cit.,* pp. 71-72.

Premises for Law

Arlene F. Gallagher

Teachers are responsible for reading the rules and regulations in the 1974 Revised Handbook.

Teachers will keep accurate records of attendance in the Official Daily Register.

Teachers will keep a daily planbook and substitute folder, the latter to be located in the department office.

Rules and directives are familiar to anyone who has functioned in an educational environment. Every school, no matter how open or "free," has guidelines for procedures and human behavior. Although at times irksome and seemingly arbitrary, these guidelines are necessary. Each of us would like to have some influence in their establishment, especially in those irritating instances when there is no apparent purpose for the regulation. Children experience similar frustration, especially because our answers to their questions of "Why can't I?" or "Why do I have to?" are often unsatisfactory.

Social relationships require guidelines, either explicit or implicit. We each need and want to know what is expected of us and what we can expect of others. In complex societies, some of these guidelines become formalized as law. Law regulates human behavior in almost every aspect, both person-to-person and person-to-environment. An appreciation of the need for regulations presupposes an acceptance of the premises that underlie those regulations. Unfortunately, too often we assume that the premises are understood.

ARLENE F. GALLAGHER is Assistant Professor of Education at the College of Our Lady of the Elms, Chicopee, Massachusetts.

Young children readily accept the need for rules in their lives. They are quick to object when someone doesn't play "fair" or cheats in a game. The elementary school becomes an ideal place for children to begin asking questions about why we have laws and what purposes they serve.

I propose that at the elementary level social studies instruction should encourage examination of those premises that support the law. We often are so busy gathering information that we fail to establish relationships between those pieces of information. We know a lot about trees but never get a look at the forest. With a relatively new area of study, such as law-focused education, it would be easy to fall into the traditional "tree-study" approach. This article will present some of those premises that the author believes are particularly significant to the study of law, coupled with some classroom strategies designed to examine those premises.

The premises that underlie law in American society can best be identified by asking several questions about law. First, what is the purpose of law? Second, how is this purpose exemplified in the characteristic action (function) of law and the characteristic features (nature) of law? Third, how is this purpose achieved or defeated by the legal processes? The following activities are designed to enable elementary-aged pupils to focus on how and why law regulates relationships.

Law in Your Daily Life

The Sign Walk. The purpose of the sign walk (or ride) is to have pupils observe how many laws and rules regulate their *daily* lives. The task is to make extensive lists of signs that govern human behavior. When the lists are brought into the classroom they should first be classified according to these, or your own, categories:

- Signs that regulate your behavior with respect to the environment.
- Signs that regulate behavior between people.
- Signs that protect the environment.
- Signs that protect people.

Some signs, of course, will fall into more than one category. No problem. Hopefully there will be some argument about the purposes of some of these signs. Which signs are most important and which are least important?

Individualized Field Trips. Individualized field trips provide excellent opportunities for gathering data on laws. Send your pupils in groups of one, two, or three to the following places:

- the public library
- a local supermarket
- another classroom
- a park or recreation area (bowling alley, skating rink)

Their task will be to observe and determine what factors are regulating human behavior and why that specific environment has specific regulations. Again, what purpose do these regulations serve? Were most of the people in that environment observing regulations? Why do you think people comply with regulations even when there isn't anyone forcing them to do so? This question should lead your discussion to another premise about law—the assumption of voluntary compliance.

Law rests upon an assumption of voluntary compliance. It has to assume that most people are going to play according to the rules. This is a familiar assumption that we all make in many of our daily activities. When you drive a car or play a game, you assume that others will do so by the rules. If we had to assume that no one would play or act according to the rules, it would be impossible to leave the safety of our homes, let alone play games or transact business.

All societies have some means by which to govern themselves. These means of governing reflect the values of that society. Law encompasses a set of prescriptions that have been established by a society about those things which that particular society believes are important.

No Vehicles in the Park: A Simulation

A basic value in our society is individual safety. We believe that people should be secure in the feeling that they will be safe from bodily injury. Many of our rules and regulations arise because we value safety. The following simulation is concerned with a statute that evolved because people wanted to be safe in a specific environment. The statute regulates behavior. This simulation was developed in cooperation with Leigh Taylor, Associate Dean of DePaul University College of Law.

The purpose of the activity is to have pupils participate in the adjudication of several cases that are alleged to be in violation of a statute. It places every participant in a judge's position. The statute reads, "No vehicles in the park." Individual cases are presented and judges are asked to rule upon each one by determining whether the statute has been violated. Violation of the statute carries a minimum fine of five dollars and a maximum fine of fifty dollars.

Announce to your class that every pupil in the room is a judge. Explain that there is a neighboring community where no vehicles are allowed in the park. You are going to present a series of cases that may be violations of the statute. Different judges will be called upon to determine whether the case is, in fact, a violation. Each judge will have to make a determination based on the facts presented. Be sure to identify each student as "Judge Smith, Judge Jones, etc.," in order to emphasize his or her role.

First Case

An automobile drives through the park. It is stopped by a police officer. After checking license and registration, the officer asks the driver why she is driving through the park and if she knows about the statute prohibiting vehicles. The driver says she knew about the statute but was in a hurry to cross town and went through the park as a shortcut.

Call upon a judge to adjudicate the case. Remind your pupils that the verdict can range from a "not guilty" to a fine on a scale from five to fifty dollars.

Second Case

A garbage truck is stopped by a police officer for driving through the park. The driver states that he knows about the law and usually he did not drive into the park to pick up refuse. However, this day there was an unusual amount of garbage and he couldn't carry it all by hand.

Call upon another judge.

Third Case

An ambulance is stopped by a police officer for driving through the park. The ambulance did not have its siren operating or its lights flashing. The driver explains that an accident had occurred and the ambulance was called to pick up an old person. The person is believed to have had a heart attack.

Call upon another judge.

Fourth Case

A group of bicycle riders from the "Fresh Air Is Fun" Club are stopped by a police officer while cycling through the park. The cyclists say they are on a day-long bicycle outing from another town and were unfamiliar with the statute. Several members of the group argue with the officer stating that the law is stupid because the paths are wide enough for riders and walkers.

Call upon another judge.

Fifth Case

This case involves an eight-year-old girl who is riding her tricycle through the park. An officer stops her and tells her she can't ride her tricycle in the park. The little girl continues to ride it, telling the officer it's a silly rule and she doesn't care.

Call upon another judge.

Sixth Case

A group of citizens in the community decides to place an old World War II Army tank on a pedestal in the middle of the park. The tank will be transported on a flatbed truck. Before doing so, a representative of the group calls the Police Department to ask if this is a violation of the statute about vehicles.

Call upon a judge to render an opinion.

By this time your class should be asking questions about what the statute means and how a vehicle is defined. If not, you can add your own cases, including roller skates, wagons, etc.

Conduct a discussion, using the following questions:

• Why would a community want a law about vehicles in a park?

- What is the purpose of a park and how does the statute protect that purpose?
- Is the purpose of the park related to the purpose of the statute?
- If you were legislators rather than adjudicators, would you want to change this statute?

Our legal system requires a delicate balance between competing interests. In the functioning of government the balance is between various institutions and their purposes. The elementary pupil needs to see the links and relationships between the legislature, the judiciary, the executive, law enforcement, and corrections. What is the purpose of each process? Why are the processes separate? Why shouldn't the lawmakers also be the law enforcers? It would certainly make life easier for the police officer if he/she could decide the punishment on the spot. What would be the dangers in operating this way? What is society valuing and protecting by separating lawmaking from law enforcement? Some of these answers are clearer to students when the following premise is examined.

Law is not justice; it is the vehicle to attain the goal of justice. If law and its processes become the end, *how* things are done then becomes more important than *what* things are done. Consider what would happen if a teacher emphasized handwriting to the extent that what was written was ignored. The skill of writing is a vehicle toward the end of communication just as law is a vehicle toward the end of justice.

What, then, is justice? Justice is that which provides for the welfare and happiness of people, both individually and collectively. For elementary pupils, this concept is most easily translated as fairness. It is difficult to discuss fairness without examining specific situations, for what is fair in one instance may be unfair in another. Is it fair to allow one vehicle in the park and not another? Surely we would all allow the ambulance in the park if the welfare of an individual were at stake. We would sacrifice the welfare of the people, who wanted the park free from the disturbance of vehicles in this instance, for the life and limb of a single person.

Is it fair to treat pupils differently? Is it fair that some get different attention than others? We must think so, because many of our educational programs are designed to consider individual differences. Our legal system provides for equal protection under the law for all members of society. This does not mean that individuals cannot be treated differently, but rather that different treatment cannot be arbitrarily administered. The equal protection clause forbids distinctions that are inadequately justified, unreasonable or arbitrary.

The following hypothetical incident develops this concept. Your pupils will probably offer other examples to discuss.

What's Fair? A Role Play

Recess is a favorite "subject" at Porter Elementary School. Everyone looks forward to it. One day, Milton, a sixth grader, looks out the window during social studies. He notices that the first graders are outside for their morning recess. "Boy, they sure are lucky to have recess twice a day," Milton says to Joan, who is sitting next to him. "It's really not fair," said Joan. "How come they get recess twice and we only get it once?"

Milton, Joan, and several other students decide to complain to the principal.

Role play a discussion between the students and the principal, and then discuss the following:

• What was the issue in this case?
• What justification did the principal give for the difference in recess time?
• Was the explanation reasonable?

This exercise stresses the idea that the quality of justice is dependent on the closeness of its relationship to law. As the concept of justice changes, so too must the law.

Rules in our daily lives are adjusted as our own notions of what is fair or what should be regulated change. Remember when female teachers had to be unmarried? Remember when teachers were not permitted to visit local establishments that served alcoholic beverages? Rules change as society changes.

Summary

In attempting to clarify statements about the nature and function of law, one is confronted by a number of characteristic features that seem paradoxical. These can be examined in terms of the premises previously stated. To review briefly:

• Law reflects social values.
• Law is a means to govern human behavior.
• Law assumes voluntary compliance.
• Law is a means to justice.

Given these premises the following statements are not paradoxes, but are complementary features of a legal system that balances and protects social interests.

Law is both stable and changing. Law protects individuals from coercion and at the same time it coerces. Law gives us freedom and at the same time it takes away, or at least limits, our freedom. Law is independent of man (we are a government of law and not men) and at the same time it is dependent on man for legislation, enforcement, and adjudication. Law reflects or mirrors society, but at the same time it affects and changes society.

A Simulation To Launch a Study of Law and Consumerism

Timothy Little

"We ought to teach youngsters more about the premises, nature, and functions of law in our society than we have in the past."

"Consumer education should be made a significant part of the social education of American children."

Variations of both prescriptions cited above are common in today's social studies literature and in the popular press as well. Commercially-developed student materials on law and consumerism are beginning to appear with increasing frequency. Indeed, both topics seem to be gaining acceptance as significant elements in the modern-day social studies curriculum. The simulation that follows incorporates elements from both the law and consumer areas into a single classroom exercise. Entitled *Truth in Advertising*, it is designed to provide a law/consumer sampler for middle and upper elementary youngsters. With regard to law, the simulation is designed to apprise students of the existence of rules created to foster fair practices in the marketplace. In its consumer dimension, the simulation is designed to assist students in developing a frame of reference with which to assess advertising that they encounter.

Truth in Advertising: A Simulation of the Federal Trade Commission

Objectives of the Game:

After playing *Truth in Advertising*, students will be able to:

1. describe, in rough fashion, the role of the Federal Trade Commission in protecting the public against deceptive advertising practices;
2. develop a personal definition of deceptive advertising;
3. identify advertisements in the media that might contain potentially misleading claims or promises.

TIMOTHY LITTLE is Associate Professor of Education at Michigan State University, East Lansing.

Introduction

Does the Federal government in Washington attempt to protect the American public against false or blatantly misleading advertising? The answer is yes. Several Federal agencies or commissions exist that are responsible for monitoring and/or regulating advertising nationally. Among these agencies are the Federal Food and Drug Administration and the Post Office Department. Probably the agency with the most responsibility for ferreting out false advertising in many kinds of businesses, however, is the Federal Trade Commission.

Created by the Congress in 1914, the FTC was and is broadly charged with overseeing and umpiring the operation of businesses in the United States. Specifically, it attempts to maintain conditions in which fair competition can take place. In addition to investigating mergers, price discrimination, and the like, the FTC is also empowered to investigate promises and claims made in national media advertising. It is this function of the Commission that will be simulated.

The Simulation in Brief

Simply stated, the game is designed to place pupils in the roles of FTC commissioners, "prosecuting" attorneys from the Commission, and lawyers appearing to defend a given advertisement charged with being untruthful or misleading. There are five commissioners appointed by the President of the United States who govern and administer the FTC. They also serve as the final review board for the Commission and hear advertising cases that have been decided at lower levels of the FTC and appealed. Such appeals may be made by either "prosecuting" attorneys or the advertiser. Decisions to stop an advertisement are determined by majority vote of the commissioners and have the force of law. These decisions may only with some difficulty be appealed to the Federal courts.

It is this final review proceeding that the *Truth in Advertising* simulation re-creates. While a great deal of case law has been developed by the Commission in the area of deceptive advertising, such cases commonly revolve around at least two standards: (1) Does the ad contain clearly false claims?, and (2) Taken as a whole, does the ad give a misleading impression to the public? Typically, attorneys for both the Commission and the advertisers plead their "cases" before the five commissioners in a courtroom fashion. The process, therefore, lends itself readily to simulation.

Simulation Instructions for the Teacher

1. The game can be played by 7-30 students.

2. In order to maximally involve the students, divide the class into up to 6 groups of 7-9 students each. Assign each group a "hearing room" location within the classroom.

3. Each group will separately and simultaneously simulate the full Commission in a final hearing. (Each group should be arranged according to the Commission hearing room.)

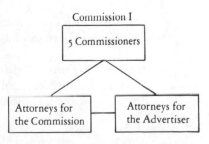

4. Five students within each group should be recruited to assume the role of commissioners. Their task will be to render a decision as to whether or not the advertisement in question is, in fact, false or deceptive and should be prohibited.

5. One to three students within each group should take on the part of Commission staff lawyers. Their task is to examine the facts of the complaint as presented and to argue that the ad should be prohibited. Basic to their success will be the degree to which they can convince a majority of the commissioners that the practice in question is untruthful or grossly misleading.

6. One to three students within each group should be assigned similarly to take the part of attorneys representing the advertisers. Their goal is to establish that their client's advertisement is, in fact, neither untruthful nor *grossly* misleading.

7. The teacher should assume the role of official recorder for all of the "mini-commissions."

8. The official recorder should pass out the role cards (included in the Appendix) and go over each participant's task with the class at large.

9. Pass out copies of the complaint sheet for Hearing #1 found in the Appendix (see p. 117) to all class members. All of the "mini-commissions," therefore, will be trying the same case simultaneously.

10. Give the opposing lawyers 5-6 minutes to prepare their "case" and to delegate spokesmen for each side. During this period, the teacher should meet with all of the "mini-commissions" as a group and again stress the grounds upon which the decision to allow or to disallow the ad are to be made (i.e., not on the advertisement's cleverness nor taste nor values appealed to, but upon its truth and/or potential to mislead).

11. Convene all of the mini-hearings simultaneously. The teacher should stretch her/his authority as official recorder to include that of timekeeper as well. As noted on the role cards, *Truth in Advertising* is played according to the schedule listed below:

Statement of Complaint—FTC Attorneys—5 minutes maximum
Defense Presentation—Advertiser's Lawyers—5 minutes maximum
Questions by the commissioners and their vote—10 minutes maximum

12. The teacher should use a stopwatch or sweep second hand wristwatch to enforce the time limit. With such limits the pace is forced, both paralleling the pressure of cases faced by the real Commission and preventing the simulation from dragging.

13. Ask each Commission in turn to report its vote to the class at large and each commissioner to explain his/her vote.

Debriefing Truth in Advertising

As in most educational simulations, a debriefing session is crucial to deriving maximum classroom benefit from *Truth in Advertising*. Therefore, on the day following the mini-FTC Commission hearings on the Roundrim Bicycle Company case, you should inaugurate one or more of the following activities.

1. Discuss with the class the nature of the FTC as watchdog of the marketplace. Consider how it is like and unlike a court, and/or a police department. (For a concise description of the procedures by which the FTC operates as well as its limitations, see "Following the FTC" cited in the bibliography.)

2. Ask each student to develop her/his own definition of what constitutes deceptive advertising. How is their definition similar to or different from the two-part definition provided on the *Truth in Advertising* role cards?

3. Discuss with the class whether the FTC should concentrate its attentions upon investigating advertisements that may be flatly untrue or whether it should also investigate ads that, though literally true, may tend to mislead. Ask students to give reasons for their answers.

As another example of a possibly misleading advertisement, consider the following: "Blotto Acne Remedy helps fight skin blemishes." Note that the ad does not claim that the product will clear up skin blemishes entirely; rather Blotto *helps* fight blemishes. The technique is called "weasel wording" and it is very common in advertising today.

Follow-up Activities

After playing *Truth in Advertising*, students commonly will view advertisements in a new light and display a high level of interest in their composition. You can build upon this interest in several ways.

1. Students can be asked to bring in samples of print advertising from magazines and newspapers. The objective? Twofold. On the one hand, to provide possible "cases" for hearings before the mini-FTCs. Should the students isolate an advertisement that they feel is possibly misleading, they can easily draft a "complaint" modeled on the Roundrim Bicycle Company complaint sheet and hold hearings. The second motive for gathering a number of ads falls in the province of balance. It is rather important that students become aware of the fact that while ads are obviously designed to sell, the large majority clearly are not designed to deceive. The ratio of straightforward to questionable advertisements that emerges from a student survey of print advertisements should make this point clearly.

2. Student rehearings of advertisements that were actually investigated by the FTC can add a fascinating new dimension to the *Truth in Advertising* simulation. Unlike hypotheticals, such cases provide students with a referent set of standards for judging an ad: How do their judgments compare and contrast with those of the "real" FTC? Obtaining the data necessary for such a rehearing is not difficult. *Consumer Reports* magazine frequently includes a section titled "On the Docket." Designed to keep consumers informed regarding the actions of regulatory and court agencies in the consumer area, the section commonly contains condensations of FTC investigations and

actions. Rewriting the "facts" of such a case into a complaint format for use with youngsters isn't difficult. Alternate sources of data concerning FTC investigations exist as well. These include other consumer-oriented periodicals in addition to the "Law" and "Business" sections of weekly news magazines. Finally, there are the *Federal Trade Commission Decisions* published by the Federal Trade Commission itself. Held by many major libraries, the *Decisions* provide the FTC "case hunter" with an endless supply of complete and highly detailed investigatory data.

3. Playing *Truth in Advertising* alerts youngsters to the existence of rules designed to put limits on advertising techniques. It also sensitizes them to the potential for mischief in advertising. Following the game students should be asked to ponder the definition of a "good" advertisement from the standpoint of the consumer. Once they have settled on some consumer-oriented criteria for a "good" ad, students can be asked to create some advertising that meets those criteria. A very effective way to achieve this calls for each student to cut out the picture of a particular product from an existing ad, paste it on a blank sheet of paper, and then modify the original text in order to transform it into a "good" ad. Information concerning specifications, price, durability, versatility, and safety will commonly appear in such efforts. Finally, the students can be asked to debate whether or not it might be desirable to require, by law, that all advertising contain certain basic information about products, and if so, what information? Students who have played *Truth in Advertising* and worked through the supplementary activities should have little difficulty mustering reasons in favor of such a proposal.

Major points that might be brought up by opponents of the proposal could include: (a) Would such full disclosure requirements intrude on a company's rights to advertise freely?, and (b) Would advertising be transformed into dull, catalog listings that wouldn't help sell products at all?

Summary

Truth in Advertising is a simulation with limited objectives. It is designed to be a catalyst—to illustrate and provide student examination of the place of government rule-making in American advertising. Students do need to be taught about the place of rules in our society. They also need training to become competent consumers early on. Hopefully, *Truth in Advertising* can provide a small first step toward achieving these larger goals in your social studies classroom. (Appendix on p. 117).

Bibliography

Brown, Mary Anne Symons. "Following the FTC," *What's New in Home Economics.* September 1973: 19-21.

The Federal Trade Commission. *Federal Trade Commission Decisions.* Washington: U.S. Government Printing Office (published annually).

Wagner, Susan. *The Federal Trade Commission.* New York: Praeger Publishers, 1971.

Appendix
for Truth in Advertising Simulation
COMPLAINT SHEET

Hearing #1

In the matter of the Roundrim Bicycle Company.

The Federal Trade Commission hereby charges the Roundrim Bicycle Company and its advertising agency with falsely claiming in TV ads that a Green Flash bicycle would enable its purchaser to outperform other bicyclists equipped with alternate brands of bicycles. Specifically, the Commission challenges as false and misleading the following statement, which is used to conclude Green Flash TV commercials. "The Green Flash 10 speed—it can make *you* the fastest biker on the block."

TRUTH IN ADVERTISING

Role Card—FTC Attorney(s)

Your task is to argue before the 5 commissioners that the advertisement named in the complaint is either untruthful or is seriously misleading. Look carefully at the ad itself. Are claims or promises made or strongly implied? If so, is the product likely to live up to them? In the 5 minutes you will have to present your argument, try to establish that a reasonable person would likely interpret the ad in such a way as to be misled.

Hearing Schedule:

Statement of Complaint	____	FTC Attorneys	____	5 min. max.
Defense Presentation	____	Advertiser's Lawyers	____	5 min. max.
Questions by the commissioners and their vote			____	10 min. max.

TRUTH IN ADVERTISING

Role Card—Roundrim Bicycle Company Attorney(s)

Your task is to argue before the 5 commissioners that the advertisement your company used doesn't lie to the public, nor is it grossly misleading to the *average* person.

Hearing Schedule:

Statement of Complaint	____	FTC Attorneys	____	5 min. max.
Defense Presentation	____	Advertiser's Lawyers	____	5 min. max.
Questions by the commissioners and their vote			____	10 min. max.

TRUTH IN ADVERTISING

Role Card—FTC Commissioners

You and your 4 fellow commissioners should read the complaint before you carefully. Listen closely to the arguments offered by the attorneys for both sides. Ask questions of the attorneys during your deliberation session. You will then be asked to vote on whether or not the ad in question constitutes deceptive advertising.*

* (Remember the standards commonly used by the FTC in ruling on whether an ad is deceptive or not include:

1. Does it contain clearly false statements?
2. Does it, as a whole, tend to mislead the common man?)

A simple majority vote of your Commission will determine whether or not the ad should be allowed in use. Do not reveal your vote until the official recorder (your teacher) calls upon you to do so as a Commission. Reveal your vote then and give one or two reasons why you voted as you did to the class.

Hearing Schedule:

Statement of Complaint	____	FTC Attorneys	____	5 min. max.
Defense Presentation	____	Advertiser's Lawyers	____	5 min. max.
Questions by the commissioners and their vote			____	10 min. max.

Career Development as Self Development: Humanizing the Focus for Career Education

Lorraine Sundal Hansen and W. Wesley Tennyson

It was in the late 1960s that *career* again became a prominent theme in education and caused educators to begin to re-examine their practices. The decade has been described as a time of a growing search for self and for human liberation. That search suggests that "today, more than ever, human experience is essentially a process of choosing and deciding among possible stimuli and courses of action" (Kroll et al., 1970). With increasing self-awareness, individuals have become more insistent upon choosing, even creating, the goals and means they consider to be of value to themselves and to society. Acquiring the skills for choosing seems imperative for individuals to manage the complexities of today's environment, whether the choice relates to partner, family, community, or work—the latter being one of the significant ways in which individuals interact with that environment. Formation of such interactive and choice process skills begins early in the elementary years.

Factors Leading to the Career Education Movement

Just as Sputnik provided the impetus for the discipline-centered curriculum changes of the 1960s, which sought to improve subjects through such projects as Science Mathematics Study Group, PSSC, Project English, and Project Social Studies, a number of concerns about the schools' inability to deliver in ways that maximize individual growth and development continued to present themselves throughout the decade. Among the problems not accommodated by the earlier curriculum revisions were the lack of meaningful relationships between school and the larger community; thoughtful challenges of the

LORRAINE SUNDAL HANSEN and W. WESLEY TENNYSON are Professors of Educational Psychology at the University of Minnesota, Minneapolis.

traditional work ethic, mid-life career changes, and concerted efforts to achieve balance among multiple life roles; limits on occupational opportunity created by a tight labor market and the need for alternative occupations and more flexible exit and re-entry opportunities throughout life; the information deficit created because of an open, rapidly-changing society in which it is difficult to know the options available or the means to achieve them; and, finally, the special needs of bypassed populations, especially women, handicapped, and minorities who have been outside the opportunity structure and lack the positive self concepts, the knowledge of life-style options, and the sense of agency that will allow their career to develop.

With time these problems will change or be replaced by new career development concerns, and it is obvious that individuals must learn to anticipate change and become flexible in inventing new patterns of career problem management.

Conceptions of Career Education

Career education is one response to a society in which purposeful choosing is imperative if change is to be managed in ways that facilitate personal development. But philosophies vary greatly in their focus, some almost ignoring the career development of the individual, others making it the core of their approaches. There are today at least four different philosophical persuasions held with regard to career education, not discrete but over-lapping categories with major points of emphasis on either *job, work, self,* or *life.* They are briefly presented here on a narrow-to-broad continuum.

Perhaps the most narrow conception is one that equates career education and vocational education or training for an occupation. This view has been perpetuated in part because of the fact that career education from its formal inception received its major financial support from vocational funds. Focus is on matching person to *job* and developing employability skills. There are probably few who philosophically support this view, but it is visible in the shape of programs being developed where career education is implemented through vocational centers, learning centers, and placement centers.

A bit farther along the continuum is a conception that puts *work* as the central focus of career education. In this view, work is defined as activities engaged in for immediate income or production. Career is viewed as external to the individual—the sum total of one's work experiences. Career education is that part of the total educational program that deals specifically with "education for work." Programs reflecting this position emphasize awareness and exploration of and preparation for economic roles in the work force. There is a heavy input of information about occupational roles providing students at all levels with units and experiences that increase their knowledge of the jobs people hold and the work done. The information often is presented within the framework of occupational clusters and could more appropriately be called "occupational education."

Still farther along the continuum is a point of view that says that *self* is the primary focus of career education. Those holding this position would define work broadly to include certain non-paid as well as paid activities. Career is defined as a process internal to the individual—a time-extended working out of a purposeful life pattern through work undertaken by the individual. Adherents to this position view the community and the world of business and industry as a resource for experiences leading to self-clarification. Career education content and experiences are infused throughout the curriculum, in all subjects, in ways to help the individual see how the knowledge or basic skills taught are used in the community and contribute to personal development. The process of career development provides the core underpinning for this approach to career education.

The right of the continuum reflects the position of those who see career as a way of looking at total education, as education for *life* and living. A major restructuring of the curriculum, a complete reform of the school is advocated. This position suggests that career education be concerned with all the life roles one may play—work, leisure, family, community. It would focus the entire instructional and guidance effort upon life career development.

Needed: A New Delivery System

The position espoused in this article is that of career education as self development. While traditional delivery systems for facilitating career development (e.g., occupational units, career days, and one-to-one counseling) may have been appropriate in their time, new systems are needed today that relate ongoing instruction to personal and community experience. Such systems must draw upon the resources of students, teachers, counselors, parents, and business-industry-labor personnel in providing a comprehensive program. To provide the rudiments of such a system, a University of Minnesota faculty and student team[1] has endeavored to conceptualize a K-post-high career development curriculum schema (CDC). This article centers on the elementary grade components of the schema.

Strongly influenced by theories and research of Piaget, Erikson, Havighurst, Super, and others, the University of Minnesota team has developed a model around the broad concept of career development as self development. Space allows only a brief description of the career development principles undergirding the model, the dimensions that provide the broad instructional goals, and the career management tasks that form its core. The team has defined *career development* as part of human development within the context of work, paid and unpaid. Career education is seen as the *teaching, counseling,* and *community* interventions to facilitate that development.

Theoretical Framework and Rationale

Career development is a process of integrating two constructs: self and the world of work. Tiedman (1961) defines it as "self development viewed in relation with orientation, exploration, decision making, entry and progress in educational and vocational pursuits." Ginzberg et al. (1951) describe it as "a continual process of working out a synthesis or compromise between the self and the reality opportunities and limitations of the world."

Choosing and entering an occupation is an important part of career development, but occupation is only one part of the vessel of career. In career development education, the emphasis is more on the process of career decision-making than on the decision itself; on career patterns over a lifetime rather than choice at a point in time; on psychological as well as logical aspects of work; on developmental stages rather than on once-for-all decisions; and on self development rather than on just occupational information.

The concept of career includes both occupation and the life style surrounding it. The way persons view themselves determines to a great extent how they view life, especially that part of life called career. A keystone of career development theory is Super's precept that in choosing an occupation one is, in effect, choosing a means of implementing a self concept (1957). Thus self concept is a powerful determinant in occupational choice, and formation of the self concept assumes principal importance in the development of the individual. Kroll et al. (1970) indicate that abilities and motivations for realistic self-evaluation can be fostered and developed with the individuals. This series of reintegrations of self concept begins very early in life and continues into adulthood. Just as self concept affects career choice and behavior, so career has a profound effect upon the self (Antholz, 1972). Career development is the process by which the reconciliation of the individual and his or her work environment takes place. It requires understanding of self, of environmental alternatives, and of ways of relating the two. It also requires assessment of the ways in which work relates to other important aspects of life, e.g., family, leisure, community participation, as well as to one's values and needs.

Career development is subject to the principles of general human development; i.e., it is similar for all, it proceeds from general to specific, it is continuous, it proceeds at different rates, and it progresses through fixed and sequential stages (Hurlock, 1956). The development of human beings is at the core of the career development program; that is why the CDC team preferred to start with the self, with the individual, rather than with the external world.

Super's precept of multipotentiality—that each person has the potential for success and satisfaction in a number of occupations—attacks the assumption of an ideal occupation for every worker and that guidance must help the individual find the true fit. The multipotentiality concept frees individuals from the fear of making the "wrong" choice (a view that pervades the traditional Parsonian approach or matching theory). It also increases the options available to them. The individual's responsibility and thus control are no longer centered on a crucial single decision point but extend throughout his or her career life and may cover several decision points from early childhood throughout life (Antholz, 1972).

The management of one's career or maximizing the individual's control over his or her own life and future is an important tenet of career development. Tiedeman calls this "sense of agency," the power to direct one's future and determine what he or she is to become. This means that individuals must obtain the skills with which to choose and plan, that they must learn *how* to choose as well as *what* to choose.

The commitment with tentativeness concept is integral to a model that is based on changing individuals in a changing society and that recognizes the importance of chance or random factors in career decision-making.

This theoretical framework for the Career Development Curriculum offers a basis for looking at the development aspects of occupational behavior, its relationships to other life roles, and a new dynamic dimension or construct related to self and work called vocational or career maturity. This framework would appear to be very closely related to social studies curriculum with its focus on the relationship of the individual and community especially in the elementary school.

Value Assumptions

A number of value assumptions undergird this conceptual model:

(1) Personal or self development consists of mastering all the skills and understandings normally taught in English, social studies, mathematics, and other subject matter areas, but it also entails a process of self discovery that can be facilitated through career exploration. Vocation and the work world offer one of the most natural frameworks for clarifying values and meanings about oneself.

(2) Occupational motives, worker attitudes, and other vocationally relevant behaviors are the result of a complex process of development. A systematic exposure to the options and expectations of industrialized and post-industrial society is vitally important in the socialization of the young person. However, the expectations should be cast as problematic situations to which the student can react, fashioning his or her own range of responses, with clear awareness of the consequences of each.

(3) A world growing more complex each day requires that students be provided a broadened base for experiencing the realities of life and living. The need is for more of an experience-based curriculum in a reality-bound context.

(4) Curriculum construction should focus upon *developing* the individual's abilities and aptitudes, rather than perpetuating a tradition that too often has tended to focus on aptitudes already developed rather than those not yet tapped.

Dimensions of Career Development

Ten broad dimensions of career development give further definition to the CDC concept. Stated behaviorally, they provide a broad framework for practice and might serve as instructional goals. They are presented in Figure 1 (see p. 123). Implications of these dimensions for the elementary grade social studies curriculum are stated below:

Figure 1
Dimensions of Career Education

The student will:

1. identify values, interests, abilities, needs, and other self characteristics as they relate to occupational roles. (self dimension)
2. explore occupational areas and describe opportunities, potential satisfactions, required roles of workers, and other related dimensions. (occupational information dimension)
3. describe the psychological meaning of work and its value in the human experience. (psychology of work dimension)
4. describe modern work structure, and work environments, and organizational characteristics. (organizational dimension)
5. tell how the individual's role in work is tied to the well-being of the community. (social contribution dimension)
6. demonstrate planfulness in striving to achieve occupational goals and objectives. (planfulness dimension)
7. demonstrate through work-relevant behavior that one is acquiring a concept of self as a productive person in a work-centered society. (work ethics dimension)
8. describe that relationship that exists between basic skills, marketable skills, and interpersonal skills and the jobs one can reasonably aspire to in adult life. (school-work relationship dimension)
9. demonstrate possession of a reasonable degree of basic skills, knowledges, and behavioral characteristics associated with some type of work or occupational area. (occupational preparation dimension)
10. demonstrate through work-relevant behavior an ability to learn, adjust to, and advance in one's chosen occupation. (work adjustment dimension)

1. *Self Dimension.* It says that the major concern is with the self development of human beings, that the schools must utilize the stimuli provided by occupational experience and career exploration to help learners come to a clearer understanding of themselves and their developing self-characteristics. For the elementary school this means helping the child begin to recognize his or her unique qualities.

2. *Occupational Information Dimension.* This is directed at helping students to acquire information about the world of work and community and to use that information in decision-making. Teachers who use career information and experience in relating their subject to the world of work and to human career patterns find this to be an effective way of motivating students to learn. Included are experiences with and information about the organization of the work world, labor force structure and trends, emerging occupations and career patterns, psycho-social information about jobs, and educational-occupational alternatives. At the elementary level it means helping children become aware of the human-ness of workers, of the stereotyping that limits options, and of the vast array of options available.

3. *Psychology of Work Dimension.* Here the focus is on what one writer has called "psychological man at work," the psycho-social aspects of a job and its impact on the individual. The aim is to have the learner consider how work fits into his or her life and how it relates to other aspects of life. Elementary children can begin to look at how people view their work and its meaning in the life of adults they know.

4. *Organizational Dimension.* This dimension alerts students to the fact that they live in an organizational world and that they may be affected by the communication patterns, power structure, peer relationships, and authority relationships of both work and non-work organizations. It suggests that many of the problems and conflicts experienced in life stem from the way individuals try to manage their work organizations (including the school) or are managed by them. The elementary social studies curriculum might have children begin to study their school environment as a social system.

5. *Social Contribution Dimension.* It is designed to enhance the individual's life by showing the importance of one's work to the community and its well-being. Students are assisted to discover the social significance of their own work and the work of others. The social studies curriculum might have children interact with senior citizens about their life cycle and also have pupils look at their own contributions to the welfare of school and family.

6. *Planfulness Dimension.* This is based on the assumption that individuals may have more control over their lives if they are willing to do some planning rather than merely let things happen by chance. It reflects interest in career maturity and the desirability of instilling in students what Super has called "planfulness" or what the CDC calls "career management." The social studies curriculum can facilitate this by creating ways for children to choose and make decisions about their daily activities and to become aware of themselves as decision-makers.

7. *Work Ethics Dimension.* It is directed at developing those attitudes and dispositions charactistic of a responsible worker. It is not intended to glamorize or push the traditional work ethic but rather to help students examine how work and leisure fit into their lives and ways in which the work ethic is changing. Interviews with people about what work means to them or study of how much time is consumed by work, family, and leisure activities provide vehicles for examining this dimension. Children might also look at ways in which work can *change* society.

8. *School-Work Relationship Dimension.* It attempts to help students see the relationship between present school subjects and future roles and goals. The elementary curriculum can do this in a number of ways, by having children talk with adults about how they use various subjects in their work and leisure, by helping them see relationships between certain abilities and worker roles.

9. *Occupational Preparation Dimension.* While it is most closely related to vocational education and stresses beginning levels of skills and competencies, it recognizes that all subjects contribute in some ways to the

development of vocational skills. Helping children begin to see how basic skills are incorporated in a variety of life roles is a natural goal of the elementary curriculum.

10. *Work Adjustment Dimension.* Although most closely related to post-high objectives, it can also apply to exploratory jobs during the high school years. It implies not merely adjusting the worker to the status quo but helping him or her learn ways to improve the work environment if incompatible with one's needs, values, and goals. This dimension is probably not as relevant to the elementary curriculum except as children are helped to see that being a student is part of career and that the "job" of student should be satisfying and growth-producing.

These dimensions clearly support the view that career development and personal or self development are part of the same package and the CDC team's belief that work, representing one major way in which the individual interacts with his or her environment, offers a promising vehicle for self examination and clarification.

Career Management Tasks

Drawing from theory and research on human development, the Career Development Curriculum team further refined a set of sequential career management tasks and translated them into performance and enabling objectives. The tasks connote a developing capacity of individuals to construct their experience and control their environment. Recognizing the limitations of behavioral objectives and the problems inherent in writing them, the team nonetheless decided to use a framework of terminal performance objectives to indicate desired outcomes and enabling objectives to suggest means for achieving performance objectives. The work of Tyler (1950) and Mager (1962) influenced goal formulation.

The career management tasks and performance objectives form the core of the Career Development Curriculum. Management tasks for K-9 are presented in Figure 2. Although development is continuous and school organization varies, it is both convenient and defensible to utilize as stages the traditional common divisions of the schools: K–3, 4–6, 7–9. These levels can be used as indicators and general guides but not as hard and fast stages of development. This kind of developmental conceptual base provides a framework from which a local needs assessment could be conducted, priority needs and goals established, and creative learning activities developed. Career exploration experiences would be tied to management tasks but, recognizing varied levels of career maturity, not rigidly prescribed. (See p. 126).

Together the dimensions, tasks, and objectives can provide a stimulus for teachers to create their own strategies and programs to meet local needs. A detailed explanation of the rationale for selection and placement of the career management tasks can be found elsewhere (Tennyson et al., in press).

Figure 2
The CDC Career Management Tasks (K-9)

Career Management Tasks of the Primary Years
1. Awareness of self
2. Acquiring a sense of control over one's life
3. Identification with workers
4. Acquiring knowledge about workers
5. Acquiring interpersonal skills
6. Ability to present oneself objectively
7. Acquiring respect for other people and the work they do

Career Management Tasks of the Intermediate Years
1. Developing a positive self concept
2. Acquiring the discipline of work
3. Identification with the concept of work as a valued institution
4. Increasing knowledge about workers
5. Increasing interpersonal skills
6. Increasing ability to present oneself objectively
7. Valuing human dignity

Career Management Tasks of the Junior High Years
1. Clarification of a self concept
2. Assumption of responsibility for career planning
3. Formulation of tentative career goals
4. Acquiring knowledge of occupations, work settings, and life styles
5. Acquiring knowledge of educational and occupational resources
6. Awareness of the career decision-making process
7. Acquiring a sense of independence

Implications of Management Tasks for Elementary Social Studies

The career management tasks have been derived largely from the work of Piaget and Erikson with corroboration from other developmental psychologists. Important components of the adult work personality find their first points of development during the early school years: becoming aware of overt difference and uniqueness, developing a sense of control over one's life, learning to assume responsibility for one's actions, learning to interact with others and present oneself objectively, acquiring respect for others and the work they do, and developing effective work habits. Career development education accommodates those goals of social studies that have to do with information-processing skills (e.g., problem-solving, decision-making, value clarification), psychological and social problems of individuals, environmental understanding, and concepts of human dignity and acceptance of others.

The CDC model has led to production of illustrative learning packages at several levels, teacher guides that represent the broad context of career development in such titles as "Life Styles and Work," "Self Concept Exploration," "Women and the World of Work," "Values Identification,"

"Significant Others," and "The Social Contribution of Work." It has also served as the conceptual base for the national career development television project called *bread and butterflies* (Agency for Instructional Television, 1974). It is intended that learning activities designed to promote career maturity might be incorporated at different levels and in diverse subjects starting in the elementary school, so that as students grow and develop they will have a systematic set of career exploration experiences that will help them to clarify goals; to obtain the skills, knowledge, and attitudes to achieve them; and to learn who they are, what they value, and how they define themselves in relation to others and to society. Career development, it would seem, is most compatible with the self-in-society goals and the inquiry process of the social studies curriculum. It is also potentially a most viable integrating base and unifying concept for the work of educators.

References

Agency for Instructional Television. *bread and butterflies*. A project in career development for nine-to-twelve-year-olds. Bloomington, Indiana, 1974.

Antholz, Mary Bee. *Conceptualization of a Model Career Development Program. K–12*. Unpublished Master's Thesis, College of Education, University of Minnesota, 1972.

Ginzberg, Eli; Ginsburg, Sol W.; Axelrod, Sidney; and Herma, John S. *Occupational Choice: An Approach to a General Theory*. New York: Columbia University Press, 1951.

Hurlock, Elizabeth B. *Child Development*. New York: McGraw-Hill, 1956.

Kroll, Arthur M.; Dinklage, Lillian B.; Lee, Jennifer; Morley, Eileen; and Wilson, Eugene H. *Career Development: Growth and Crisis*. New York: Wiley & Sons, 1970.

Mager, Robert F. *Preparing Instructional Objectives*. Palo Alto: Fearon, 1962.

Super, Donald E. "The Individual and His Environment." Paper presented at Ohio Conference on Guidelines for Implementing Career Development through Curriculum, K–12, Ohio Department of Education, Ohio State University, June 6, 1971.

_____ *The Psychology of Careers*. New York: Harper, 1957.

Tennyson, W.W.; Hansen, L.S.; Klaurens, M.K.; and Antholz, M.B. *Teaching and Counseling for Career Development*. St. Paul: Minnesota Department of Education, in press.

Tiedeman, David, "Decision and Vocational Development: A Paradigm and Its Implications," *Personnel and Guidance Journal*, 40:15–21, 1961.

Tyler, Ralph W. *Basic Principles of Curriculum and Instruction*. Chicago: University of Chicago Press, 1950.

Footnotes

[1] Professor Mary Klaurens, along with the authors, has guided the development of this career development curriculum system.

Developing Racial Tolerance with Literature on the Black Inner-City

James A. Banks

When white suburban children read that 47 blacks lost their lives in the explosive Detroit riot of 1967, and that an unarmed black teenager was gunned down by a white policeman in the Algiers Hotel amidst that disturbance, their emotions are not likely to be deeply aroused because such cold statistics and incredible incidents seem remote from their lives and experiences. It is only when we are well acquainted with an individual or people that we suffer intensely when they are hurt or harmed. In literature, children can read about individuals from different cultures and subcultures, come to know them as human beings, develop intense feelings for them, and experience agony when they are exploited or mistreated.

Young readers are saddened when Lonnie is murdered by a white racist and David Williams is attacked by a white mob in *Whose Town?* They react strongly to these incidents because author Lorenzo Graham builds his characters so successfully that children feel that Lonnie and David are their pals. When Lonnie is killed, children lose a cherished and delightful friend. They are enraged when David is beaten, because no sensitive child wants to see his pal beaten mercilessly, especially when he has done nothing to warrant attack. Some children conclude that limp and starving Zeke, a black ghetto child vividly and sympathetically portrayed in *The Jazz Man,* dies at the end of the story and weep because Zeke captures young children's hearts. Henry in *Durango Street,* Jethro and Fess in *The Soul Brothers and Sister Lou,* and Jimmy in *Dead End School* are other memorable characters of the black ghetto who evoke deep feelings and concern in young readers.

Given the immense racial crisis which pervades the nation, it is imperative

JAMES A. BANKS is Professor of Education at the University of Washington, Seattle.

that we help "culturally sheltered" children to develop positive attitudes toward persons who are different from themselves racially and culturally. An acquaintance with different cultures and groups *can* contribute to the development of the kind of tolerance so desperately needed in our highly polarized society. Since most American children live in tightly segregated communities, they have little opportunity to interact and to become acquainted with people of different races and groups.

Literature can help bridge the gap by acquainting children with people who belong to other racial and ethnic groups. However, like actual social contact, familiarity with other groups through literature *can* help develop racial understanding and tolerance, but *may* also reinforce stereotypes and misconceptions. A child who reads *The Jazz Man* may feel intensely negative toward Zeke's parents because they desert him, and conclude that all black parents in the inner-city are irresponsible and heartless. If inappropriate teaching strategies are utilized, literature will enhance rather than mitigate the development of racial bias.

To use such a book as *The Jazz Man* effectively in social studies, the teacher *must* help children see how characters such as Zeke's parents are the victims of harsh and painful discrimination. Zeke's father is unable to find a meaningful and challenging job; his mother deserts the family when she becomes disillusioned with her husband's working situation. Father turns to drinking when his wife leaves because he feels that he has failed as a man. He physically escapes from Zeke's life. With carefully structured questions, and by leading the children to factual informational sources on the black inner-city, the teacher can help children develop empathy and concern for both Zeke and his parents. The teacher could ask the children questions based on why Zeke's father can't find a good job, and why his mother buys groceries daily, and why the family lives in a dilapidated apartment. After carefully researching these kinds of questions, the students will discover that the real villain in the story is neither of Zeke's parents, but a society which discriminates against poor and black people. The teacher could ask the children to think of actions which could be taken by the larger society to eliminate the kinds of problems encountered by Zeke's family. They should also be encouraged to predict possible consequences of the actions they propose.

Other aspects of black ghetto life portrayed in children's literature might reinforce stereotypes without careful and effective teacher guidance. Most of the families depicted in children's novels lack a father, the home is crowded, mother works as a domestic and is the dominant family member, formal education is not often encouraged, and the family attends a storefront church. It is extremely important that the teacher help the child understand *why* these conditions frequently *do* exist in the black ghetto. However, it is imperative that children become aware of the extent of these conditions in the inner-city. For example, while nearly one-fourth of the black families in America are headed by females, a highly significant three-fourths are headed by men.[1] Recent educational literature suggests that most black parents *do* want their children to attain a formal education, but that they are often unaware of ways to actualize their aspirations.[2] If maximum benefits are to accrue from the utilization of realistic fiction in the social studies, the teacher must encourage students to ascertain the extent to which "realities" portrayed in literature can be generalized to the actual world in which they live. When children read about riots in *Northtown,* they should make a survey of the cities in which riots have actually occurred, and determine the degree to which Mr. Graham's description of racial violence and conflict reflects factual information.

Children will be unable to fully understand and appreciate the American black experience unless they are acutely aware of the devastating effects of slavery on both the black man and his master. The legacy of slavery is still manifested in the black inner-city. Literature can help children gain insights into American slavery. In her beautiful yet poignant biography, *Amos Fortune: Free Man,* Elizabeth Yates vividly describes how Amos Fortune, an African prince enslaved in America, emerges from an overwhelmingly dehumanizing experience "humanized" and perhaps more human because of it. At times children may find this book excruciating beyond tolerance, but perhaps it is this kind of grim realism which helps us attain deeper insights and empathy. The stark realism which permeates this book would be difficult to portray in a social studies textbook.

Julius Lester's *To Be a Slave* is a highly selected and edited collection of documents dictated by former slaves which includes helpful editorial comments. The former slaves' vivid descriptions of suicides, merciless beatings, and the huts in which they lived will evoke intense emotions and reactions. This description of the scars inflicted upon an escaped slave will give children some feeling of what it was like to be a slave:

> My friend desired me to look at his back, which was seamed and ridged with scars of the whip and hickory, from the pole of his neck to the lower extremity of his spine. The natural color of his skin had disappeared and was succeeded by a streaked and speckled appearance of dusky white and pale flesh color, scarcely any of the original black remaining.[3]

At the turn of the century, most black Americans lived in the Southern states which had made up the Confederacy. Then after that, black people began an exodus to Northern cities to escape the poverty, violence, and discrimination which they experienced in the South. The jobs which opened up in Northern cities during World War I and the prevalence of lynchings and other violent acts in the South were cogent factors which pushed the black man northward. Blacks poured into Northern cities again during World War II when jobs were prevalent in defense industries.[4] *South Town, North Town,* and *Whose Town?* by Lorenz Graham will acquaint children with the problems faced by a typical black Southern family, and how the Williams attempted to solve them by migrating North. *South Town* is a poignant, gripping, yet realistic story about the family's painful experiences with racism in a Southern community. The book is replete with examples of harsh, overt, and unrelenting incidents of bigotry. The book is extremely powerful because the characters are completely believable.

In *North Town,* the Williams discover, like many other Southern black migrants, that the North is no promised land. Their small house is in a slum, David no longer has a room of his own, and he gets into trouble with the police because he lives in a "bad" neighborhood. The family gradually discovers that prejudice "Northern style" is more covert and subtle but no less insidious than Southern racism. The adjustments which David and his family must make in North Town and the disillusionments which they experience epitomize the problems encountered by the black Southern migrant in the Northern city. The reader will sympathize with David's awkward attempts to adjust to a racially-mixed school which is covertly racist, and admire his courage as he leads the family through a major catastrophe. While most children's books on the black inner-city portray a fatherless home, this one depicts a closely-knit family whose greatest strength and power lie in a strong, loving, and understanding father. For this reason, it should be given special emphasis.

In the third and most outstanding book in his trilogy, *Whose Town?,* Graham effectively and poignantly describes the black revolt of the 1960's as manifested in fictional Northtown—which could be Newark, Detroit, Chicago or any other American city in which riots have occurred. In candid detail, he relates how the racial tension in Northtown results in brutal and unprovoked attacks against blacks, killings, and finally a riot when a small black boy is drowned by a white mob at a public pool. The author makes it clear that the pool incident merely triggered the riot, but that it had deeper causes. Gross unemployment, constant indignities and white racism, which permeated the city, were the root causes. The teacher could ask the children to compare this description of the riot in Northtown to newspaper accounts of outbreaks in cities such as Los Angeles, New York, Detroit, and Chicago in the 1960's:

> Gradually the crowd fell back. The people began moving toward the east side. They left behind a block of stores and business places about half of which had been smashed open and several of which had been burned. Merchandise was strewn in the street. Some of it was carried away by looters. David could not tell how many had been arrested. Some who had been hurt were carried off in ambulances and police cars. Others whose heads were bruised and whose faces were bloody were helped away by friends.[5]

Other harsh social realities are revealed in this seminal and gripping novel. The white man who kills Lonnie in cold blood is freed because of what the jury dubs "justifiable homicide." Children could compare this slaying with the Detroit Algiers Hotel incident. When David is attacked by a white mob, he, rather than the attackers, is jailed and humiliated. Mr. Williams' perpetual unemployment disrupts the family, forces Mrs. Williams to work as a domestic, emasculates him, and turns him into a bitter and disillusioned man. The strength and power which he evidences in the earlier novels are dissipated. Children can study factual informational sources on the inner-city to validate the reality of Mr. Williams' experiences. This novel vividly illuminates the powerlessness and alienation of the black community, and indicates how the black migrant's dream of finding a heaven on earth in Northern cities was almost completely shattered in the 1960's. *Whose Town?* is destined to become a classic in children's literature. In it, Mr. Graham attains the acme of his literary career.

One of the characteristic groups in the inner-city is the gang. Novels whose setting is the black ghetto can help children understand why boys sometimes join gangs, the needs they satisfy, and how a gang can be transformed into a constructive group when gang members are encouraged and helped to satisfy their group needs in more legitimate ways. Frank Bonham studied a number of gangs in Los Angeles and embodied what he learned in *Durango Street,* an interesting story about Rufus Henry and the Moors. When he is released from a camp for delinquent boys, Rufus and his sister are attacked by the Gassers, a local gang. After his attack, Rufus realizes that he must violate his parole and join a rival gang if he is to survive in his neighborhood. Young readers will sympathize with Rufus as he longs for a father, and will share his triumphs as he leads the Moors to street victories and finally into more constructive pursuits. In using this book, the teacher could ask the children to think of ways Rufus might have solved his problems without joining the Moors. They may conclude that he had few other alternatives.

Kristin Hunter's powerful novel, *The Soul Brothers and Sister Lou,* is a story about 14-year-old Louretta Hawkins, and her friends the Hawks, a Southside gang. A strong person, Lou persuades the Hawks to use their group efforts constructively. However, their attempts to pursue legitimate activities are continually frustrated by the local police, who perpetually harass them and brutally kill Jethro. The author skillfully and effectively handles police brutality and other violent acts which take place on the "rough" Southside. When reading this book, the class could study the causes of police brutality in the black ghetto and use factual sources to study actual cases. This book will also help the reader attain many insights into black family life in the inner-city. *The Soul Brothers and Sister Lou* has many strong characters and memorable incidents which will help the child develop empathy for ghetto residents. Fierce but brilliant Fess, talented and lonesome Blind Tom, shy and sensitive Calvin, and Lou, who searches relentlessly for her black identity, will deeply impress the reader.

Poetry by black American writers can be used in the social studies to help children develop empathy and understanding of the black experience and life in the inner-city. Most black poets express their feelings, emotions, and aspirations in their poetry. They have been preoccupied with themes dealing with oppression, freedom, and the meaning of blackness in America. In "Montage of a Dream Deferred," Langston Hughes asks what happens to a deferred dream and implies that it explodes. When studying race riots, this poem would be especially appropriate. The teacher could ask the children what dreams of black people have been deferred, and in what ways have they exploded. Claude McKay's anguished and evocative poem, "If We Must Die," can also stimulate a discussion on race riots. McKay penned this poem when riots broke out in our cities in 1919.

An infinite number of beautiful, poignant, and revealing poems are available for use to teach children the facts of ghetto life. *Bronzeville Boys and Girls* by Pulitzer Prize winning poet Gwendolyn Brooks is a collection of poems about children in the inner-city. This book includes happy, sad, as well as thoughtful reflections by urban children which reveal their feelings and emotions. *On City Streets,* edited by Nancy Larrick, is a collection of poems about the inner-city which urban children helped to select. The book includes captivating photographs which enhance the appeal of the poems. Stephen M. Joseph's *The Me Nobody Knows: Children's Voices from the Ghetto* includes poetry and prose written by children who live in the inner-city. In their accounts they reveal their fears, aspirations, and a limited, but eventful, world.

American Negro Poetry by Arna Bontemps, *I Am the Darker Brother: An Anthology of Modern Poems by Negro Americans* by Arnold Adoff, and *The Poetry of the Negro* by Langston Hughes and Arna Bontemps are excellent and comprehensive anthologies of black poetry. Poetry can evoke interest and help children gain deep insights into the moods and feelings of black inner-city residents.

Our very existence may ultimately depend upon our creative abilities to solve our urgent racial problems. The flames that burned in Watts, the blood that ran in Detroit, and the willingness of black leaders to chance assassination by taking strong stands on social issues indicate that the black American is willing to pay almost any price to secure those rights which he believes are his by birthright. The reactions by the white community to the black man's new militancy have been strong and intense. A "law and order" cult has emerged to stem the tide of the black revolt.[6] Since our major social problems grow from the negative attitudes which whites have toward blacks,[7] we must modify the racial attitudes of whites if we are to create the democratic society that we verbally extol. When used effectively, literature can help white children in our sheltered suburban areas to develop racial tolerance and a commitment to the eradication of social injustice.

Children's Books Cited

Arnold Adoff, *I Am the Darker Brother: An Anthology of Modern Poems by Negro Americans* (New York: The Macmillan Company, 1968). Illustrated by Benny Andrews.

Frank Bonham, *Durango Street* (New York: E. P. Dutton and Company, Inc., 1965).

Arna Bontemps (editor), *American Negro Poetry* (New York: Hill and Wang, 1963).

Gwendolyn Brooks, *Bronzeville Boys and Girls* (New York: Harper and Row Publishers, 1965). Illustrated by John Kaufmann.

Natalie Savage Carlson, *The Empty Schoolhouse* (New York: Harper and Row Publishers, 1965). Illustrated by John Kaufmann.

Robert Coles, *Dead End School* (Boston: Little, Brown and Company, 1968). Illustrated by Norman Rockwell.

Lorenz Graham, *North Town* (New York: Thomas Y. Crowell Company, 1965).

Lorenz Graham, *South Town* (Chicago: Follett Publishing Company, 1958).

Lorenz Graham, *Whose Town?* (New York: Thomas Y. Crowell Company, 1969).

Langston Hughes and Arna Bontemps (editors), *The Poetry of the Negro 1746-1949* (Garden City: Doubleday and Company, 1949).

Kristin Hunter, *The Soul Brothers and Sister Lou* (New York: Charles Scribner's Sons, 1969).

Stephen M. Joseph (editor), *The Me Nobody Knows: Children's Voices from the Ghetto* (New York: Avon Books, 1969).

Nancy Larrick (editor), *On City Streets* (New York: Bantam Books, 1964). Illustrated with photographs.

Julius Lester, *To Be a Slave* (New York: The Dial Press, Inc., 1968). Illustrated by Tom Feelings.

Mary Hays Weik, *The Jazz Man* (New York: Atheneum, 1967). Illustrated by Ann Grifalconi with woodcuts.

Elizabeth Yates, *Amos Fortune: Free Man* (New York: Dutton and Company, Inc., 1950). Illustrated by Nora Unwin.

Footnotes

[1] James A. Banks, "A Profile of the Black American: Implications For Teaching," *College Composition and Communication*, vol. 19 (December, 1969), pp. 288-296. See also Andrew Billingsley, *Black Families in White America* (Englewood Cliffs, N.J.: Prentice-Hall, Inc., 1968).

[2] Robert L. Green (editor), *Racial Crisis in American Education* (Chicago: Follett Educational Corporation, 1969).

[3] Julius Lester, *To Be a Slave* (New York: The Dial Press, Inc., 1969), p. 124.

[4] James A. Banks, *March Toward Freedom: A History of Black Americans* (Palo Alto: Fearon Publishers, 1970).

[5] Lorenz Graham, *Whose Town?* (New York: Thomas Y. Crowell Company, 1969), p. 194.

[6] James A. Banks, "Racial Prejudice and the Black Self-Concept," in James A. Banks and Jean D. Grambs, *Black Self-Concept* (New York: McGraw-Hill Book Company, 1972).

[7] *Report of the National Advisory Commission on Civil Disorders* (New York: Bantam Books, 1968).

Global Education in Elementary Schools: An Overview

Charlotte J. Anderson and Lee F. Anderson

This nation needs . . . an internationally informed citizenry—both in and out of school—that is adequately aware of its relationship to the rest of the world, prepared to support as well as criticize the tough decisions which leaders must make, and capable of contributing to the necessary dialogue of a functioning democracy and an emerging world order.—Stephen K. Bailey, "International Education: An Agenda for Global Interdependence," *The College Board Review*, Vol. 97, (Fall, 1975).

Introduction

Over the past several years, a still small but growing number of individuals and organizations in many nations of the world has been working to improve the quality of children's international or global education. In the course of these efforts, several critical issues or questions have emerged which require continuing examination. In this article we shall comment briefly on two of these issues. They can be summarized as follows:

WHAT IS ADEQUATE GLOBAL EDUCATION?

WHAT SHOULD BE THE OBJECTIVES OF GLOBAL EDUCATION?

What Is Adequate Global Education?

Global education in elementary schools is generally treated in two ways. One conception treats global education as the study of foreign peoples and

CHARLOTTE J. ANDERSON is Assistant Professor of Education and LEE F. ANDERSON is Professor of Political Science and Education at Northwestern University, Evanston, Illinois.

cultures. The other conception treats global education as the study of the foreign policies and international relations of national governments.

We believe that while these conceptions of global education may not be inaccurate, they are inadequate. Obviously, global education involves students in one society studying about the geography, history, and culture of people living in other societies. It is also obvious that global education involves the study of the foreign policies and the international relations of nation-states.

Conceptions can be correct, however, and at the same time be incomplete or inadequate. In our judgment, both of these prevailing conceptions of global education suffer serious weaknesses.

Global Education as the Study of Foreign Societies and Cultures

This conception appears to suffer at least three serious deficiencies. It builds a "we-they" or "us-them" dichotomy into the very heart of the educational enterprises; this, in turn, reinforces children's tendencies to perceive the world in ethnocentric terms and to stereotype other societies and peoples. Obviously, this is the very antithesis of the ends which most teachers and schools believe should be served by world affairs instruction. Moreover, dividing the world into "things American" and "things non-American" for purposes of their study obscures the degree to which studies of American families, communities, and states, along with the study of American history, can and should have an international dimension.

Most importantly, the concept of global education as education about foreign peoples and cultures obscures the global character of human experience in the contemporary world. One of the most visible hallmarks of our time is the historically unprecedented scale and degree of human interdependence at the global level. The earth has ceased to be a piece of cosmic real estate on whose surface live relatively scattered, autonomous, and isolated groups of *Homo sapiens*. As Robert Harper observes, "Throughout most of history, mankind did exist in separate, almost isolated cultural islands . . . now most of humanity is part of a single worldwide system."[1]

The "systemness," the "unity," the "oneness" of the modern world is evidenced in a wide variety of ways. It is witnessed in the interpenetration of international and domestic systems, with the consequent eradication of boundaries between domestic and foreign affairs. It is evidenced in the rapidly expanding volume of private or nongovernmental transactions among nations. It is seen in the growing number of both governmental and nongovernmental transnational organizations. It is manifest in the developing web of military, economic, political, and ecological interdependencies. It is witnessed in the convergence of social organizations and technologies in the world's large-scale, mass societies. And it is evidenced in the internationalization of contemporary social problems, including the management of violence, the control of disease, the maintenance of environmental health, and the promotion of economic well-being, social justice, and human rights.

Inherent in the emergence of a world system are far-reaching implications for the way children and young people are taught about the world. Perhaps these implications can best be understood by noting that, in the study of any phenomena, one can focus either upon the parts or upon the whole. For instance, we can study a forest or we can study the individual trees that make up a forest. We can study homes or neighborhoods, flowers or gardens, rocks or the quarry. The choices we make are a function of our purposes. If our aim is to understand trees as such, then we need pay little or no attention to whether the trees are part of a forest. On the other hand, if our purpose is to understand a forest, then we must also study trees; but in this case the parts must be studied in the context of a larger whole.

Whether to focus on the parts or the whole becomes a particularly critical issue with the emergence of a world system. What is the kind and quality of understanding that we wish to develop in students? Do we wish simply to develop some knowledge of the world's different regions, societies, and cultures? Or do we want to develop some understanding of the world as a totality, of the world as a global system? In our judgment, the latter should be our goal.

We believe that the task before us is to transmit "to the next generation a rich image of the 'total earth.' "[2] If this is the task, then the conception of global education as education about foreign societies and cultures is inadequate, for it obscures the fact that all of humanity is part of a planet-wide system.

Global Education as Education about the Foreign Policies and International Relations of the Governments of Nation-States

This conception of global education suffers from a serious defect because it obscures the actual and potential involvement of individual citizens in world affairs. By focusing almost exclusively on the international behavior of national governmental officials, this conception fails to illuminate many facts about international life which are important for future citizens to understand. For example, it obscures the fact that many sub-national governments, such as the governments of states and cities, are involved in transnational relations. More importantly, it obscures the fact that countless nongovernmental groups are deeply involved in international affairs. These include religious groups, business organizations, labor unions, educational institutions, families, scientific and professional associations, and cultural organizations, to name but a few. Also, it obscures the activities and work of the many intergovernmental international organizations.

By obscuring these aspects of international life in the modern world, the concept of global education as education about the foreign policies and the international relations of national governments fails to provide future citizens with an awareness and understanding of the many ways they are and can be involved in transnational processes, institutions, and problems.[3]

A More Adequate Approach to Global Education

If, as we have argued, the prevailing approaches to world affairs instruction are grounded in inadequate conceptions of global education, then it is reasonable to ask what a more adequate conception might be. It seems to us that it is fruitful to view global education as education for responsible citizen involvement and effective participation in global society.

This conception of the nature of global education consists of a set of interrelated propositions. First, it asserts that the scale and scope of human interdependence has for the first time in human history reached a point where we can speak of the emergence of a planet-wide or global society. Second, the conception asserts that individuals are members of global society as well as being citizens of particular local communities and nations. Third, the formulation asserts that individuals must be educated for membership in global society in much the same sense that they are educated for membership in sub-global communities. Fourth, this conception of global education asserts that schools, including elementary schools, have a responsibility, along with other educational agencies, to prepare individuals for responsible involvement and effective participation in global society.

Viewed in this way, global education is perhaps best seen as an extension and enlargement of the school's traditional, time-honored responsibility of preparing children for responsible and effective citizenship. In the past, the schools have been charged with preparing young people for citizenship in families, communities, states, and nations. With the emergence of a global society, this historic mission of the schools is extended to encompass preparation for citizenship in planet-wide society. We must continue to try to prepare children for citizenship in local communities and nations, but now we must also educate them for responsible involvement and effective participation in global society.

What Should Be the Objectives of Global Education?

In the previous section of this article, we briefly critiqued the prevailing approaches to global education and outlined what we feel is a more adequate approach. Specifically, we argued that it is useful to view global education as education for responsible citizen involvement and effective participation in global society.

Implicit in this conception are four types of competency that need to be developed within students if they are to eventually become responsible and effective participants in global society. The promotion of these competencies constitutes four overarching objectives that we believe can and should be served by world affairs instruction at all levels of formal education.

Competence in Perceiving One's Involvement in Global Society

As individuals, each of us is involved in global society in a variety of basic ways. Biologically, we are involved in global society because we are members of a single, common species of life, and hence we share with all humanity many commonalities. Ecologically, we are involved in the world system because we are a part of the earth's biosphere, and hence inescapably linked to our planet's material and energetic structure. Culturally, we are involved in global society because we are enmeshed in the human-created environment we call culture; and in the modern world, human culture has become a global environment. The technologies, the institutions, the languages, and the beliefs that make up human culture link us, our communities, and our nation to people, communities, and nations elsewhere in the world. Through these cultural linkages, we influence the lives of people elsewhere in the world; and they, in turn, influence our lives. Historically, we are involved in global society because much of the culture that surrounds us is an amalgamation of technologies, languages, beliefs, and institutions initially created by members of our species who lived elsewhere in both space and time; and, conversely, much of the culture surrounding others is of our creation. Psychologically, we are involved in the world system by virtue of the fact that the world external to our nation is an object of our perceptions, attitudes, and beliefs. Reciprocally, we are the object of the perceptions, attitudes, and beliefs of others. And we and others have self-conceptions of ourselves and our relations to the world, along with perceptions, attitudes, and beliefs about relations among ourselves and relationships to the natural environment.

We do not "naturally" perceive these dimensions of our involvement in global society any more than we "naturally" perceive the relationship between color and form in a painting. We must learn to see the ways in which we are linked to the world external to the boundaries of our communities and nation. The development of such a perceptual competence is one of the major objectives of global education, and that development must begin in childhood.

Competence in Making Decisions

The emergence of a global society is affecting our decision-making life in two significant ways. One, the impingement of the external world on our lives is creating new conditions to which we, both as individuals and as members of American society, must adapt. This process involves decisions about change in life styles, in our attitudes toward the external world, and in our self-conceptions. Two, the decisions we make as individuals, as well as the collective decisions made by the groups to which we belong, increasingly affect the well-being of both the 94 percent of humanity that lives outside of the boundaries of the United States and the well-being of yet-to-be-born generations. In brief, the boundaries of our decision-making life are expanding in both space and time. Issues that were once matters about which we could make decisions with an eye only to their local and short-term consequences are becoming decisions that have both transnational and transgenerational consequences.

For these reasons it seems to us imperative that the nation's schools seek to improve the decision-making competencies of future citizens. The emergence of a global society demands a citizenry capable of creatively adapting to historical forces over which they have little control, and also capable of activity that takes into consideration the transnational and transgenerational consequences of the decisions made by individuals, private groups, and the governments of our cities, states, and nation.

Competence in Making Judgments

In the years ahead, the quality of life enjoyed by the human species will be determined in large part by the actions taken by private organizations and governments in respect to a set of interrelated global problems. These can be characterized in summary fashion as: (1) problems in the management of cultural diversity, (2) problems in the management of conflict and violence, (3) problems in the management of cultural change, (4) problems in the management of inequalities, (5) problems in the management of population growth, and (6) problems in the management of human-biosphere relations. The kinds of actions taken in respect to these problems by governments and by private organizations will be substantially influenced by the quality of judgments made about these problems by thousands—indeed, millions—of individuals in this nation and elsewhere in the world. Thus, the development of the analytical skills and emotional capacities associated with competent judgment-making must be one of the major objectives of global education in schools.

Competence in Exercising Influence

In a global age when worldwide interdependence makes itself felt in the daily lives of most citizens, it is critical that individuals learn to exercise some control and influence over the transnational problems, institutions, and social processes that impinge upon their well-being and the well-being of other members of the human species. Schools, we believe, can assist individuals in developing some competence in exercising influence within the context of global society by developing their ability to see how they can exert influence: (1) through lifestyle decisions, (2) through occupational or professional activities, (3) through social action, (4) through political activity, and (5) through modelling and other kinds of educational activity.

Footnotes

[1] Robert Harper, "Geography's Role in General Education," *Journal of Geography*, 65 (April 1966), 182.

[2] Kenneth Boulding, "What Can We Know and Teach about Social Systems?" *Social Science Education Consortium Newsletter*, 56 (June 1968), 1.

[3] For a very good discussion of the ways individual citizens are involved and can be involved in world affairs, see Chadwick Alger, "Foreign Policies of United States Publics," The Mershon Center, Ohio State University, January 1975.

Man: A Course of Study An Exemplar of the New Social Studies

John G. Herlihy

Most of the social studies curricula in use today are a content sequence that basically follows the guidelines of the Commissions of the National Education Association, American Historical Association, and the Carnegie Foundation of the first three decades of the twentieth century. Basal social studies texts emphasize history with some attention to government, economics, and place geography. District social studies curricula guidelines traditionally have contained headings such as: Ancient History, Egypt, American Discoverers, Latin America, and American History. Since World War II, there has been some widening of the curriculum through such offerings as: The Non-Western World, Africa South of the Sahara, Global Geography, and area studies. Even these options strongly reflect the position of history as "king" of the social studies and also of a set body of content information as the basis of the courses.

In the late 1950's and early 1960's, many critics of school program began to challenge this emphasis on content/information and began to seek alternative methods. Jerome Bruner's report of the 1959 Wood's Hole Conference, *The Process of Education*[1] is a key example. That seminal work indicated the direction of the "new social studies"—the emphasis on how (activity) scientists think rather than on the knowledge (product) that they have generated. Problem solving, inquiry, discovery, inductive processes, and higher order thinking became essential features of the new instructional programs.

Since the ideas of *The Process of Education* had a profound effect on the scope, development, and direction of the curriculum reform movement,

JOHN G. HERLIHY is Assistant Dean, Division of Educational Studies, College of Arts and Science, the State University of New York at Geneseo.

Bruner felt the need to provide concrete illustrations of the ideas and principles enunciated in his landmark work. During the 1964-1965 school year, Bruner took a leave as Director of the Center for Cognitive Studies at Harvard University and became deeply involved in designing and constructing a curriculum to illustrate and exemplify his views. From 1964-1969, he and a number of other scholars worked with Education Development Center (EDC) (formerly Educational Services, Incorporated) of Cambridge, Massachusetts to develop a one-year upper elementary social studies curriculum called *Man: A Course of Study* (MACOS).

EDC received financial assistance for this new venture in the social studies from the National Science Foundation (NSF) and from the Ford Foundation. These agencies were interested in supporting the curriculum development movement in the social studies and in introducing the work of leading scholars in emerging areas such as territoriality, aggression, communication, and social organization. NSF supported the introduction of MACOS in schools and colleges by funding a set of installation and dissemination centers until 1971. The author was the director of one of these centers from 1969-1972. Since that date, Curriculum Development Associates has been the commercial disseminator of the course.

The themes and content of the MACOS curriculum are drawn from anthropology, social psychology, and biology. The actual subject matter (salmon, herring gulls, baboons, followed by an in-depth study of the Netsilik Eskimos) of the curriculum presents an opportunity for students to compare human behavior patterns to those of other animals. The behavioral relationships among topics emerge through the instructional techniques of contrast and comparison. For example, child-rearing practices, one of the five major recurring themes of the curriculum, is first introduced by studying the salmon, whose parents die before the young are born. Throughout the curriculum this concept is revisited in each topic with more information, with greater depth, and with greater insight. By this designed pattern of information release, concepts such as life cycle, adaptation, innate behavior, learning, parental care, social structure and communication are introduced, developed and expanded in increasing stages. This organizational pattern illustrates Bruner's notion of concept formation—the spiral curriculum.

At each level of investigation, students are provided with information in a variety of formats. MACOS contains twenty-six booklets (not textbooks), sixteen movies (many are natural sound ethnographic records), filmstrips, records, problem sheets, photomurals, data cards, simulations, etc. This variety and range of instructional resources provide many paths for learning and can allow for multiple learning styles and modes. The variety of informational input sources enables most students to participate and to contribute in many aspects of group work. These built-in features assure individual participation and greater breadth and depth of contributions from each group. This instructional procedure is designed to promote the testing of ideas and the exchange of information.

MACOS generates conditions whereby students are involved in the investigation of questions on the cutting edge of knowledge. The present state of information on some of the topics (aggression, territoriality, social organization of baboons) does not provide definite responses. Students are provided rich background materials that enable them to carry out the role of a scientific investigator. They use the skills of observation, recording data, making inferences and testing these in a group setting. As Bruner said, "We . . . try to encourage students to discover on their own. Children surely need to discover generalizations on their own."[2] Considerable emphasis and reward is placed on the "processes" of analyzing, questioning, hypothesis making and testing, inferring, screening relevant information, thinking fluently, flexibly, originally, and elaboratively. Thus, ". . . the classroom can become for the teacher, as well as for the student, the setting of a teaching-learning experience that relies more on the excitement of the processes of inquiry than on the mastery of the specifics of the subject."[3]

The developers of MACOS curriculum made a basic assumption about the power of a concept: an organizing principle as a key force in a learning situation. Thus content becomes a vehicle through which students use information as a means to organize their mental processes and are able to apply this new concept in another setting. The Netsilik Eskimos are studied not for themselves, but rather as a means for students to apply the new analytical tools and skills they have been developing. The study of the social organization of baboons also enables students to study and examine powerful organizing ideas such as role, hierarchy, dominance, power, communication, and the interrelations of the various members of a baboon troop. The contrast and a comparison of these forces in a baboon troop with those in a human society provide interesting differences—how deviance is treated, how much dissonance from a part the whole group can tolerate. Other questions that arise are: What is a society, how does it function, and what is the "social cement" that holds a group together? These powerful organizing ideas enable students to form, apply and test generalizations. These tools and skills help students to approach new content with the ability to examine, organize, analyze and form tentative hypotheses. This ability to generalize, to see relationships, to make applications, and to make a preliminary analysis from content is one of the goals of MACOS and the "new social studies."

In a MACOS classroom, the teacher is a co-learner with his students. The processes, the intuitive leaps, and the excitement of discovering encourage both pupils and teachers to be actively involved in the classroom. A MACOS Teacher's Guide states, "If education [is] to become more than just a process of feeding student reified information, then we must be concerned that teachers experience not only the complexity, but also the productivity of alternative ways of approaching a topic."[4] Therefore, both teachers and students need to assume new roles in the classroom.

In looking at a MACOS classroom in operation, the role/behavior of teachers and pupils as well as classroom appearance are clear. Teaching strategies become more dialectic and child-directed rather than didactic and adult-directed. Group work, problem sheets, movies, simulations, etc., stress the idea of "messing around with stuff."[5] The students are responsible for their own learning, and teachers are engaged as active learners with students in the classroom. The teacher discourages pupil appeals to her as an authority and works to make the learner involved and responsible for his own learning.

Other teacher and pupil behaviors in evidence are: a tolerance for ambiguity, open-ended questions that may not have an end point, a non-enforced consensus of student responses, and an apparent conflict between value systems. Students in these activities will demonstrate deferring judgment, testing ideas, and dealing with novel or unusual situations.

Teachers also must become skilled in group work, in diversified instructional strategies, and in interpersonal communication skills. Student self-assessment and feedback techniques are operational systems; not objectives, monitored and evaluated by the teacher in the classroom.

The social interaction and the excitement of learning through inquiry take place in group work. In these student-student interactions, not only the testing of ideas takes place, but also the group processes that let students act on openness, decision making, and mutual cooperation.

The MACOS curriculum fosters an attitude of openness toward one's own and other cultures, values, and people. The rationale for studying the Netsilik Eskimos is to help children understand and empathize with people of different cultures in order to help them discover themselves.

Basic assumptions about content, the learning environment, the role of the teacher, and of students are radically different in the MACOS curriculum than in most traditional programs. As an exemplar of the "new social studies," MACOS stresses the interrelated nature of knowledge by combining the methodologies of many disciplines in one instructional package. Students also have more responsibility for their own learning, the rate of learning, and the evaluation of the learning as they are the manipulators of the variety of instructional resources.

In summary, MACOS illustrates the rationale and operations of the "new social studies" by emphasizing the "processes" of learning and by the social interactive nature of learning experiences. The traditional social studies curricula dealt with transmitting content areas through verbal procedures—text and lecture. In contrast, pupils in MACOS and the "new social studies" are active, mobile, audible, and follow multiple paths for information.

Footnotes

[1] Jerome S. Bruner, *The Process of Education* (New York: Vintage Books, Random House, 1960).

[2] Jerome S. Bruner, *Man: A Course of Study*, Occasional Paper #3 (Cambridge, Mass: The Social Studies Curriculum Program, Education Development Center, Inc. [formerly Educational Services, Inc.], 1965), p. 30.

[3] "Seminars for Teachers," *Man: A Course of Study* (Cambridge, Mass: Education Development Center, Inc., 1967), p. 1. Materials disseminated by Curriculum Development Associates, Washington, D.C.

[4] *Ibid.*

[5] David Hawkins, "Messing About in Science," *Science and Children* II (Feb. 1965): 5.

Evaluating Textbooks for Elementary Social Studies: Criteria for the 'Seventies [1]

Arthur S. Nichols and Anna Ochoa

There is no influence in American schools which does more to deter-mine what is taught to pupils than does the text-book. Yet this impor-tant factor in our educational system has until recent years altogether escaped critical study. [2]

—*Charles H. Judd*

Judd's statement of over half a century ago may still have meaning today. While the textbook's influence in determining the curriculum may have decreased, only in recent years has the critical study of textbooks been considered a worthy and acceptable professional task. This article will present one set of evaluation criteria. . . .

The *evaluation* of textbooks is not the same process as the *selection* of textbooks. The process of evaluation results in judgments concerning a book's worth in terms of stated criteria; the process of selection results in a decision to use specific text material with an identified student population. Selection takes into account factors other than those dealing with the validity of textbooks; for example, cost, durability, and type size. The actions of social studies educators often fail to make this distinction clear. Frequently, selec-tion and evaluation are either assumed to be identical or it is assumed that the latter process is accomplished through the former one; that is, a decision to use a book *per se* is a judgment of a book's validity as an instructional medium. Reviewing the traditional principles of selection will therefore indicate the standards that social studies educators have previously applied to textbooks.

ARTHUR S. NICHOLS is Associate Professor of Education at California State University, North-ridge. ANNA OCHOA is Associate Professor of Education at Indiana University, Bloomington.

Spalding[3] has described two traditional approaches used in the selection process: the *score-card formula* and the *master-teacher conception*. The score-card formula assumes that by rating a book on specific characteristics an objective measure of a book's worth can be established. Such characteristics may include format, authorship, readability, content coverage, and publisher. The master-teacher conception views the book only as a "tool" to be modified and used by the teacher in any way he sees fit. Both of these approaches have one common characteristic: they do not investigate the relationship between the student and the printed word. One approach focuses on the book and the other on the teacher. Neither focuses on the student; and, consequently, they do not investigate what the pupil will learn. The textbook cannot be primarily evaluated on the basis of its qualities as a book, or its flexibility in the hands of a teacher. It must be evaluated on the basis of what effect it may have on children.

New Criteria for the 'Seventies

The criteria that are used to evaluate textbooks are necessarily derived from the philosophy and goals that have been defined for a social studies program. For example, if social studies educators place high priority on developing appropriate attitudes with respect to their definition of citizenship education, they will look for examples of those attitudes in any textbook considered for classroom use. The content and learning activities provided in the textbook should be consistent with the goals that are held for social studies programs. Some writers do not define the philosophical base from which they derive their evaluation criteria. The authors of this article do not take a neutral stance. They have assumed that one cannot discuss the characteristics of a "good" social studies textbook without first defining their objectives for a "good" social studies program. The criteria for textbook evaluation presented here are derived from the learning goals and purposes that the authors hold for social studies education. If the reader finds that he supports similar goals for learning in social studies, he will probably find these criteria useful in evaluating textbook materials.

Briefly stated, the social studies program that is advocated here has, at a minimum, two essential components: a knowledge and an intellectual component. The knowledge base is organized around the persistent social issues that man continues to face in the last half of the twentieth century. Higher level thinking skills and decision-making characterize the intellectual component.

I. The Knowledge Component

A. *Social Issues: Does the knowledge presented in the textbook support the understanding of complex and persistent social issues?*

A safe prediction for the children who are or will be enrolled in the elementary schools of this decade is that their adulthood will be characterized by increasingly complex social issues. Some of these issues are likely to be extensions of current and historic conflicts; other issues have yet to be identified. The problems inherent in continuing technological development, expanding urbanization, increasing population, and growing environmental pollution can be safely predicted for the year 2000. If educators are genuinely concerned with developing a generation of socially competent adults who can skillfully address such problems, elementary social studies textbooks need to be organized around these pervasive social issues.

B. *Interdisciplinary, Conceptual Organization: Does the textbook emphasize conceptually organized knowledge from many disciplines and fields of study?*

Textbook authors traditionally have defined a range of topics for which they provide a vast array of factual knowledge. Recently, content coverage is being replaced by organizing knowledge around disciplinary concepts and generalizations. This new emphasis enhances the development of highly transferable verbal symbols that contribute to the pupil's intellectual management of social phenomena and problems. Social issues cannot be studied from the perspective of a single discipline; the complexity of such issues requires the definition of a broad knowledge base that includes the natural sciences and the humanities as well as the social sciences.

C. *Recency: does the knowledge presented reflect the most recent scholarly findings?*

Many publishers consult scholars who represent one or several social science disciplines in an attempt to ensure the accuracy of their social studies materials. This provides a valuable service to educators, who cannot be expected to have current knowledge of recent findings in several separate disciplines. With respect to the recency and accuracy of knowledge, educators need to rely heavily on the judgments of scholars. If publishers have built this factor into the development of their materials, the credibility of the text is increased. If not, school systems might employ scholars as consultants to review textbooks that are being considered, rather than risk using materials that present outdated or erroneous knowledge.

D. *Bias: Is the information in the textbook objectively presented?*

Bias in textbooks is usually demonstrated in one of two ways. One form is chauvinistic in its extolment of the glories and accomplishments of American society while avoiding both the presentation of significant social problems and interpretations that are critical of the American past and present. The second reflects the norms and values of the white, middle-class strata of society. Although representatives of minority groups have been somewhat successful in their efforts to influence publishers to produce textbooks that reflect cultural diversity, progress along these lines has been extremely slow. In too many instances the inclusion of minority group history represents another kind of tokenism to which these groups are subject. Textbooks may add a section, an entire chapter, or include some illustrations that shade faces in darker hues. None of these practices are sufficient for materials that will be used by youngsters who will, in all probability, face the consequences of minority group problems for the rest of this century.

II. The Intellectual Component

A. Analytic Mode: Can the textbook serve as a basis for inquiry?

Information presented in most textbooks is primarily descriptive. It seeks to answer who, what, when, and where questions. The why and the how of social phenomena are often left unanswered. Textbooks can present interpretive data in many ways. Case studies, pictorial essays, graphs, maps, and primary source data may be used to confront the learner with the causes and consequences of social forces. With such data readily at hand, children can be asked to develop hypotheses with respect to the following questions: Why did this happen? Could this happen today? What implications does this information have? In this manner a textbook can provide a powerful springboard for inquiry.

B. Higher-Level Questions: Do the questions presented in the textbook support the use of intellectual processes above the memory level?

Social studies textbooks have overemphasized low-order memory-level questions. Questions need to be written that encourage the learner to explain, interpret, and translate data in ways that are meaningful to him. Thoughtfully written higher-level questions can lead the learner to apply his information to new situations, to recognize bias and gaps in information, to establish relationships between data, and to identify the elements of what he sees and reads. Such questions entail higher-level thinking processes that are essential to the development of intellectually competent young people. When these kinds of questions are integrated with the organization of a textbook, the textbook promotes intellectual growth. Textbooks that present questions that are limited to memory harness the intellectual growth of the learner to the rote level.

C. Decision-Making: Can the textbook function as a basis for decision-making?

Decision-making is a vital dimension of intellectual development. At a minimum this process involves the identification of alternatives, a prediction of consequences, and the presentation of evidence. Textbooks can facilitate the development of decision-making skills in at least two ways: by raising open-ended questions that engage the learner in a comparison of alternatives and by presenting data that facilitate knowledgeable and analytical approaches to these questions. Examples of questions that facilitate decision-making are: Should welfare programs in our community be changed? What rules should there be in our classrooms? What can be done to maintain a pure water supply? In the process of deriving answers to these questions, pupils are able to clarify the values they hold with respect to important social issues. To provide an adequate knowledge base for the intelligent treatment of such questions textbooks can present background information, unfinished stories, a range of interpretations on a given issue, and can also identify sources of information that will widen understanding of the question.

D. *Establishing a Direct Relationship with the Learner: Does the textbook consistently demonstrate the relationship between the knowledge presented and the immediate life-space of the learner?*

The connection between the reader and the information presented in textbooks is seldom made clear. Pupils are asked to study the coffee growers of Brazil, the War of 1812, or the regions of the United States and relate this information in some manner to their own backgrounds, problems, or aspirations. Yet, the conditions that prevail in other nations or in other regions of the United States as well as the conditions that accompany war or other social issues can be compared to problems faced in the youngster's own peer group, family, school, or community. A thoughtfully developed textbook will relate remote events and places to the personal experiences of the learner.

(At this point in the original article, the authors used the above criteria to evaluate two social studies textbook series).

Concluding Comment

This article has had a limited objective. It has presented criteria reflecting one point of view toward the social studies. Other criteria can be developed representing other points of view. All such philosophically-based standards examine the internal validity of a textbook series; that is, the criteria are standards of the series' consistency with respect to a given position regarding social studies education. Such evaluation is a necessary, first step in any selection process.

Footnotes

[1] This article was originally published in 1970. At that time, concern with civil rights as they applied to racial groups was extremely salient. The issue of women's rights had not yet surfaced. Consequently, the criteria set forth in this article do not focus on discriminatory treatment of females in student materials. Clearly, in the late seventies, this issue cannot and should not be ignored. A sense of social responsibility requires that learning materials be free of the stereotypic portrayal of women that has pervaded this society for far too long.

[2] Charles H. Judd, "Analyzing Text-Books," *The Elementary School Journal*, XIX (October, 1918), p. 143.

[3] Willard B. Spalding, "The Selection and Distribution of Printed Materials," in Lee J. Cronbach (ed.), *Text Materials in Modern Education* (Urbana: University of Illinois Press, 1955), pp. 166-87.

SECTION III
Instructional Environments

The concluding section of this book centers on instructional environments—on the locales where social studies learning occurs. Although the following articles approach this topic from a wide variety of perspectives, they tend to reflect one central theme: The social studies program is only as good as the social studies teacher. Once instruction begins, it is the teacher who assumes responsibility for what is taught, how it is taught, and how effectively it is learned. Although all of us would accede to this proposition, too few teachers are willing to acknowledge that they do have the power to create within and outside the classroom stimulating and exciting learning environments that enable learning to flourish. If the following articles can help teachers to better use their creative talents to this end, they will have served their purpose.

What environments are most conducive to social studies learning? The initial article, by Ryan, distinguishes between the *formal* and *hidden* social studies curricula, and demonstrates how the one is as real and meaningful to the student as the other. Armento and Goetz maintain that it is virtually impossible for the individual teacher to create an environment that facilitates individualization of learning; accordingly, they offer a proposal for "integrated teaming." A third environment is advocated by Perrone and Thompson, who present a rationale for applying the open education philosophy to social studies instruction. The fact that they buttress their proposal with examples of successful programs in various communities should be of significance to skeptics.

The concluding articles in this section provide another perspective on learning environments. Spodek reviews the theoretical bases for teaching intellectual skills to young children, assesses current social studies programs, and then offers concrete proposals for change. Rogers then reacts to Spodek's comments by presenting a series of challenges to early childhood educators.

Implementing
the Hidden Curriculum
of the Social Studies

Frank L. Ryan

Frequently, in discussing "new" social studies programs, "new" content in the forms of key concepts and ideas from the social sciences is emphasized. In addition, emphasis is placed upon the procedures or methods of inquiry a social scientist might employ to produce such understandings.[1] Collectively, we might refer to the concepts, ideas, and methods of inquiry of the social studies curriculum as the *formal* curriculum. However, equally important to the formal curriculum are the ways in which the teacher strives to implement the newer programs.

Let us think of the formal curriculum as analogous to a new 747 transcontinental jetliner, standing on the runway and poised for takeoff. Obviously the plane is not yet serving any of its main functions, one of which might be to transport passengers from some beginning point, such as New York, to some terminal point, such as Paris. Nor will the plane's function be served until a person, or, probably more correctly, groups of persons come along who understand its operation and inner workings, the type of fuel it requires, its maintenance requirements, its instrumentation, and the procedures necessary to get the craft airborne. In similar fashion, the materials of "new" social studies programs are conspicuously displayed in numerous schools—but frequently there is no one around to "get them off the ground." The essential ingredient missing is the teacher's role in establishing those learning environments which allow the newer social studies programs to take off.

Let us then intellectually gather all of the mannerisms, procedures, and ways of dealing with students that a teacher might use when implementing a

---

FRANK L. RYAN is Professor of Education at the University of California, Riverside.

lum—a curriculum, by the way, which becomes just as real to the students as the formal curriculum of concepts, ideas, and procedures of inquiry. It is the nature of the hidden curriculum which will determine whether or not the formal curriculum gets properly fueled and takes off. More directly stated, the formal curricula of new social studies programs are never implemented unless the hidden curriculum involving the teacher's role is "right." Students learn from both curricula—the hidden as well as the formal.

Philip Jackson, drawing from one of his studies conducted in an elementary school setting, estimates that teachers can engage in as many as 1000 interpersonal interchanges each day.[2] The hidden curriculum can be thought of as what happens between teacher and students during these daily interchanges. The characteristics of this curriculum are reflected in the responses to such questions as: What kinds of questions are being posed? How are students asked to respond to the questions? How does the teacher react to the students' responses? Which students do the responding? What are the nonresponding students doing?

Let us now translate such questions into a specific description of a classroom environment established for teaching social studies. In this particular instructional situation, the students are in neat rows of desks facing the front of the classroom. Students take out their social studies textbooks, and the main part of the lesson consists of having various students (usually the better readers) take turns reading aloud to the rest of the class. The day's reading is followed by a short discussion period in which the teacher asks a series of questions which are ordinarily at a recall level. The teacher's role now becomes one of soliciting from the students the facts of the day's reading. Now we all know that some students are better than others at recalling information, and there is evidence available to indicate that we will call on the "better" students most often.

What is it that the students are learning from the hidden curriculum of this lesson's environment—that is, in addition to the facts from the formal curriculum? Believe it or not, the students are learning quite a few things from the hidden curriculum. Specifically, chances are excellent they are learning that:

- facts are the most important part of a social studies program (facts might even *be* the program).
- the best way to acquire understandings (that is, if you want to receive praise from the teacher) is to "pay attention" to the readings, acquiesce to the rest of the class, and allow all learnings to go unchallenged.
- the primary usefulness of facts (or any knowledge from the social sciences) is their recall for the teacher upon a second's notice.
- social studies (and therefore the social sciences) is essentially a bland mixture of information, books, and maps that must be swallowed unquestionably and can be anticipated with the same enthusiasm as spoonfuls of cod liver oil.
- only certain students are expected to understand all of the social studies curriculum.

Of course, such learning outcomes are completely incompatible with the intent of the newer social studies programs. To return to the analogy of the 747, we can conclude that even the "new" program, if linked to the hidden curriculum described above, will never get off the ground.

We can even think of the hidden curriculum as having a "classroom learning spirit"—and like most spirits, it becomes a little difficult to nail into place and describe. However, the following teacher behaviors would probably lead to the establishment of the learning spirit required for newer social studies to flourish.

There is a utilization of higher-level questions. A survey of research on teacher questioning practices conducted by Hoetker and Ahlbrand[3] indicated that for at least the past fifty years, teachers most frequently have posed questions to students at the recall, memorization level, and that this trend still persists. If the social sciences were a mere summation of a series of facts, then a predominate use of recall questions would be satisfactory. However, such an assumption is invalid. Nor is the nature of knowledge in the social sciences such that we have the instructional right to treat it as though we are dealing with "recallable" absolutes. The purpose of the investigative activities of social scientists is not to collect facts as end-products, but rather as intermediate data from which to make further statements about man's behavior. The higher level questions[4] when posed by the teacher can involve students in making statements about the knowledge they have assimilated. Thus, the student is allowed to think about what he is intellectually acquiring.

There is a solicitation of multiple and varied ideas from the students. The teacher "allows" all student responses and considers them as starting points for further learnings. Ordinarily the higher level questions do not have a "correct" response, but are assessed on the bases of such characteristics of the response as its plausibility in relation to the posed question, originality in terms of the student's previous thinking experiences, and the supportive rationale which argues for its acceptance by the listener.[5] An instructional implication is that the teacher is receptive and supportive of all ideas.

Caution is exercised not to sway student opinion through expression of teacher self-opinion. For many students the opinions of teachers can carry a particularly powerful clout. For the student to disagree with the teacher becomes a David-Goliath affair (without the happy ending), and most students will simply withhold their own responses rather than commit intellectual suicide. The teacher might better concentrate on eliciting various student opinions, rather than indoctrinating students with his own.

Opportunities are provided for students to express their own ideas, and to react to the ideas of others. Frequently, students become so engrossed and enchanted with their own responses that they are oblivious to the ideas expressed by others. Teachers can have students react to the response of other students. For example, one student might indicate that he would favor a Boston Tea Party if he had been around at that point in history. The teacher might then ask another student to react to such a response and ask any further questions he desired. The teacher would be supportive of students' attempts to be open-minded to those responses.

Students are encouraged to examine the reasons behind their own responses. Implied in responding to higher level questions is a supporting rationale. Students must be urged to offer the supporting reasons for their responses and allow others to react to their reasons as well as to their responses.

The assumption is made that the student's response is a reflection of his best thinking for the present. It is certainly the unique student who doesn't want to make a coherent, defensible, provocative classroom contribution in the presence of his peers. It would also be the unique student who didn't feel the pangs of failure when one of his responses resulted in some form of ridicule from his teacher or peers. Teachers can support the students' efforts at responding, and use such responses as starting points for further thinking.

There is a willingness of the teacher to relinquish "center-stage." Recently, John Wayne was characterized in a feature article in a national magazine as possessing the type of magnetic stage presence that automatically rendered him center-stage as soon as he entered to play a scene. It is easy for teachers to become the John Waynes of their classrooms, and the gatekeepers of all activity. The teacher so cast decides what questions will be asked, what will be the "acceptable" responses to the questions, who will talk, who will listen, and what will be the discussion topics. Flanders' research[6] indicates that most teachers dominate the talking activity for their classrooms. However, students should be encouraged to ask questions as well as respond to them and should not feel forced to channel all of their inquiries through the teacher. Similarly, teachers can "allow" the noise of small discussion groups and role-playing situations, and even allow some groups to conduct discussions without constant teacher interjections.

Students are allowed to generate, as well as receive, knowledge. Traditionally there has been an emphasis in social studies instruction on having students acquire a series of understandings—to "cover the content." Ordinarily this coverage has been at the factual, recall level of understanding. Newer programs continue to reflect the acquisition of understandings by the students, but characteristically, higher forms of understanding, such as concepts and pervasive ideas, are emphasized. However, besides acquiring understandings, students must also be allowed to work with the kinds of data social scientists use when *generating* understandings. In other words, students should be inquirers as well as receivers of understanding. The instructional expectation is that student-inquirers can begin to acquire insights relative to the nature of knowledge, such as: its tentativeness, the calculated risks involved in making inferences, and the necessity to scrutinize carefully all data sources. This means that students must have opportunities to collect the data of the social sciences, to make inferences from those data, and to acquire those intellectual tools which allow them to check on the adequacy of their inferences.

For example, the author has described a lesson elsewhere[7] in which students are given aerial photographs of the same location at two different points in time. Students are asked to identify data from the photographs and make statements around the concept of "land-use change" for the location shown. Thus, in essentially the same manner as a social scientist—the geographer in this case—the student employs data to generate understandings, rather than receive the end products of someone else's investigation.

The above list of characteristics is indicative, rather than exhaustive, of the types of teacher characteristics and behavior that would set the stage for new social studies programs to take root. Learning expectations from such a hidden curriculum would include the following:

• knowledge is continuously evolving through the generation of new knowledge as well as the reinterpretation of previous knowledge.

• the social scientist interprets evidence to make inferences about man's behavior, but frequently, different interpretations can be given to the same evidence.

• every student can think, and therefore can meaningfully participate in the various facets of a social studies curriculum.

• people must be open to the ideas of others, including those ideas which are at variance with their own.

Implementation of the hidden curriculum just described is, however, not always easily attainable, especially when it requires an erosion of some "other" behaviors we have acquired. For example, in using the aerial photograph lesson previously described, who can precisely predict what the students will come up with as they identify data and make statements about those data? Sometimes this lack of predictability of student behavior during such lessons will lead to feelings of teacher insecurity, and certainly in a textbook-read-recite instructional environment there is little that is relegated to the unpredictable. However, it is important that the teacher become a model for inquiry and investigation for the student, and forego the more traditional role (admittedly at times alluring) that has the teacher cast as an infallible dispenser of knowledge.

Although teachers may at times have too few opportunities to offer input into the formal curriculum, each teacher is solely responsible for the learnings of the hidden curriculum. Also, instructional implementation of any formal curriculum is ultimately characterized by the hidden curriculum the teacher has concurrently chosen to follow; one does not "fly" without the other.

Footnotes

[1] Ryan, Frank L. *Exemplars for the New Social Studies.* Englewood Cliffs, N. J.: Prentice-Hall, Inc., 1971.

[2] Jackson, Philip H. *Life in the Classroom.* New York: Holt, Rinehart and Winston, Inc., 1968.

[3] Hoetker, James and William P. Ahlbrand, Jr., "The Persistence of the Recitation," *American Educational Research Journal,* 1969, 6(2), 145-67.

[4] Ryan, *Exemplars,* pp. 122-130. The author identifies and gives examples of five higher (than recall) questioning categories: relationship, application, educated guess, synthesis, and opinion.

[5] Ryan, Frank L., "Description of a Scheme for Analyzing the Questioning Activity of Students and Teachers," *College Student Journal,* in press.

[6] Flanders, Ned A., "Intent, Action, and Feedback: A Preparation for Teaching," in Amidon, Edmund J. and John B. Hough (editors). *Interaction Analysis: Theory, Research, and Application.* Reading, Massachusetts: Addison-Wesley Publishing Company, 1967, p. 104.

[7] Ryan, *Exemplars,* pp. 56-62.

Let's Get It Together: A Case for Integrated Teaming

Beverly Jeanne Armento and Judith Preissle Goetz

In the raptness of such few moments,
A ring of softly intent faces surrounds
my private being;
I am united with myself.

Together, with self, with others, with the world: intellectually, emotion-ally, physically. This is a goal which many who teach children would like to realize, a genuine goal, both for students and teachers. Given a clearly explicit philosophical structure, a group of teachers functioning as an in-tegrated team, and a flexible learning environment, we believe that it is a goal within reach. The purpose of this discussion is to explore these three constituent elements.

The "Together" Component: A Philosophical Structure

What are the elements of a curriculum that will achieve the above goal? What assumptions should be made concerning what we are about? We believe the philosophical characteristics of such a curriculum would include facilitation of the child's total growth (cognitive, affective, and effective), intellectual honesty, a balance of pedagogical factors, individualized instruc-tion grounded in personal choice, and the integration of subject-matter areas.

The intellectual and social milieu of the classroom will be one in which the child can feel a sense of worth as a successful, capable human being. He will be encouraged to develop creatively as a thinker, a feeler, and a doer. Complex, legitimate learning is based upon risk-taking and will only flourish

BEVERLY JEANNE ARMENTO is Assistant Professor of Education at Georgia State University, Atlanta. JUDITH PREISSLE (KASPER) GOETZ is Assistant Professor of Social Science Education at the University of Georgia, Athens.

when the total environment is supportive of the child's initiative, curiosity, and spontaneity.

Intellectual honesty will pervade in choice of topics and depth of inquiry. Gut-level problems facing children and adults in our society—the value-laden areas of poverty, war, racism, rats, sex-role standards, etc.—will be confronted openly and realistically. Children can and will deal with issues using comparative, analytic, and evaluative skills. To do otherwise is morally hypocritical and perhaps psychically damaging.

The construction of learning environments includes a balance of several pedagogical factors. Objectives are designed for the total child, and include cognitive, affective, and effective dimensions. Teaching strategies can then be chosen as appropriate to particular goals, drawing from a range of directed to nondirected activities. Multimedia approaches will then be chosen for the appropriateness to objectives as well as for their support of sensory and psychomotor skills. Varieties of social experience, from solitary activity to large group interaction, will be incorporated into the program. And finally, various levels of intensity should be allowed for ranging from casual, spontaneous dabbling to highly-concentrated mastery.

Individually-matched learning activities for skill and specific concept development are essential in beginning "where the children are" on any number of process dimensions. Furthermore, children should have choices of learning options. Even those objectives to be met by everyone can be achieved through student choice of differing content, media, and final products.

Integration of isolated aspects of subject matter will be necessary in order to promote the transfer of learning and the sense of integrated environment. Reality does not occur according to academic disciplines!

The "Let's" Component: An Integrated Team

The design, construction, and implementation of a curriculum based on these elements is a challenging task. Can one teacher do it alone? We've seen only a few. It is our contention that it can be done more successfully, more effectively—perhaps, and even more joyfully—by a group of teachers who have freely chosen to combine forces: an integrated team.

The integrated team is a number of teachers—varying in interests, experiences, and talents—who share *equal* responsibility for building a learning environment. It is essential that it be composed of individuals who are committed to the idea of teaming. Roles, functions, and goals of the entire group are formulated, implemented, and evaluated *consensually*. This means that all planning and decision-making is by group consensus. While members may be playing different roles at a particular time, each person can and will play all roles available to the team as a whole. There should be a team-chosen leader (ideally, this will rotate); however, his tasks will be procedural and administrative rather than authoritative.

How is it that such a group, the integrated team, will be able to accomplish the goal more effectively? What are the potential benefits of this group?

• *Teaming can be creative.* The total learning environment can be improved, and learning options can be greatly multiplied. Have you ever brainstormed an idea with a friend and suddenly realized that together you have formed a totally new, creative idea? The integrated team holds great potential for just such interaction.

• *Teaming can be a helping relationship for professional and emotional support.* For the staff members, there is an equal commitment to a common purpose that binds them together. This opens the arena for the sharing of expertise and materials as well as for peer feedback on teaching performance. It also provides a bedrock of emotional strength, encouraging to students and teachers alike. Working with children can often be a tiring, emotionally draining, and perhaps lonely task. The unit of the integrated team carries the potential for supporting and reinforcing its individual members.

• *Teaming creates more options for significant child/adult relationships.* Each child has a complex of human personalities from which to draw in terms of human interaction, and the variety and depth of available relationships are greater. Consultation and guidance can be more easily and more frequently arranged. Lack of empathy from one staff member can usually be compensated for by adequate understanding from another.

• *Teaming can be a vehicle for social and educational change.* Teaching teams change the organization social structure of a school from isolated-independent to interdependent and powerful decision-making sets. The intellectual climate of a healthy team[1] has the potential of producing innovations from within the schools; i.e., teachers can become innovators in addition to adopting educational advances from outside sources. Building intense communication systems enables faster flow of information about the tools for using new ideas; the strength of a consensual demand ought also to speak to academicians and producers of curricular materials to influence the nature of future products.

• *Teaming can be a unique resource for social education.* The functioning processes of the team offer students both a source for learning about human interaction and a model of human cooperation for task accomplishment. The team offers a model also for group and individual decision-making. It provides multiple examples of conflict, confrontation, and resolution. It can be, essentially, a laboratory resource for examining human behavior.

• *Teaming can provide a viable arena for risk-taking.* Teaming increases the degree of interdependence and communication among teachers, and it is thus wrought with intense personal and professional risk-taking. Members must be open, flexible, trusting of each other, and able to function effectively in an atmosphere characterized by divergent value systems. The common goal, that of helping children learn, provides the basic group adhesion, strengthened by mutual respect and affection. There should be at least one person on the team who (either through training or talent) is highly sensitized to interaction processes; i.e., there must be someone aware enough to be able to "read" and verbalize his understanding of the emotional situation and who takes leadership in clarifying and promotion of the human framework.

"Let's Get It Together": A Plan for Action

Regardless of whether one teaches in a self-contained classroom or as part of a team, the essential process of goal-setting, diagnosing, implementing, and evaluating the entire learning environment remains constant. However, as total team size increases, classroom variables also are multiplied and the situation becomes more complex.

The success of any team depends greatly upon its coping effectively with these four group processes: (a) detailed coordination of personnel, resources, schedules, and children; (b) consensual agreement on all facets of decision-making; (c) equal and shared responsibility of all team members; and (d) continuous communication, with new information and feedback effecting changes in all aspects of the team system.

Let us now consider the basic process cycle inherent in all teaching-learning situations. The major focus will be to explicate those behaviors particularly unique to teaching teams attempting to develop a flexible learning environment.

Goal Setting. What concerns, interests, conceptions, and/or misconceptions do the children have? What thinking and social skills have they mastered? What realities from the child's social environment does the teacher wish to take into account? What general type of program or set of activities seems to be appropriate to all of the information?

With which major concepts or issues will the children deal? What are their component parts? What are some examples and non-examples of the concepts? Could they be examined equally well in different contexts? Which of these contexts would be interesting to one's students? How can the teacher find out? Could these different contexts offer choices to students?

> *Example.* A hypothetical team of four adults, 120 children in a family grouping, ages 6-12; the adults have noticed a prevalence of ethnocentric, stereotyped thinking by the students regarding peoples and places in the world. They plan to devise a unit on "Me—Others: Alike or Different?"
>
> Concepts include physical and behavioral characteristics, basic needs, personal preferences, roles, institutions, etc. The variable is the cultural context within which one analyzes aspects of the concept and then applies them to his own life. This context or "content" flexibility enables one child to examine roles of a Bushman mother as compared to his own, while another child compares and contrasts the roles of an early pioneer mother, a seventeenth-century English-woman, and a modern woman.

What should the children be better able to do after the unit?

How much active involvement will children have in planning this unit? How will this be facilitated? (We might suggest here that teams establish a plan which would promote the counselling and guidance function of the teacher and of peers, as well as serve as a vehicle for student voice in decisions.) One might match each student with a home teacher with whom he relates particularly well. Individuals can turn to this person for help with out-of-school problems. The group as a whole can meet regularly for planning-helping seminars. In addition, one could establish adult-monitored, peer interaction teams wherein children can assist each other. It would be important that these kinds of decisions and agreements be made by the total team consensus.

Diagnosing. Where are the students regarding the chosen ideas and skills? What is the range of concepts, and thinking, and social skills with which children will deal? What data are available or can be collected to facilitate matching of activities to skill needs of each child? Would a pretest and/or a sociogram be useful? Which team member will volunteer to adapt or construct appropriate informational devices and present these for group examination and alternation at "Tomorrow's" meeting?

Preparing a Learning Environment. Team brainstorming and agreement on basic activities are essential first steps. What alternative strategies and activities can be devised to meet the goals? How will these in turn be matched to each individual child? What learning options will be created? What range of activities and options is necessary for the obvious variety of skill, interest, social, and learning differences of the children?

What human and material resources in the school and the community can be utilized? What is available and what must be constructed?

At this stage, a fact-finding mission will probably be in order, and team members could disperse to locate and evaluate the applicability of all textbooks, library resources, films, filmstrips, records, tapes, overlays, vertical file materials, study prints, games and simulations, concrete and manipulative realia, strategy suggestions from various professional sources, popular music, poetry, art, programmed materials, and parts of reading and study skill kits.

Armed with an initial set of resources and basic ideas, the team is now ready to organize core inputs for the total learning environment. We suggest grouping the primary activities into some sensible construct; for example:

Discussion activities, or those depending upon *social interaction* of children; sharing ideas; listening to another's point of view; clarifying values; engaging in divergent, creative thinking; brainstorming alternative strategies; simulating and gaming; focusing on smallgroup behavior and human interaction skills.

Individual skill development activities, focusing on each child and his own concept and skill strengths and needs. Matching activities to the child is all-important here. Almost any available audiovisual material, textbook segment, programmed material, etc. could be adapted to learning centers or individual learning packets. The content of these activities should pertain to the major topic.

Extending activities or those that allow a child to delve into another aspect of the concept or problem, to apply an old skill in a new way, to become tantalized by a new idea. For instance, the child locates information on animals hunted in his section of the country; he writes, draws, charts, or graphs what these animals have in common with one another.

Implementing. This includes decisions on who will do what, where, and when.

Room Arrangement: What are the space options available to the team? Mark off general zones for discussion activities, individual and extending activities. Which resources and furniture should be in each area and how could it be initially set up? What "props" are needed for the various activities: easel and wet area; tape recorders; table tops for spreading out; etc.? Does the room arrangement ease movement of groups and individuals?

Grouping: What criteria will be used? When the criteria change, how will the groups change? What means of record-keeping, self- and group evaluation will be maintained? How can children form peer and older/younger tutorial teams? Children are to be encouraged to choose among learning options: are they supported and helped in this process?

Scheduling: Our hypothetical team meets for 90 minutes three times weekly for social studies. That time is organized into three 30-minute modules. During each module, the three major types of activities—group, individual, and extending—occur simultaneously. Children are grouped into six heterogeneous groups, and they "rotate" to a different activity each module. Initially, flexibility can only be attained through structure—all children and adults must know basically what alternative options are available and how to function within each choice.

A prime factor at this stage is sensitivity to the students and to the intrateam processes. Plans are not always realized; direction changes according to student interest and our revised perceptions of their needs. Flexibility is essential!

Evaluating. How far did we go? What adaptations were made or should be made along the way? Where is each child relative to his major and minor goals? What concerns, interests, conceptions and/or misconceptions do children now have? Where are we going from here? (and, of course, here we go again).

Children spend approximately 740 hours a year in the classrooms. During this time, they need to be preparing for 21st-century adulthood, developing their own unique talents and abilities, and creating a purposeful, meaningful life style within a mobile, social environment. We are convinced that the structure presented here enables students to effectively accomplish these tasks. Consider it.

Footnotes

[1] For dimensions of organizational health, see Matthew B. Miles, "Planned Change and Organizational Health: Figure and Ground," in *Change Processes in the Public Schools*, Center for the Advanced Study of Educational Administration, University of Oregon, Eugene, Oregon, 1969.

Social Studies
in the Open Classroom

Vito Perrone and Lowell Thompson

Interest in Open Education has grown enormously over the past three years. As an educational movement it has reached a state where responsible educators must examine it seriously. Reforms in the British primary schools are to some degree responsible for the interest in Open Education in the United States. But to a larger degree, interest is growing because of the belief that schools are failing children. The critique that schools are responsible for the "mutilation of the child's spirit . . . of spontaneity, of joy of learning, of pleasure in creating, of a sense of self"; as places that are too often "grim, joyless . . . oppressive and petty . . . intellectually sterile and esthetically barren . . . lacking in creativity . . .",[1] is finding an increasingly responsive audience.

That such a critique is gaining support must discourage many educators who have, over the past decade, devoted so much energy to curriculum reform. Excellent materials have been produced and are being used successfully in *some* schools by *some* teachers and children. But they have brought little change of significance to *most* teachers and children. Silberman noted that while there is considerable discussion about such things as the structure of the disciplines, learning how to learn, developing basic concepts and "Postholing," the reality is that "the great bulk of students' time is still devoted to detail, most of it trivial . . . and almost all of it unrelated to any concept, structure, cognitive strategy . . ."[2] John Goodlad reported recently, on the basis of his rather extensive study of the elementary school, that:

> Rarely did we find small groups intensely involved in the pursuit of knowledge
> . . . rarely did we find individual pupils at work in self-sustaining inquiry . . . we

VITO PERRONE is Dean, Center for Teaching and Learning, and LOWELL THOMPSON is Associate Professor of Education at the University of North Dakota, Grand Forks.

are forced to conclude that much of the so-called educational reform movement has been blunted on the classroom door.[3]

The basis for the curriculum reform efforts—from mathematics and science to the social studies—was the sense that enormous gaps existed between what was known and what was part of the existing school program. It became more than that. Inquiry (and/or discovery) became the key teaching-learning strategy in the reform movement. As Jerome Bruner said: "The ideal was clarity and self-direction of intellect in the use of modern knowledge."[4] Unfortunately, curriculum reformers assumed that children—regardless of ethnic, economic, or social background—would be motivated to learn as a result of new curricula. That the school as an institution needed significant changing was not sufficiently questioned.

As a part of the New Social Studies, concern about fostering the values of democracy increased greatly. Reading materials became relevant to contemporary issues. Minority people found their way into the curriculum. America's political and social institutions were dealt with more critically. At the same time, schools remained fundamentally authoritarian institutions. It seems abundantly clear today that such institutions do not encourage initiative and responsibility. Sensitivity and a belief in the dignity of the individual are not taught in settings where children are not treated with dignity. A sense of community is not fostered in settings where competition is paramount, where failure is expected, where alienation is encouraged. Personal value systems are not extended in settings where children do not confront situations that require judgments and decisions, where a variety of learning options are not available.

In many ways Open Education, unlike the curriculum reform of the past decade, is raising questions about the nature of childhood, learning, and the quality of personal relationships among teachers and children. It challenges many assumptions about schooling, its organization, and its purpose. Rather than develop an extended philosophic statement on Open Education,[5] we have chosen to provide here only a brief outline to establish a context for our discussion of the social studies. The major curriculum concern in the open classroom is not so much the specific content of instruction as it is *the process* by which it is taught and the conditions under which children learn. In this regard, we believe that it is particularly important that:

Children be able to initiate activities, that they are self-directing and able to take responsibility for their own learning.

Children exhibit intense involvement, where their curiosity leads to concern and commitment.

Children continue to wonder and imagine.

Children are willing to face uncertainty and change in the process, be able to cope with complexities they have not specifically been taught to manage.

Children are open, honest, and respectful of themselves, adults, and other children, and are learning responsibility as an integral part of freedom.

Classrooms that are responsive to the foregoing will and should develop their own unique character. Still, they tend to have many common attributes. The following is a list of characteristics which we look upon as important:

1. An atmosphere of mutual trust and respect among teachers and children.

2. The teacher acts as guide, advisor, observer, provisioner, and catalyst, constantly seeking ways to extend children in their learning. The teacher views himself as an active learner and typically works without a predetermined, set curriculum.[6]

3. A wise assortment of materials for children to manipulate, construct, explore, etc., thus providing rich opportunities to learn from experience. Materials will have diversity and range with very little replication.[7]

4. Learning through play, games, simulations, and other autotelic activities is legitimized. Childhood is respected.

5. Activities arise often from the interests children bring with them to school.

6. Children are able to pursue an interest deeply in a setting where there is frequently a variety of activities going on simultaneously.

7. There are few barriers between subject matter areas and a minimum of restrictions determined by the clock, thus providing a fluid schedule that permits more natural beginning and ending points for a child's learning activities.

8. Children's learning is frequently a cooperative enterprise marked by children's conversations with each other.

9. Older children frequently assist younger children in their learning.

10. Parents participate at a high level in the classroom sharing in children's learning. They also assist children outside the classroom where much of the children's learning takes place.

11. Emphasis is on communication, including the expressive and creative arts.

What must be readily apparent from a review of the foregoing classroom characteristics is that social studies, whether history, geography, political science, anthropology, or economics, is not looked upon as a discrete area separate from reading, language arts, science, mathematics, art, and music. The use of a single textbook doesn't fit. A curriculum that outlines specifically what will be studied at each grade level does not confront openly children's questions, concerns and views of reality.

Teachers in open classrooms constantly look for starting points. In addition, they develop themes which have the potential for sustained interest and individuality. What are the possibilities around a theme of *printing?* Hertzberg and Stone described the activities they observed in an English primary school.

Some children were spending much time in school and local libraries, finding out how books are printed. Others were attempting to restore an old printing press brought by the teacher. Illuminated manuscripts were being examined; technology was being discussed; a small group decided to print its own newspaper . . .[8]

Children's interests in printing carried them to silk-screening, wood-block printing, potato printing, studies in advertising, alphabet systems, Egyptian hieroglyphics, and the Gutenberg Bible. The theme had been under study for a month. The possibilities for continued extension appear limited only by the imagination of children and teacher.

Social studies activities vary from classroom-to-classroom because so much depends upon the children's interests and the enthusiasm of teachers and their knowledge of the varied resources existing in the local environment. It is common, however, to see themes develop around such topics as: what people do, how people take responsibility, what life was like in earlier days (a good base for oral history), people's beliefs about war, recreating, education. It is also common to focus on human relationships. While there may be a serious class study of another country—Mexico, for example—and the room has been provisioned with maps, posters, records, films, and filmstrips, individual children's study will tend to focus on a small aspect of life. We have worked with classrooms in which some children were involved in exchanges of audio-tapes, art work, and drafts with children in Mexico City; others were preparing dramatizations of stories they had read about Mexican children. Mexican food was prepared, games played by Mexican children were learned, music popular in Mexico was available, a variety of children were learning Mexican folk dances, and Spanish was being learned through elementary language topics. Obviously, these children were *actively* involved in their learning.

How do children organize the learning in an open classroom? Individually or in small groups, children plan, along with the teacher, what they are going to study. They attempt to raise questions they are interested in pursuing. They begin to identify the resource materials they need and consider community resources that may be helpful to them. They may also plan ways of sharing their discoveries with their classmates through activities such as a dramatization, slide and tape presentation, or by developing a game or simulation that could be played by the class. They might also plan to meet with the teacher periodically to review their progress. Equipping the classroom to extend individual children's learning becomes a crucial task for the teacher. It is not uncommon to see mathematics, science, or language arts become an integral part of a child's project. The open classroom, in essence, encourages children to become significantly involved in planning what they are going to learn and how they are going to learn it. This balance between the content to be learned and the planning by students is central to much of what happens in an open classroom, especially at the intermediate level. Gordon, in his detailed analysis of the Coleman report, indicated that:

> In addition to the *school* characteristics which were shown to be related to pupil achievement, Coleman found a *pupil* characteristic which appears to have a stronger relationship to achievement than all the school factors combined. The extent to which a pupil feels he has control over his own destiny is strongly related to achievement.[9]

If a student is told what he is to learn, how he is to learn it, when his learning will terminate, and what grade he will receive, one could expect a situation that contributes little to child's sense of efficacy. If, on the other hand, a student is involved in the planning of his learning and, more importantly, in the process of evaluating his own growth, one can more readily expect to find the kind of achievement suggested by Gordon.

Meaningful Experiences

The starting points for meaningful classroom experiences may grow organically out of a particular experience the class has had; for example, a field trip, a classroom discussion, a conversation with a friend, or something as simple as an object a student brought to school to share. A group of nine- and ten-year-old-children in Fargo, North Dakota, turned a story they read together into a house-building experience. The story, about a class which built a clubhouse, prompted a similar idea—the class would build one of its own. Children greeted the idea with such enthusiasm that some visited a lumberyard and arranged to get some old plywood. They developed rather elaborate plans which involved measurement and geometry. An architect demonstrated model making, which the children then tried. They viewed a variety of films on house building. A tape-recorded lesson taught them about tools—the lever, plane, and gear. Retired carpenters in the community provided additional demonstrations. Individual children pursued many different interests in relation to the house-building project. They wrote letters telling others of their experiences. They engaged in individual projects involving Indian homes, termites, trees, creatures who live in trees, homes around the world, workers who build homes, old and modern tools, skyscrapers, doll houses, and, of course, they built the 10' × 8' × 6' clubhouse. They gave a party to thank parents and others who had helped, and presented their construction to the younger children in the school for use during recess.

Students not only have chances to structure their own learning experiences through this type of approach, but they are also able to approach learning in a more unified way, without the narrow and sometimes artificial categories of mathematics, science, English, and social studies impinging on the breadth of their possible learning experience.

Another example of the breadth of experience inherent in a seemingly inconsequential experience involved a junk motor from a Renault automobile. The motor was brought into a fourth- and fifth-grade classroom, and several boys began to take it apart. Before they were through, they learned not only the principle of the internal combusion engine, but also developed a vocabulary of key words like piston, head, cylinder, carburetor, etc. (spelling); wrote several letter requesting information on the motor (language arts); had read parts of several repair manuals (reading); had learned about fractions, the metric system, and cubic measure (mathematics); had learned something about levers and gears, power, and gases (science); and had learned certain things about France, its people, and the Renault Automobile Company, which had developed a car that set an auto speed record (social studies). These boys were "turned on" to learning, and as John Lubbock has said: "The important thing is not so much that every child should be taught, as that every child should be given the wish to learn."

"Brotherhood" became the focus for a group of sixth-grade youngsters in Minot, North Dakota. The range of activities pursued by individual children included: biographical study of individuals like Martin Luther King, Ralph Bunche, and Eleanor Roosevelt; reasons for racial discrimination; simulations on race relations; the Indians in North Dakota; new towns and integration; bias in reading materials; stereotyping; television and cultural bias; ways of promoting better relations among children in the classroom, in the school; and visual montages of man's varied relations with others.

Interest in Open Education has influenced quite directly the approach being taken by the State Department of Public Instruction in rewriting the North Dakota Social Studies Curriculum Guide. The new guide will be less prescriptive than the old, and its major focus will be upon teaching-learning strategies in preference to the more traditional scope and sequence orientation of state courses of study. The content of the social studies, then, will be determined by individual communities, schools, and teachers. This type of guide, it is anticipated, will encourage local communities and their teachers to think through and to organize the kind of social studies program that appears most appropriate.

The Department of Public Instruction will make available printed materials and human resources to individual communities and teachers as they forge ahead in the task of developing individual (and individualized) curricula. The task of the Department becomes one of assisting each community in developing a social studies program which capitalizes on the competence and creativity of each teacher, the interests of individual children, the richness of community resources, and the perceived needs of individual communities.

Much more could be said about social studies in the open classroom, especially with regard to the use of the local community as a base for intensive study. This, however, is another article. We have attempted here only to introduce the open classroom, some of its dimensions—starting with children's interests, the need for children to be actively involved in all aspects of their learning, from planning to evaluation—and its concerns for an integrative quality curriculum rather than the linear, formally-organized curriculum so familiar to most of us.

Footnotes

[1] Silberman, Charles, *Crisis in the Classroom* (New York: Random House, 1970), p. 10.

[2] *Ibid.*, p. 172.

[3] Goodlad, John, "The Schools vs. Education," *Saturday Review*, April 19, 1969.

[4] Bruner, Jerome, "The Process of Education Reconsidered," Address, 26th Annual ASCD Conference, St. Louis, Missouri, March 6-10, 1971.

[5] For a more extensive background on Open Education, readers are directed to: Barth, Roland, *Open Education*, unpublished doctoral dissertation (Harvard Graduate School of Education, 1970); Blackie, John, *Inside the Primary School* (New York: Schocken Books, 1971); Featherstone, Joseph, *Schools Where Children Learn* (New York: Liveright, 1971); Hertzberg, Alvin and Stone, Edmund, *Schools Are for Children* (New York: Schocken Books, 1971); Hawkins, Francis, *The Logic of Action* (Boulder: University of Colorado, 1969); Marshall, Sybil, *Adventure in Creative Education* (London: Pergamon Press, 1968); Murrow, Casey and Liza, *Children Come First* (New York: American Heritage Press, 1971); Plowden, Lady Bridget, et al., *Children and Their Primary Schools: A Report of the Central Advisory Council for Education* (London: Her Majesty's Stationery Office, 1966); Richardson, Elwyn S., *In the Early World* (New York: Pantheon, 1969); Rogers, Vincent, *Teaching in the British Primary School* (New York: Macmillan, 1970); Silberman, Charles, *Crisis in the Classroom* (New York: Random House, 1970); Vermont State Department of Education, *Vermont Design for Education* (Montpelier: State Dept. of Education, 1968); Weber, Lillian, *The English Infant School* (New Jersey: Prentice-Hall, 1971); Yeomans, Edward, *Education for Initiative and Responsibility* (Boston: National Assoc. of Ind. Schools, 1967). An extended annotated bibliography is available from Education Development Center, Newton, Massachusetts.

[6] We have found that the open classroom makes increased psychological demands on teachers. It also provides, as "compensation," enlarged opportunities for intellectual stimulation. Assuming the role of a learner with children frees the teacher from many of the traditional constraints of knower and dispenser of information. The teacher is more free to bring his interests into the classroom where they, too, can be extended.

[7] Much of what has come out of the New Social Studies efforts is especially helpful in open classrooms because of the inquiry base and open-ended character. We have seldom recommended any one program, generally encouraging small quantities of materials from several programs and assisting teachers in gaining understanding about their use—not only that intended but the possibilities for integration with other areas of learning.

[8] Hertzberg, Alvin and Stone, Edward, *Schools Are for Children* (New York: Schocken Books, 1971), pp. 129-130. Hertzberg and Stone have an interesting chapter related to "Steps toward Openness in Social Studies" that may be helpful to teachers in elementary schools.

[9] Gordon, Edmund, *JACD Bulletin*, Ferkauf Graduate School, Yeshiva University (Vol. III, No. 5, November, 1967).

Social Studies for Young Children: Identifying Intellectual Goals

Bernard Spodek

The first professional article I wrote for publication was titled "Developing Social Science Concepts in the Kindergarten."[1] It was based upon a doctoral dissertation of the same name which was later elaborated with the collaboration of Helen Robinson into a book titled *New Directions in the Kindergarten*.[2] The article, the dissertation, and the book that followed were written in the spirit of the curriculum reform movement of the 1950's and 1960's. It was our judgment that early childhood curricula were limited intellectually and were in as much need of reform as those suggested for older children.

At the center of this reform movement was the belief that scholars could identify basic structures of their disciplines which would provide the essential content for school programs. This belief permeated the work of the many social studies projects of this period as well as the work of program developers in other areas of the curriculum. It was felt that signifcant intellectual content could be abstracted from the scholarly disciplines that would enliven and remake school programs.

Earlier Views of Social Studies Curriculum

The ascendancy of intellectual content as the key to curriculum development was in contrast to earlier points of view in curriculum development. During the progressive era, the most pervasive and popular education movement that preceded the curriculum reform movement of the 50's and 60's, curriculum was viewed as the result of the social life that was to be reflected in the school or of the child's needs and interests, a view based upon

BERNARD SPODEK is Professor of Early Childhood Education at the University of Illinois, Urbana-Champaign.

developmental levels. Patty Smith Hill in her report on the kindergarten reflected this view of the social nature of school learning.[3] Hill characterized subject matter as a reflection of human achievement which originates and grows out of the social life and is reflected in school life. Social experience was not only the basis for knowledge but the vehicle through which knowledge was transmitted. Social learnings and the reflection of social activity in the play of children was the stuff from which a social studies program was to be built. It also provided the organizing framework for other areas of the curriculum.

Lucy Sprague Mitchell's work in social studies was a reflection of the use of child development principles as a framework for curriculum. Mitchell viewed the "here and now" as the basis for social studies programs for young children. The concrete, the familiar, even the ordinary experiences and occurrences that surrounded the young child could provide the basis for social studies learning. Mitchell made use of field trips immediately outside the school and into the community as a way of helping children to observe and understand the nature of social phenomena and organizations that could be found within that neighborhood. She had children use unit blocks and other two- and three-dimensional materials to construct representations of these phenomena and to help symbolize the observed social processes in their play. Mitchell organized a program so that young children were provided activities related to the immediate and the concrete; as they matured they would have access to more abstract and remote sources of knowledge and would deal with social phenomena further removed from them in time and space. Her book, *Young Geographers*,[4] is an excellent example of a social studies curriculum that is firmly grounded in developmental principles.

These same developmental principles became the organizing framework for the "expanding communities" approach to social studies that is reflected in so many curriculum guides and textbook series. The "here and now" is viewed as more accessible and more understandable to young children. The remote in time and space is reserved for study later in the child's elementary school career, when experience and maturity will allow the child to deal with more abstract content. Unfortunately, little attention is given in these latter programs to Mitchell's use of the immediate environment as a social science laboratory for young children.

Problems Within Current Conceptions

Just as there was dissatisfaction in the past with the use of the social life of the community as an organizing basis for social studies education and dissatisfaction with the use of human development principles as an alternative base, so there is now a dissatisfaction with the use of the "structure of the disciplines" as an organizing principle. The identification of the basic structures of the social sciences has been a more elusive task than was originally thought. There is no high degree of agreement as to what constitutes the core of each social science or even on occasion of what constitutes the field. The core, if identified, should contain basic concepts and generalizations as well as substantive knowledge, integrating theories, and methods for gathering and verifying data.

If these basic cores could be identified, there would still be the problem in curriculum development of integrating knowledge among the social sciences without losing the integrity of each source of knowledge. Other issues would also remain, relating to what portion of that core of knowledge should be transmitted to children, at what level of development, in what form, and through what method of instruction. Should young children be allowed to discover significant knowledge serendipitously or should carefully detailed programs of instruction be prespecified? Are behavioral objectives appropriate for social science education or should goals be determined only in the broadest terms?

The trends in social studies programs discussed above deal essentially with the intellectual content of the programs. There is more to any social studies program, however, than just intellectual content. Much attention is being given today to the place of values in such programs. Is there a core of values that should be transmitted to children through the social studies, or should the program be designed to help children clarify and judge the values they hold? One of the significant problem areas in our culture relates to social conflicts. Should not a core of social skills be a part of any social studies program for children, including skills in conflict avoidance and conflict resolution?

Another suggested portion of the social studies program for young children relates to the process of socialization. The elementary school has been given responsibility for the socialization of children from the moment they are enrolled. Not only are children expected to learn the student role so that they behave appropriately in the setting of the school, but schools are also used to help children become a part of the larger society. Schools maintain and transmit the traditions of the culture. They pass down the secular rituals and myths to the younger generation. They help children identify different roles and behavioral settings and teach them the behaviors that are appropriate to each role and each setting.

While it can be argued that the social studies have a special function in teaching values and social skills and in helping to socialize the child, these processes are not the function of the social studies program alone. The content of the books the young child is given for reading instruction, the songs he is taught to sing, the room arrangements and organizational patterns of the classroom, the forms of discipline the teacher uses, the joint celebration of national holidays, and even the ways in which the children are taught to enter and leave the classroom, all play a role in the teaching of these social processes, even though that role may not be made explicit. The one element that sets the social studies apart from the other aspects of schooling is the use of social science content as a source of school experience.

Relating Social Studies to the Rest of the School Program

As I write these words, one set of nagging questions continues to return to my mind: Is all of this concern for the identification of the basis of social studies content for young children merely an intellectual exercise? Has all of the prior discourse really affected practice in any real way? In spite of the work of social studies educators, in spite of the development of program and program materials and the arguments as to the appropriateness of content and method, there is little evidence that school practice has been affected in any way in recent years. It is not that schools have simply not responded to the shifts in patterns of social studies education for young children. Rather it seems that the social studies play a minor and relatively unimportant role in the kindergarten and primary programs of most schools in the United States.

Jarolimek, in a recent article, convincingly argues that the failure of the social studies curriculum reform was the result of a shift from concern with the structure, concepts and method of inquiry of disciplines to concern with cultural diversity, values and relevancy.[5] Attractive as this argument appears, I doubt if it holds true for the kindergarten-primary grades. Instructional programs at these levels seem no more culturally relevant today than they were ten or twenty years ago.

A recent study by Judith Evans assessed the patterns of school programs in traditional American, and British and American Open classrooms. The traditional American classrooms were identified as exemplary ones. In these traditional classrooms students were observed engaging in reading activities 65.9% of the time, in math activities 12.6% of the time, and in unspecified books and worksheets 14.5% of the time. Science activities were engaged in 0.4% of the time. While there was no social studies categorized by the observers, the "other" category (which might include social studies) included only 4.1% of the student's time. Patterns in the open classrooms observed in England and the United States were significantly different.[6]

The kindergarten and primary grades in American elementary school are essentially skills oriented. The teaching of reading, writing and arithmetic instruction fill most of the instructional time available. Those areas of the curriculum that are not themselves skills oriented are either given scant attention by teachers and other school personnel, avoided entirely, or used in some way to further the teaching of skills. Given the present orientation of the schools, any proposal to modify current social studies programs would have little if any impact on the schools. Teachers have neither the time nor the inclination to invest vast amounts of effort in modifying part of their programs that are not considered important in the first place.

Given this skill orientation of early schooling, the classic "textbook reader" approach to social studies will probably continue. Teachers can use these textbooks to help children cover the areas of knowledge deemed important in the social studies. At the same time they are affording their children opportunities to practice reading skills. If the children are expected to write reports, more often than not they will use other books, encyclopedias and library books, as a source of information, basing reports on excerpts from these books. Again the skills of reading and writing will be practiced by the children.

Newer, more intellectually oriented social studies programs will become a necessity in the early years of the elementary school only if the nature of the total school experience changes. The moves towards newer approaches to the social studies identified with the progressive education era resulted from the need to redefine all of school content based on a totally new orientation. The social studies became a focal element of the program when the social life of the community was viewed as the basis for the total curriculum. The child-centered approach to schooling supported social studies education which was more than the reading of textbooks since the entire curriculum was viewed as activity based. The social studies were as important as other areas of the curriculum—perhaps even more important, for a social studies topic could become the integrating factor for all the children's school work when projects or units were the organizing scheme.

Given a school where intellectual goals are valued, intellectual activities will become a part of the curriculum. Given a school in which knowledge is viewed as resulting from a child's interaction with his environment, children will be given opportunities to abstract information through such interactions, using mental operations to transform facts and percepts into ideas and concepts. In such a school new social studies programs will have to be generated.

What is presently being called "open education," I believe, represents this type of school. As teachers have moved towards open education in the primary grades, they have moved away from the characteristic skill orientation of most traditional programs. This should not suggest that skills are not taught in these classrooms. Rather in an open classroom children learn skills in the context of broader intellectual activities. Reading instruction in such schools utilizes language experience as a medium for learning. Mathematics involves using measuring and other quantitative techniques that are integrated into other portions of the program. Science activities allow for a certain amount of "messing about" with materials as well as for careful observations. "Open" social studies programs will need to be generated that are consistent with the rest of the program of open education and which might provide an integrative force so necessary for the integrated learning of the open classroom.[7]

A Framework for Developing Intellectual Goals

While newer social studies programs will make use of the knowledge base of the social sciences, it is doubtful that the "structure of the disciplines" approach would provide the appropriate framework, not only for the reasons cited earlier but also because no one social science can serve this necessary integrative function. Piaget, however, has developed a framework for developmental epistemology that might provide a useful framework for the task.

Kamii[8] has described a Piagetian framework for cognitive goals of early childhood education which can provide the basis for an organizing scheme for social studies, as well as criteria to judge the appropriateness of materials and activities. According to Kamii, cognitive objectives can be organized into physical knowledge, social knowledge, logical knowledge, and representation. She suggests that, according to Piaget, physical knowledge, social knowledge and logical knowledge are structured from different sources of feedback. Logical knowledge receives its feedback from the internal cognitive structures of the child, social knowledge from people, and physical knowledge from objects.

While these categories can help us identify the knowledge base of school programs their use should not suggest that knowledge should be transmitted within separate categories. Knowledge needs to be developed in an integrated way as the child, for example, uses logico-mathematical structures to act upon physical knowledge and then represents the product in order to communicate it to others.

Physical knowledge results from the child's experience with external reality. The child's experiences with things provide him with information about the nature and attributes of objects. This knowledge, an outgrowth of empirical observation, can be discovered by the child alone. Social knowledge cannot be discovered in the same way since it is arbitrary in nature. Essentially it must be told to children, although the telling may take different forms.

Logical knowledge consists of logico-mathematical knowledge and spatio-temporal knowledge. The former includes developing classification systems, seriations, and numerical constructions. The latter includes ways of organizing objects in space and time. Concepts like *in* and *out*, or *above* and *below*, as well as concepts of *before* and *after*, are included in this form of knowledge.

Representation occurs on three levels as indices, symbols and signs. Symbols and signs are abstract representations. Symbols include pictorial representations and maps as well as imitation as in dramatic play; signs include representations on a language level.

Social studies programs contain goals in all four of these cognitive areas, but goals for each distinct area must be achieved in ways that are different from those in other areas. The collection of data from firsthand experience, observations, sense impressions, and other information gained from the world of experience, is essentially physical knowledge. While the child is less dependent upon physical knowledge as he matures, he continues to need to abstract information from the physical world as the basis for intellectual operations, and validate the results of these operations in the physical world. No reading of printed matter, viewing of film or listening to the accounts of others can provide this form of knowledge for the child. It is this form of knowledge that is too often lacking in current social studies programs.

Social knowledge, however, can be appropriately transmitted in these ways. Telling can occur in many ways, by a teacher recounting her experiences or reading from a book or using the rich sensory experiences of the media. Much of telling is nonverbal as well, for our actions, our stances, and our visual expressions often tell children what is right and what is wrong, what is acceptable and what is taboo. Social knowledge also requires intellectual (logico-mathematical) operations to become meaningful to the child.

Logico-mathematical knowledge requires the child to use his thought processes to act upon the information he is told or that he gathers from his experiences. The child organizes knowledge into classification systems, developing concepts that allow him to view a group of objects or actions as equivalent, thus bringing order to the world and allowing him to act appropriately with novel objects and in new settings. He must also learn to place events into a temporal order, an essential ingredient of historical thought, and learn to place things in space at appropriate distances and directions, an essential ingredient of geographic thinking.

Expression becomes an important part of the social science program since it requires representation. Some of these representations will be in art forms. Others can be forms of dramatic play. Language can be used in writing and telling reports or creating dramatic presentations.

Reviewing Social Studies Programs

Early childhood curriculum is derived from many sources, including organized knowledge, developmental theory and learning theory.[9] Values provide the screen through which we sift abstractions from these sources that we use as we invent educational programs and activities for children. We judge the worth of each program by recourse to these values. Certain forms of knowledge, skills or attitudes are judged better than others because they are consistent with our view of man in general, and of the kind of person we want to result from our educational program in particular. We judge the effectiveness of our programs by an assessment of the change that takes place in children who are involved in these activities. Hence, we use pupil outcomes as a basis for educational evaluation. The range of outcomes we assess may be limited by our ability to observe and record them, or our ability to specify all that we wish to accomplish.

The Kamii/Piaget framework can help us identify the intellectual goals of various social studies programs, practices and materials. Whether these goals are worthy or whether they are ever achieved is a judgment that must be made based upon other sources, but with such a framework we will be better prepared to know what we are looking for.

A great number of textbook-based social studies programs at the primary grade level, for example, are essentially concerned with the transmission of social knowledge. The content of these programs, as well as their basic medium, is useful in that it tells children about their social world and much of what is told in these programs cannot be discovered unaided by children.

Such programs, however, do not help children develop conceptual or representational knowledge, for there is nothing intellectual required of the children except to assimilate the knowledge in the books. Such social studies programs are very limited.

Some of the newer social studies programs have goals that go beyond the transmission of social knowledge and also include a concern for representational knowledge. Multimedia programs such as MATCH[10] provide not only books, but films and manipulative materials that show different representational forms and help children develop their own representations of social phenomena as well.

Other social studies programs have been conceived with goals that include not only social knowledge and representational knowledge, but logico-mathematical forms of knowledge as well. *Our Working World,*[11] for example, helps children use the classification systems of economists in organizing information about the world (e.g., differentiating between "consumers" and "producers," and, within the latter category, "producers of goods" and "producers of services," based upon the characteristics of the activities of individuals). The Taba Social Studies Program[12] also has as its goals the development of logico-mathematical forms of knowledge in children. The social scientific frameworks of these two programs are different from one another and judgment about the comparative worth of the two programs could be made based upon the scope of social science knowledge of each program. Neither of these programs, however, provides the children with the social science equivalent of physical knowledge. Only representations of the empirical knowledge of others is presented through books and other source materials, or through dramatic representations.

Social studies programs for young children with goals in all four intellectual areas can be developed. The kindergarten units of the University of Minnesota *Project Social Studies*[13] as well as Mitchell's *Young Geographers,* cited earlier, are examples of programs thus conceived. In both instances children are involved in direct observation of social phenomena. They are given opportunities to act upon the data collected through these observations, structuring information in time and space as well as using classification schemes and numerical constructions. Social knowledge is also transmitted to children in these programs and a range of representational forms are used, including pictures, maps and stories. In addition, the children are asked to construct their own representations through play as well as through the use of signs and symbols.

Programs broadly conceived to include this range of intellectual goals are especially important for young children. Not only are the programs richer but, because these areas of intelligence are interrelated, they have greater potential for enhancing development. Young children cannot handle abstract hypothetical thought systems, though they can handle similar ideas in concrete form. The presence of firsthand data sources provides the children with the opportunity to gather a wide range of information through many senses and to grasp intellectual processes they could not understand in most abstract form. The involvement of children in representational activity requires uses of logical processes. It also allows children to represent ideas as simple as well as abstract forms. An idea that cannot be put into words by a young child can be represented in a picture or through dramatic play.

Such programs are necessarily activity based. They require the child not only to observe his world, but to act upon it in some intellectual fashion. This may require the use of field trips outside the classroom to gather information firsthand. It could also use the social processes in the classroom as the basis for the study of social phenomena, or the use of the child's home background as a source of social study. The immediate environment, the "here and now" taken in its original sense, would become important.

Programs such as these could be prespecified, as suggested above. They could also make use of unplanned occurrences. Once a teacher knows what he wishes the children to learn and has some idea of what kinds of resources might be most useful, he has greater freedom in selecting activities as the basis for educational programs. Children's interests could play a more important role in determining topics to be studied. Harris provides an excellent example of how local occurrences were used in an English primary school as the basis for environmental studies.[14]

Summary

In these few pages I have attempted to review the bases for social studies programs for young children that have developed through the years. I have also suggested that one of the reasons for the lack of intellectual quality in social studies programs, as well as for the absence of any social studies programs, may be due to the nature of traditional early childhood classrooms. Social studies programs might flourish more readily in open classrooms. In such classrooms, not only would intellectual goals be supported, but the social studies might even provide a medium for program integration. New programs of social studies, possibly prescribed, possibly emergent, would need to be created which would include as goals the development of physical knowledge, social knowledge, logico-mathematical knowledge and representation. Prototypes of open social studies programs are available in the tradition of social education.

Footnotes

[1] Bernard Spodek, "Developing Social Science Concepts in the Kindergarten," *Social Education*. Vol. 27, No. 5, May, 1963.

[2] Helen F. Robison and Bernard Spodek, *New Directions in the Kindergarten*. New York: Teachers College Press, 1965.

[3] Patty Smith Hill, "Second Report," *The Kindergarten*. Boston: Houghton Mifflin Co., 1913.

[4] Lucy Sprague Mitchell, *Young Geographers*. New York: John Day Co., 1921 (Reissued: New York: Agathon Press, 1971).

[5] John Jarolimek, "In Pursuit of the Elusive New Social Studies," *Educational Leadership*. Vol. 30, No. 7, April, 1973.

[6] Judith T. Evans, "An Activity Analysis of U.S. Traditional, U.S. Open, and British Open Classrooms." Paper presented at AERA Meeting, Chicago, April, 1972.

[7] For statements of theory and practice of Open Education see: Charles Rathbone, editor, *Open Education*. New York: Citation Press, 1971, and Ewald B. Nyquist and Gene Hawes, editors, *Open Education*. New York: Bantam Books, 1972.

[8] Constance K. Kamii, "Evaluation of Learning in Preschool Education: Socio-emotional, Perceptual-motor Cognitive Development," in B. S. Bloom, J. T. Hastings and G. F. Madaus, editors, *Handbook on Formative and Summative Evaluation of Student Learning*. New York: McGraw-Hill Book Co., 1971.

[9] Bernard Spodek, "What Are the Sources of Early Childhood Curriculum?", *Young Children*, Vol. 26, No. 1, October, 1970.

[10] Frederick H. Kresse and Ruth Green, *Materials and Activities for Teachers and Children* (MATCH). Boston: American Science and Engineering, n.d.

[11] Lawrence Senesh, *Our Working World*. Chicago: Science Research Associates, 1964.

[12] Hilda Taba, *Elementary Social Studies*. Palo Alto: Addison-Wesley, 1967.

[13] Edith West, "K-The Earth as the Home of Man," *Minnesota Social Studies Curriculum Project*, Minneapolis: Green Printing Co., n.d.

[14] Melville Harris, *Environmental Studies: Informal Schools in Britain Today*. New York: Citation Press, 1971.

Reaction

Vincent Rogers

Let me begin by describing some activities that took up a good deal of the schooltime of a group of four eight- and nine-year-old children over a three- to four-week period last June.

A dead owl was found in the woods by two of the children. They, with two of their friends, brought the owl to school. After some discussion with the teacher, it was agreed that the four would boil the owl, get rid of flesh and feathers, and examine the skeletal structure of the bird. This was done. The bones were carefully organized, then mounted with wire on black construction paper. This experience led to a further study of the lifeways and habits of owls. Since a simple reference book had mentioned that owls eat a great many mice, owl pellets were gathered, opened and examined. Tiny bones were found, verified as mice bones, categorized into shoulder bones, leg bones, etc. and also carefully mounted. A short but very specific book was written and illustrated by the four children concerning the habits of owls, and two of the children made a lovely "batik" of an

VINCENT ROGERS is Professor of Education at the University of Connecticut, Storrs.

owl sitting in a tree. During the course of this study, the children shared some of their findings with other children in the school. The younger children were particularly moved by the older children's guesses about how the owl had met its death (its head was badly bruised by a blow that could have been made with a stone or stick) and considerable discussion followed (in which the teacher played a significant role) concerning the cruelty of those who killed wantonly, and that killing owls was against the law.

I have taken the time to describe this very real incident because I think it illustrates in concrete terms much of what Dr. Spodek was describing in more theoretical ways in his paper. The Kamii-Piagetian framework emphasizing physical, social, and logical knowledge and representation comes to life in this simple classroom description.

I have no quarrel with that schema as a way of conceptualizing the intellectual goals of early childhood education. Nor would I quarrel with the major implications Dr. Spodek draws from this analysis for the direction social studies education for young children might or should take in the United States.

I think I would, however, emphasize some points more strongly, and perhaps de-emphasize others—largely on the basis of my acceptance of a number of important ideas that I have come to believe about the ways in which children learn.

For example, it seems to me that Piaget's notion that knowledge is not a *copy* of reality—rather, that "to know is to modify, transform or act upon"—is of vital importance to our thinking about the education of young children. Equally important is his caustic observation that teachers who believe that they are "making themselves understood and that they are understanding" when they *talk* to *classes* of children are guilty of pedagogical "illusions."

There is little doubt in my mind that knowledge is a very personal thing; that each learner brings to a given experience his own particular set of predispositions and that the ensuing "learning experience" is finally synthesized into something that, again, is unique for each individual.

Most importantly, and of particular relevance to this discussion, is the significance of wholeness or unity in children's learning. Certainly one of the great errors of the curriculum movement of the 1960's was the tendency to isolate the disciplines and give added support to traditional, piecemeal approaches to learning. Children do not deal (voluntarily!) with "social studies" or "social science" questions. They view the world in a more wholistic way, and the questions they raise (if they are genuinely *children's* questions) deal with concerns that are difficult to categorize exclusively as "geography," "sociology," "economics," etc. Certainly the questions raised during the "owl experience" described earlier were partly social studies, partly science, partly skill development, partly art, partly ethics, etc. The sort of analysis or "framework" presented in Dr. Spodek's paper is an exceedingly useful way to examine the experiences of children for possible growth in a number of directions *and* for planning, in broad general ways, new experiences for children. If, however, it encourages teachers and curriculum workers to compartmentalize learning in a *new* way, we are perhaps back where we started in the 1960's.

For me the big question is: How do we change the *total* school experience for children? How do we encourage more complete learning experiences for children that demonstrate the intertwining of ideas and the development of process skills *in context?*

Dr. Spodek seems more hopeful than I that prescribed materials and programs—although admittedly far better conceived, planned and organized than the materials and programs that emerged during the 1960's—would be effective. I am doubtful about this. I think materials of all kinds *can* be useful to teachers and children in particular circumstances. The key to their effectiveness will depend, however, upon the degree to which classroom teachers become free enough, flexible enough, spontaneous enough, and *confident* enough to use materials and experiences in ways that recognize and take seriously some of the basic ideas about learning that I outlined above.

I would place my emphasis, then, as one deeply concerned about improving the social education of young children, on attempts to help teachers to see children and their learning in new ways *and* in providing opportunities for teachers to grow, to experience, to live richly and fully.

To what extent do either pre-service or in-service programs provide such opportunities? To what extent do teachers, in their day-to-day professional lives in schools, have the opportunity to create, inquire, and decide? What sorts of restraints do we put upon classroom teachers? Do we encourage them to believe in themselves, recognizing that truly individualized teaching and learning can only take place where teachers have the freedom to make day-to-day curricular (and other) decisions that affect the learning of each child? In a word, what are we doing to help teachers become truly professional?

To summarize, then, I am in agreement that the Kamii-Piagetian framework for cognitive goals is a useful conception for teachers and curriculum workers. I emphasized, however;

1. the importance of creating learning situations in which children have opportunities to act upon, modify, or transform knowledge;
2. the dangers inherent in approaches emphasizing talk or verbalization;
3. the need to see learning as highly personal and idiosyncratic;
4. the need for wholeness or unity in children's learning;
5. my concerns about placing too much faith in social studies "programs" as ways of achieving such goals, or, to put it another way, the need for a greater variety of social studies materials that can be used in far more individualized ways by classroom teachers;
6. the overriding importance of the classroom teacher (as opposed to materials and programs), his or her understandings, competencies, freedom, spontaneity, flexibility and personal and professional self-image in achieving the intellectual goals outlined in Dr. Spodek's paper.

Location of Author's Articles in *Social Education*

Author	Volume No.	Issue	Pages
Anderson, Charlotte J.	41	January, 1977	34–37
Anderson, Lee F.	41	January, 1977	34–37
Armento, Beverly Jeanne	36	April, 1972	457–459, 464
Armstrong, David G.	40	March, 1976	164–167
Banks, James A.	34	May, 1970	549–552
Ellis, Arthur K.	39	Nov./Dec., 1975	493–496
Fraenkel, Jack R.	37	November, 1973	674–678
Fulda, Trudi A.	39	January, 1975	24–28
Gallagher, Arlene F.	39	March, 1975	156–158
Goetz, Judith Preissle	36	April, 1972	457–459, 464
Hansen, Lorraine Sundal	39	May, 1975	304–309
Hawkins, Michael L.	41	March, 1977	224–228
Herlihy, John G.	38	May, 1974	442–443, 455
Herman, Wayne L., Jr.	41	March, 1977	232–236
Hoffman, Alan J.	39	Nov./Dec., 1975	489–492
Jantz, Richard K.	39	January, 1975	24–28
Johnson, David W.	39	Nov./Dec., 1975	493–496
Kelly, Kevin P.	39	Nov./Dec., 1975	484–486
Larkin, James M.	38	Nov./Dec., 1974	698–710
Lee, John R.	39	Nov./Dec., 1975	487–488
Little, Timothy	39	March, 1975	159–162
Nichols, Arthur S.	35	March, 1971	290–294, 304
Ochoa, Anna	35	March, 1971	290–294, 304
Perrone, Vito	36	April, 1972	460–464
Rabozzi, Mario D.	41	March, 1977	229–231
Rogers, Vincent	38	January, 1974	45–46
Ryan, Frank L.	37	November, 1973	679–681
Savage, Tom V., Jr.	40	March, 1976	164–167
Shirts, R. Garry	35	March, 1971	300–304
Simon, Sidney B.	35	December, 1971	902–905, 915
Spodek, Bernard	38	January, 1974	40–45
Tennyson, W. Wesley	39	May, 1975	304–309
Thompson, Lowell	36	April, 1972	460–464
Wheeler, Ronald	39	Nov./Dec., 1975	484–486
White, Jane J.	38	Nov./Dec., 1974	698–710

Book design and production by Joseph Perez
Typography by William Byrd Press
Printing and binding by Waverly Press